Volume 10

Business, Government and Society

Business Administration Reading Lists and Course Outlines

Compiled by Richard Schwindt, *Simon Fraser University*,
August 1990

NOTE TO THE USER

This is the third compilation of the Business Administration series of reading lists and course outlines. It is gratifying that acceptance of the series has warranted a new, completely revised set of volumes.

The intention is to disseminate as quickly and as efficiently as possible information on what is currently being taught, and how it is being taught in leading business schools. It is recognized that there is a trade-off between rapid diffusion and polished appearance. The former has been emphasized. I hope that users of these volumes will agree with this decision, recognizing that nearly all of the outlines and syllabi pertain to courses given within the last year.

These volumes will be useful to both individual teachers and curriculum committees when revising existing courses and creating new ones. They will also be helpful for librarians responsible for acquisitions in the business area. But, as before, there is a less modest goal. Between publication in academic journals and integration into mainstream textbooks, scholarly research passes through the transition stage of classroom exposure. Hopefully, these volumes will facilitate that transition.

From time to time this series will be updated, expanded and revised. Suggestions and submissions of new and updated materials, especially in emerging or unconventional areas, are encouraged and appreciated.

ACKNOWLEDGEMENTS

I thank Mr. Dixon Low, for his very competent research assistance, and my colleagues, Professors Barry Gibbs, Robert Rogow and Bert Schoner, for compilation assistance in their respective areas of expertise. I particularly want to thank Professor John Herzog both for help with the finance volumes and for hours of discussion on past, present and future trends in business education. The cover was designed by the Division of Audiovisual Education, Duke University, and the volumes were printed by Multiprint, Inc., New York.

Richard Schwindt, *Simon Fraser University*

© Eno River Press, Inc. 1990. All rights reserved. No part of this publication may be reproduced, stored in a retrieval system, or transmitted, in any form or by any means, electronic, mechanical, photocopying, recording or otherwise, without the prior permission of Eno River Press.

Eno River Press, Box 4900, Duke Station, Durham, NC, 27706

ISBN for this volume: 0-88024-122-5
ISBN Eno River Press for this series: 0-88024-127-6
Library of Congress Catalog Number: 90-082700

VOLUME 10

BUSINESS, GOVERNMENT & SOCIETY

Mitchel Abolafia, *Cornell University*
   Cultural Analysis of Business 5

James A. Brander, *University of British Columbia*
   Government and Business 8

R. Chatov, *State University of New York at Buffalo*
   Legal Environment of Management 11

R. Chatov, *State University of New York at Buffalo*
   The Modern Corporation and the Coming of Managerial
   Capitalism 15

R. Chatov, *State University of New York at Buffalo*
   Government and the Firm 18

Earl Cheit, *University of California, Berkeley*
   Social and Political Environment of Business 20

Edwin M. Epstein, *University of California, Berkeley*
   Business Ethics and the Corporate Social
   Policy Process 25

Gerald Faulhaber, *University of Pennsylvania*
   Management in the Regulatory Environment 29

Murray Frank, *University of British Columbia*
   Business and Government 33

Thomas Kerr, *Carnegie Mellon University*
   Managerial Environment 36

George C. Lodge, *Harvard University*
   Comparative Business-Government Relations 85

Alfred A. Marcus, *University of Minnesota*
   Business, Government, and Macroeconomics 105

Alfred A. Marcus, *University of Minnesota*
   Social Issues in Management 120

David D. Martin, *Indiana University*
   Business, Government and the World Economy 128

D. Nickerson, *University of British Columbia*
   Public Policy Analysis 130

Eli Noam, *Columbia University*
    Conceptual Foundations of Business 136

Seth Norton, *Washington University*
    The Managerial Environment 147

O. Ornati and L. Zicklin, *New York University*
    The Non-Market Context of Employment Decisions 155

Kurt Parkum, *Pennsylvania State University*
    Business in a Global Society 161

Bohumir Pazderka, *Queen's University*
    Economics and Public Policy 166

Sam Peltzman, *University of Chicago*
    Economics of Regulation 172

William A. Sax, *Duke University*
    Business Ethics 188

Walter D. Scott, *Northwestern University*
    Organizational Challenges and Decisions 191

William Stanbury, *University of British Columbia*
    Business-Government Relations in Canada: A Strategic Approach 199

George J. Stigler, *University of Chicago*
    Public Control of Economic Activity 213

Richard S. Tedlow, *Harvard University*
    The Coming of Managerial Capitalism 218

Richard Vietor, *Harvard University*
    Managing in the Regulated Environment 221

A. Vining, *Simon Fraser University*
    Business, Government and Society 236

David Vogel, *University of California, Berkeley*
    Social and Political Environment of Business 239

David Vogel, *University of California, Berkeley*
    Business and Public Policy 244

Murray L. Weidenbaum, *Washington University*
    Business, Government and the Public 248

L.J. White, *New York University*
    Market Organization, Antitrust, and Regulation 251

JOHNSON GRADUATE SCHOOL OF MANAGEMENT
Cornell University

Professor Mitchel Y. Abolafia
530 Malott Hall

Tue. Thur.: 1:00 - 2:15
Room 224

CULTURAL ANALYSIS OF BUSINESS
NBA 671
SPRING 1990

The course examines the culture of business. An understanding of differences in behavior, values, beliefs, and norms between firms, industries, and nations is increasingly important to competitive success. The course is divided into two parts. In the first part, students study the theory and methods of cultural analysis. In the second part, they apply the theory and methods to the study of Wall Street culture, including the areas of trading, sales, and merger and acquisition. Students engage in exercises and projects to develop their skills as cultural analysts.

The course format is that of a graduate seminar. Each class session will be an open class discussion of topics in the readings. Students are expected to come to class prepared to participate.

Openers: Every student will be responsible for presenting a short analysis of the limits or advantages of two of the readings over the course of the semester. A two page paper, describing the argument, will be handed in at the time of each presentation.

Midterm: There will be a Midterm Exam (25% of grade) based on course concepts on 3/1.

Field Project: The Field Project (50% of grade) will be an analysis of some aspect of the culture at JGSM or in the wider university community. This will be a fieldwork project requiring interviews and observation. You may study rites, ceremonies, sagas, physical setting, symbols, or any other cultural form. The project may be done in teams. There will be a proposal, a progress report, and a class presentation in the final weeks of class.

Exam	- 25%
Project	- 50%
Participation	- 25%

DATE	TOPIC	ASSIGNMENT
PART ONE:	**Theory and Methods in Cultural Analysis**	
1/23	Introduction to Cultural Analysis	Handout in Class
1/25	What Is Cultural Analysis?	Geertz - The Balinese Cockfight
1/30	Doing Cultural Analysis I: Rituals and Ceremonies	Trice and Beyer: Studying Original Cultures, Deal and Kennedy: Rites and Rituals
2/1	What is Organizational Culture?	Ott: Appendix to Chapter 1 and Chapter 2
2/6	How Culture Shapes Business	Sutton: Chapter 8 and Chapter 14. The Functioning of A Competitive System and the Institutional Framework
2/8	Doing Cultural Analysis II: Methods	Spradley: Cultural Meaning, Whyte: Interviewing in Field Research
2/13	How Culture Forms	Kunda: Chapter 3 Tech. Culture Codified
2/15	Culture and Emotion I	Van Maanen and Kunda: Real Feelings, pp. 52 - 70
2/20	No Class Session	
2/22	Culture and Emotion II	Hochschild: Chapter 6, pp. 89 - 118
2/27	International Comparison: Culture and Personality	Crozier: Chapter 8
3/1	Exam	

6

DATE	TOPIC	ASSIGNMENT
PART TWO:	**Cultural Analysis Applied to Wall Street**	
3/6	Socialization	Lewis: Liar's Poker Chapters 3 & 4
3/8	Market Structure	Abolafia - Structured Anarchy pp. 129-141
		Mayer - Chapter 2 pp. 27-49
3/13	Trading Culture I	Abolafia: Constructing Market Culture
		Kroll - The Professional Trader pp. 34 - 59
3/15	Trading Culture II	Brooks: Chapter 5 The Trading Game
		Bruck: My Master is My Purse
	3/20 and 3/22 SPRING	BREAK
3/27	Trading Culture III: Data Analysis	To be given out before class
3/29	Sales Culture: Data Analysis	To be given out before class.
4/3	Market Crisis I	Lefevre pp. 240-284
4/5	Market Crisis II	Brooks: Meltdown pp. 50-88
4/10	Market Crisis III	Abolafia - Enacting Market Crisis
4/12	Takeover Culture I	Eccles & Crane: Doing Deals, Chapter 1 & 2
4/17	Takeover Culture II	Bruck, Chapter 6 & 10
	4/19 - 5/3 CLASS PRESENTATIONS	
5/3		Final Papers Due in Class

Commerce 394: Government and Business

(Sections 012 and 013)

Professor Brander
Office: H.A. 252   224-8483
Office Hours: Tue, Thurs, Fri., 2:30-3:30

Overview

This course is concerned primarily with the interaction between government and business in a modern mixed economy such as Canada's. More specifically, the course addresses the following basic questions.

(1) What should the role of government be?
(2) What factors explain actual government intervention in the economy?
(3) How does government policy affect the business environment?

In addition, an objective of the course is to provide some background knowledge of Canada's economic and public policy structure.

Reading

The required text for the course is <u>Government Policy Toward Business</u> by James A. Brander. This book is in the bookstore. In addition, there is a required readings package available for sale in the note sale office (HA 103).

Grading

30 % Midterm Exam (Thursday, February 23, 1989, in class)
40 % Final Exam
20 % Policy Analysis Essay (due Friday, March 31, 1988 by 4:30 p.m.)
10 % Assignment and class participation

Policy Analysis Essay

This project involves a critical analysis of some current policy issue relating to actual or potential government intervention in the marketplace. Begin by reading some major daily newspaper on a regular basis. (e.g. the Sun, the Globe and Mail, the Wall Street Journal. The best source for most issues will be the Globe and Mail.) Follow at least one important policy issue during the term. You may supplement your reading in any way you wish: using older news items on the topic, using weekly or monthly newspapers and journals, using notes, recordings or transcripts from T.V. or radio, and conventional library sources. The minimum requirement, however, is that you collect a strong file of current clippings from one source during the term.

Use the file you collect to write a 6 page typewritten double-spaced paper on your chosen issue. This paper should include the following elements:

1. a brief desription of the issue and why it is important
2. recent developments surrounding the issue (including
   citations to the articles you are using)

3. analysis of the pros and cons of government involvement using course material where relevant
4. your own recomendations if you wish (you are not required to draw definitive conclusions)
5. brief comments and criticisms about the way the media have handled the issue.

Item 3 (analysis) is the most important of these elements.

Submit your clippings file of original clippings with the essay.

It may take some time to determine which issues will generate ongoing public debate. You should, therefore, start following the news now so that you have a topic within the next few weeks.

Outline

The course will start by emphasizing the conceptual framework of policy analysis. This framework draws heavily on basic economics. The rest of the course will emphasize application of this framework to particular policy areas, with some further development of the basic theory.

Topics

1. Introduction
2. Basic Economic Concepts
3. The Philosophical Foundations and Normative Rationale for Policy
4. The Positive Theory of Government
5. Firms and Markets
6. The Canadian Business Environment
7. International Trade Policy
8. Canadian Competition Policy
9. Regulation in Canada
10. Public Enterprise
11. Externalities and Environmental Regulation
12. Stabilization Policy
13. Fairness, Ethics and Public Policy

Readings
(All reading are in the text or the readings package. The readings indicated by the word "chapter" refer to the text.)

1. Chapter 1.

2. Chapter 2.
   "The Economics of Incentives, An Introductory Essay" by H. Sonnenschein

3. Chapter 3.
   "Social Responsibility and Economic Efficiency" by Kenneth Arrow
   Excerpts from <u>Capitalism and Freedom</u> by Milton Friedman (optional)*

4. Chapter 4.
   "The Lobbyists" by Tema Frank
   "Inside the Industrial Policy Garbage Can: Selective Subsidies to Business in Canada" by M. Atkinson and R. Powers
   "Thinking Strategically About Adoption and Implementation" from <u>Policy Analysis</u> by D. Weimar and A. Vining
   "Problems of Public Choice" by E.S. Phelps (optional)*

5. Chapter 5.

6. Chapter 6.

7. Chapters 7 and 8.
   "Is Free Trade Passe?" by Paul Krugman

8. Chapters 9 and 10.

9. Chapters 11 and 12.
   "Positive Steps in Transport Deregulation -- The Prairies" by D. Dawson and L. Parent
   "I would do it again" by Alfred E. Kahn

10. Chapter 13.
    "Mixed Enterprise in Canada" by E.C. Elford and W.T. Stanbury (optional)*

11. Chapter 14.
    "Risk Analysis and Relevance of Uncertainties in Nuclear Safety Decisions" by M. Pate-Cornell

12. Chapter 15.

13. Chapter 16.

STATE UNIVERSITY OF NEW YORK AT BUFFALO
School of Management

Spring 1989
MGT 403-Legal Environment
 of Management 1.S2T
Tu., Th., 2:00-3:20 PM

Prof. R. Chatov
248 Jacobs Center
Office hours:
Th., 3:30-4:30 PM

This course provides an introduction to basic legal principles governing business. We begin with a brief introduction to the history of the legal system and the nature of legal reasoning applied to management issues. This material serves as background to the examination of two fundamental areas of substantive law: torts and contracts. We then analyze the role of these topics in fields of law important to contemporary business practice: products liability and the organization and operation of the business enterprise, including partnerships and corporations. A final major component of the course focusses on the role of government in regulating business conduct and management decision-making. In this section we explore the issues of securities regulation, antitrust law, administrative process, and selected topics in international business transactions.

The text for the course is Roszkowski, __Business Law: principles, cases, and policy__. Little-Brown, 2nd Edition.

Student participation is important in learning the course material and preparing for examinations. If you can't attend classes, don't take this section. For each class be prepared to discuss the application of concepts to the questions and case problems at the end of the assigned chapters.

Week	Topic	Chapter Assignments:
1	The nature of the legal system	1, 2
2	Introduction to Contracts	7, 8
3	Contracts: consideration, capacity, and legality	9, 10
4	Contracts: assent	11
5	Contracts: form and third	12, 13
6	Contracts: performance and	14, 15
7	Torts and products liability	Mid Term 5, 20
8	Business Organizations: agency	40, 41
9	Business Organizations: partnerships	42, 43, 44

Week	Topic	Chapter Assignments:
10	Business Organizations: corporations	45, 46
11	Business Organizations: corporations (cont.)	47, 48
12	Government Regulation: antitrust	50, 51, 52
13	Government Regulation: securities	49
14	Government Regulation: environmental law and international trade	54, 57
15	Review	
May 15-19		Final Exam

Grading will be based on the following schedule:

```
            Points
Final        40
Mid Term     30
Quizzes      30
            ___
            100
```

plus extra points for in-class discussion of cases at the end of the chapters.

MGT 403 - Legal Environment of Management

Suggestions on Learning the Subject Matter in the Course

1. The text used is sophisticated and appropriate for serious seniors in a high quality management program; it requires close study but will reward you with considerable insights and knowledge about the law and the legal process in important business related areas.

2. The key to learning the material is in careful reading of the text, identifying the major principles of the law, and applying those principles to concrete situations, most importantly, to the problems at the end of each chapter. Attending classes without being prepared will result, at best, in a fragmentary--hence misleading--understanding of the material, since the class time mostly is devoted to legal analysis of problems, rather than to comprehensive lectures on the subjects.

3. Make note of areas of the text you find confusing, and ask for clarification in class.

4. Engage in class discussion because it will hone your ability to analyze problems.

5. Make brief notes or an outline of the major legal rules as you go through the text, being careful to record exceptions to those rules. Try to give summary statements of those rules in your own words to test your comprehension.

6. Think of specific situations in which the legal principles can be applied; it is good preparation for examinations to create and then answer legal problems you invent.

7. Spend some time discussing the material with other students; some people find it very helpful to form regular study groups.

8. If the applicable laws or solutions for the chapter problems are not clear to you after class discussion, ask for clarification at that time.

9. Try to identify the common legal themes running through the different subject matter areas.

10. Write out the analysis of the chapter problems prior to class; don't trust your memory to retain the information.

MGT 403 Legal Environment of Management

Suggestion On Analyzing the Problems at the End of the Chapters

1. Be able to summarize the essentials of the case problem in very few words.

2. Identify the area of law relevant to the case, and state the main legal principle involved. Note any exceptions to the main principle.

3. Relate the relevant facts to the legal principle and identify the rights of the parties.

4. Decide who will prevail in the case and why.

STATE UNIVERSITY OF NEW YORK AT BUFFALO   Dr. Chatov
SCHOOL OF MANAGEMENT   Fall 1989

MGT 695 - SEMINAR:
THE MODERN CORPORATION AND THE COMING OF MANAGERIAL CAPITALISM

Tu Th   11:00-12:20   379 Jacobs Center

The seminar focuses on business' strategic adaptation to changing economic and business conditions and opportunities in the United States. We use cases developed at the Harvard Graduate Business School by Chandler and Tedlow. The cases follow an historical sequence. The development of managerial technique thereby is related to the maturation of the national and global economies.

The transition from individual entrepreneurship to hired managers, with its attendant diffusion of economic power, has been one of the most profound changes in business activity. By examining particular cases we observe how this change occurred and how hierarchical managerial structures became employed in modern corporations. Business adaptability to new opportunities and abandonment of unprofitable activities is another theme. The relation of enterprise with government and business ideology with business practice is examined relative to regulation and antitrust. Multinational business and mergers are the seminar's final topics.

Requirements:

Because the seminar focuses on discussion and analysis of the cases, all participants have to be familiar with the assigned readings. Questions on the cases will be distributed in advance. A one page response to a question on the day's case is required; presentation of cases will be assigned; a term paper is the major basis for the course grade.

Readings:

Chandler, Alfred D., Jr. and Richard S. Tedlow, *The Coming of Managerial Capitalism*, R.D. Irwin, 1985.

Office Hours:

Tu Th: 10:00-11:00 am; 6:00-7:00 pm
Phone: 636-3226
Secretary: Mrs. Fairbanks in Rm. 234, phone 636-3293

The course outline is attached.

MGT 695, Fall 1989

OUTLINE

PART ONE
The Agrarian, Commercial Economy

Date	Day	Case Assignment
8/29	Tu	Introduction
8/31	Th	1. Benjamin Franklin and the Definition of American Values
9/5	Tu	2. Establishing the Political Base

Forging a National Economy

Date	Day	Case Assignment
9/7	Th	3. John Jacob Astor, 1736-1848
9/12	Tu	4. The Rise of New York Port
9/14	Th	5. The Second Bank of the U.S.
9/19	Tu	6. Samuel Slater, Francis Cabot Lowell, and the Beginnings of the Factory System in the U.S.

PART TWO
Economic Revolution

The Revolution in Transportation and Communication

Date	Day	Case Assignment
9/21	Th	7. The Coming of the Railroads
9/26	Tu	8. The Railroads and the Beginnings of Modern Management
9/28	Th	9. Jay Gould and the Coming of Railroad Consolidation
10/3	Tu	10. J.P. Morgan, 1837-1913
10/5	Th	11. The Railroad Problem and the Solution

The Revolution in Distribution and Production

Date	Day	Case Assignment
10/12	Th	12. Nineteenth Century Retailing and the Rise of the Department Store
10/17	Tu	13. The Integration of Mass Production and Mass Distribution
10/19	Th	14. The Standard Oil Co.--Combination, Consolidation, and Integration
10/24	Tu	15. DuPont: The Centralized Structure

| 10/26 | Th | 16. | The Emergence of Managerial Capitalism |

New Relations of Management and the Work Force

10/31	Tu	17.	Patterns of Work in Nineteenth Century America
11/2	Th	18.	Mass Production and the Beginnings of Scientific Management
11/7	Tu	19.	Organized Labor and the Worker
11/9	Th	20.	From lean years to Fat years: The Labor Movement Between the Wars

PART THREE
Twentieth Century Developments

11/14	Tu	21.	The Antitrust Movement: Symbolic Politics and Industrial Organization Economics
11/16	Th	22.	The Great Depression: Causes and Impact
"	"	23.	The Federal Government and Employment
11/21	Tu	24.	The Federal Trade Commission and the Shared Monopoly Case Against the Ready-to-Eat Cereal Manufacturers

Business Management in the Modern Era

11/28	Tu	25.	The Multidivisional Enterprise
11/30	Th	26.	The Multinational Enterprise
12/5	Tu	27.	The Conglomerates and the Merger Movement of the 1960s; Takeovers & Mergers in the '80s: Reading TBA
12/7	Th	28.	General Electric: Strategic Position, 1981

A Look Ahead

| 12/12 | Tu | 29. | The Challenge Ahead: Economic Growth, Global Interdependence, and the New Competition |

State University of New York at Buffalo
School of Management

Dr. Chatov
Fall 1989

MGT 615 GM1

Government and the Firm

Tu 7:00-9:40 p.m., Jacobs 112, 8/29-10/24
(10/24 class will run 7:00-8:20 p.m.)

Course Description:

This course is a half semester survey of some important interactions between government and private enterprise. Participants in the course will become more aware of the activities of firms as they impact on society, and should integrate these materials with those in their technical courses. The topics will include corporate autonomy and legality, takeovers and mergers, financial liability of firms for faulty products, antitrust, securities and environmental regulation, business ethics and crime, and accountants' liability to third parties.

Requirements:

Participants are expected to be able to discuss the assignments relative to the current business situation. Everyone ought to be acquainted with current topics as reported in The Wall Street Journal and based on the lectures, readings and current policy issues of importance to business-government relations.

Course Materials:

Course materials consist of a reading packet and two texts:

1. Levi, Edward H., An Introduction to Legal Reasoning, U. of Chicago Press, 1949 (Paperback).
2. Buchholz, Rogene A., Public Policy Issues for Management, Prentice Hall, 1988 (Paperback).
3. Packets available at Kinkos.

Office Hours:

Tu 10:00-11:00 a.m.; 6:00-7:00 p.m., and by appointment.
Room - 248 Jacobs
Phone - 636-3226
Secretary - Mrs. Fairbanks, Rm. 234 Jacobs; phone 636-3293.

MGT 615 COURSE OUTLINE

Date	Subject	Readings:	B=Buchholz L=Levi P=Packet
8/29	Introduction		
8/29	Public Policy & Regulation	B 1,2	
9/5	The Law & Product Liability	L pp.1-27 (Robins Case; Law Cases)	
9/12	" " " " (cont'd)	" "	
9/12	Antitrust	B 3	
9/19	Antitrust (cont'd)	B 3	
9/26	Corporate Governance	B 4	
9/26	The Securities Acts	P (Securities Act Case; Auditors' Liability)	
10/3	Business Crimes & Ethics	P	
10/3	Consumer Protection	B 8	
10/17	Pollution Control	B 9	
10/17	International Business	B 10	
10/24	EXAM		

UNIVERSITY OF CALIFORNIA
School of Business Administration

Course Information and Outline
Spring Semester, 1989

B.A. 170 - Social and Political Environment of Business
Mr. Cheit
654 Barrows Hall
642-2448

Office Hours: Wednesday 3-4; Friday 11-12 and by appointment

    B.A. 170 meets each week as a group from 12-2 in Room 1 LeConte for two hours of lecture, and in eight sections for one hour of discussion led by a section instructor.

    The four section instructors are:

        Dana Donohoe
        Office: 18 Barrows Hall
        Office hours: To be arranged in section meeting

        Kenneth Koput
        Office: 18 Barrows Hall
        Office hours: Wednesday 12-2 and by appointment

        Barbara Lombardo
        Office: 581 Barrows Hall
        Office hours: Monday 9-11

        Joanne Oxley
        Office: 18 Barrows Hall
        Office hours: To be arranged in section meeting

    The lectures will follow the topics in this course outline. The discussion sections examine issues raised in the lectures and will be shaped by your participation based on your reading.

    Reading assignments are from these books (all available in soft cover) and a reading packet (available at CopyMat):

    Robertson, James Oliver, *America's Business*

    Porter, Glenn, *The Rise of Big Business*, 1860-1910

    Reagan, Michael, *Regulation: The Politics of Policy*

    Commons, Dorman, *Tender Offer: The Sneak Attack in Corporate Takeovers*

    Berry, J.M., *The Interest Group Society*, Little Brown & Co.

    Abegglen, James C. and Stalk, George, *Kaisha: The Japanese Corporation*

    As explained below, you will be expected to read the business press.

BA 170
Mr. Cheit

- 2 -

Course Outline
Spring Semester, 1989

COURSE REQUIREMENTS

BA 170 has five requirements. All must be met to complete the course.

(1) Midterm.

(2) Final examination.

(3) Participation in sections.

(4) Two short essays (5-7 pages) whose characteristics will be described in your section meetings. The first is due on March 10. Its subject will be regulation or deregulation. The second, due before April 28, will be on corporate governance or interest groups.

(5) A journal based on your regular reading of the business press. On three occasions you will be handing in your journal for reading by your section instructor. What do I mean by the business press? Choose either (1) a daily business paper (the <u>Wall Street Journal</u> or the <u>Financial Times</u>); or (2) the business and financial section of a major daily paper; or (3) a substantial weekly business publication (<u>Business Week</u>, <u>The Economist</u>, or <u>The Far Eastern Economic Review</u>).

From your reading, you should at least once a week make an entry in your journal of one to three pages on the following schedule and topics.

Weeks 1-3	Attitudes toward and about business; views of business leaders; political reform directed at business; the American business system; capitalism in contemporary society.
Weeks 4-6	Regulation (social, economic) and deregulation.
Weeks 7-10	Corporate ownership and control; takeovers; ethics; corporate social responsibility; business political activity.
Weeks 11-15	Competitiveness; trade policy; America's role in the global economy.

How should you start? Read carefully with the knowledge that you will have plenty of latitude within these categories to choose your own issues. Read critically. News is sparse from time to time. Some news stories raise several issues. Be confident. Your skills will improve with practice.

BA 170
Mr. Cheit

Course Outline
Spring Semester, 1989

What should guide your journal entries? Use this approach:

- Identify the source or sources of a story you want to follow (print must be your primary source; radio or TV business news programs can be used only as secondary sources).
- Summarize the point or issue of the story. Note conflicting sides or viewpoints involved and their corresponding interests.
- Describe the relevance to the material being developed in our course. Does the course help to explain the issue or put it into perspective? If not, what should the course be doing?
- State your views about the matters involved. This is an important part of the work. As in all matters of opinion in the course, I am interested in a cogent statement of your views, and not whether you agree or disagree with the instructors.
- Bonus: Compare and contrast coverage of the story in two or more places (e.g., <u>Wall Street Journal</u> vs. Nightly Business Report on PBS).

In determining your grade for the course, the five requirements will be weighted as follows:

Midterm	15%
Final (exam group 9)	30%
Class participation	15%
Two Essays	20%
Journal	20%

BA 170
Mr. Cheit

LECTURE TOPICS AND READING ASSIGNMENTS

1/27   <u>Business in America: The Market System and the Corporation</u>

Robertson, *America's Business*, pp. 3-119.

Reading Packet, "Business and Government: the Origins of the Adversary Relationship."

2/3   <u>The Rise of Big Business</u>

Porter, *The Rise of Big Business*, pp. 1-101.

Robertson, *America's Business*, pp. 120-187.

2/10   <u>The Age of Reform</u>

Robertson, *America's Business*, pp. 188-254

1/17   <u>Economic Regulation</u>

Reagan, *Regulation: The Politics of Policy*, pp. 1-71.

2/24   <u>Social Regulation</u>

Reagan, *Regulation: The Politics of Policy*, pp. 85-111.

3/3   <u>Deregulation: The New Age of Reform</u>

Reagan, *Regulation: The Politics of Policy*, pp. 72-82, 154-219.

Reading Packet, "Deregulation is Another Consumer Fraud;" and "Consumers Aren't All Angels Either."

3/10   <u>Corporate Ownership and Control</u>

Commons, *Tender Offer: The Sneak Attack in Corporate Takeovers*, pp. ix-141.

Reading Packet, "The Market for Corporate Control;" "Takeovers and Stockholders: Winners and Losers."

3/17   Mid-term Examination.

BA 170　　　　　　　　　　　- 5 -　　　　　　　　　　　Course Outline
Mr. Cheit　　　　　　　　　　　　　　　　　　　　　Spring Semester, 1989

3/24　　　Spring Recess.

3/31　　　Corporate Governance

4/7　　　Social Responsibility and Ethics

　　　　　Reading Packet, "The Social Responsibility is to Increase its
　　　　　Profits;" "How Ford Put Two Million Firetraps on Wheels;"
　　　　　"Free Gifts;" and "Economic Justice for All."

4/14　　　Corporate Public Affairs and Political Activity

　　　　　Berry, The Interest Group Society, pp. 1-220.

4/21　　　Business and the Popular Culture

　　　　　Reading Packet, "The Image of Business on Prime-time
　　　　　Television;" "Press Proves an Unlikely Conservative."

4/28　　　American Business in the Global Economy

　　　　　Reading Packet, "World Shares;" "American Industry in
　　　　　International Competition: Government Policies and Corporate
　　　　　Strategies."

　　　　　Abegglen, Kaisha: The Japanese Corporation, pp. 3-180.

5/5　　　Who is Number 1? Does It Matter?

　　　　　Reading Packet, "U.S.-Japan Trade Friction: Creating a New
　　　　　Relationship."

　　　　　Abegglen, Kaisha: The Japanese Corporation, pp. 181-288.

5/12　　　Will America Compete?

　　　　　Reading Packet, "The Industrial Policy Debate Re-examined;"
　　　　　"Lessons from the Chrysler Bailout."

EFC:sl(C1)
24

UNIVERSITY OF CALIFORNIA
Walter A. Haas School of Business

Course Announcement

B.A. 279F Pro-Seminar

BUSINESS ETHICS AND THE CORPORATE SOCIAL POLICY PROCESS

Professor Edwin M. Epstein

This pro-seminar will examine the "classical" and contemporary scholarly literature arising from efforts to develop analytically useful conceptual categories both to evaluate the social performance of business organizations and those who run them and to assist corporate leadership in what has been termed the "management of values"--i.e., the incorporation of value considerations within ongoing organizational decision-making processes. Students will be exposed to three streams of literature of which have evolved over the years around the concepts of "business ethics," "corporate social responsibility," and "corporate social responsiveness" as well as burgeoning current scholarship relating to synthetic concepts such as the "corporate social policy process" which provide potentially useful integrative analytical frameworks for clarifying and augmenting the older conceptual categories. Particular attention will be paid to recent empirical research relating to corporate social performance and "business ethics" at both the individual and organizational levels, thereby familiarizing students with the problems and potential of such research.

Students will write a seminar paper on a pertinent theme. There is no final examination. Although intended primarily for doctoral students in Business Administration, the seminar is appropriate for MBAs and graduate students in other disciplines who are interested in ethical and social performance analysis, particularly in an organizational context.

Literature will be drawn from such works as:

Books:

Hoard R. Bowen, Social Responsibility of the Businessman (Harper and Row)

Raymond Baumhart, S.J., Ethics in Business (Holt)

Clarence C. Walton (ed.), The Ethics of Corporate Conduct (Prentice-Hall)

_____, Corporate Social Responsibility (Wadsworth)

Robert A. Miles, Managing the Corporate Social Environment: A Grounded Theory (Prentice-Hall)

Robert Ackerman, The Social Challenge to Business (Harvard)

Robert Ackerman and Raymond Bauer, Corporate Social Responsiveness: The Modern Dilemma (Reston)

Charles S. McCoy, Management of Value: The Ethical Differences in Corporate Policy and Performance (Pitman)

Christopher Stone, Where the Law Ends (Harper and Row)

Thomas Donaldson, Corporate Morality (Prentice-Hall)

Benjamin Morris Selekman, A Moral Philosophy for Management (McGraw-Hill)

Thomas Donaldson and Patricia H. Werhane (eds.), Ethical Issues in Business: A Philosophical Approach (2nd ed. - Prentice-Hall)

Manuel G. Valesquez, Business Ethics: Concepts and Cases (Prentice-Hall)

Barbara L. Toffler, Tough Choices: Managers Talk Ethics (Wiley)

Dow Votaw and S. Prakash Sethi, The Corporation Dilemma: Traditional Values versus Contemporary Problems (Prentice-Hall)

Peter S. French, Collective and Corporate Responsibility (Columbia)

Kenneth E. Boulding, Organizational Revolution: A Study in the Ethics of Economic Organization (Harper and Row)

Lee E. Preston and James E. Post, Private Management and Public Policy: The Principle of Public Responsibility (Prentice-Hall)

R. Edward Freeman, Strategic Management: A Stakeholder Approach (Pitman)

Morrell Heald, The Social Responsibilities of Business: Company and Community, (Case-Western)

William A. Evans, Management Ethics: An Intercultural Perspective (Martinus Nyhoff)

Kenneth J. Arrow, The Limits of Organization (Norton)

Charles W. Powers and David Vogel, Ethics in the Education of Business Managers (Hastings Center)

Lee E. Preston (ed.), Research in Corporate Social Performance and Policy, Vols. 1-8 (JAI)

Milton Friedman, Capitalism and Freedom (Chicago)

Articles

Kenneth E. Goodpaster and John B. Matthews, "Can a Corporation Have a Conscience?", HBR (January-February, 1982), pp. 132-141

Steven L. Wartick and Philip L. Cochran, "The Evolution of the Corporate Social Performance Model," Academy of Management Review, (AMR), V. 10, No. 4 (October 1985), pp. 753-769

Archie B. Carroll, "A Three-Dimensional Conceptual Model of Corporate Social Performance," AMR, V. 4 (1979), pp. 497-506

Peter Drucker, "What Are Business Ethics?" The Public Interest, No. 64 (1981), pp. 18-36

Edwin M. Epstein, "Societal, Managerial and Legal Perspectives on Corporate Responsibility, Hasting Law Journal, V. 30 (1979) pp. 1287-1320

Thomas M. Jones, "An Integrating Framework for Research in Business and Society: A Step toward the Elusive Paradigm?" AMR, (1983), pp. 559-564

Lee E. Preston, "Corporation and Society: the Search for a Paradigm," J. Econ. Lit., V. 13 (1975), pp. 434-453

S. Prakash Sethi, "A Conceptual Framework for Environmental Analyses of Social Issues and Evolution of Business Response Patterns," AMR, V. 4, (1979) pp. 63-74

Memholf Dierkes and Ariane Berthoin Antal, "Wither Corporate Social Reporting: Is It Time to Legislate?" CMR, V. 28 (1986), pp. 106-121

Lee Burke et al "Corporate Community Involvement in the San Francisco Bay Area," CMR, V. 28 (1986), pp. 196-121

Liam Fahey and Richard E. Wolkutch, "Business and Society Exchanges: A Framework for Analyses," CMR, V. 25 (1983), pp. 128-142

Charles Q. Greer and H. Kirk Downey, "Industrial Compliance with Social Legislation: Investigations of Pension Rationales," AMR, V. 7 (1982), pp. 488-492

Peter Arlow and Martin J. Gannon, "Social Responsiveness, Corporate Structure and Economic Performance," AMR (1982), V. 27, pp. 235-241

Barry Z. Posner and Warren H. Schmidt, "Values and the American Manager: An Update," CMR, V. 26, No. 3 (1984), pp. 202-216

Susan B. Foote, "Corporate Responsibility in a Changing Legal Environment," CMR, V. 26 (1984), pp. 212-228

Steven N. Brenner and Earl Molander, "Is the Ethics of Business Changing?" HBR, V. 55 (1977), pp. 57-71

Working Papers

Kenneth E. Goodpaster, "The Moral Agenda of Corporate Leadership: Concepts and Research Techniques," (HBS, 1986)

Edwin M. Epstein, "Beyond Business Ethics, Corporate Social Responsibility, and Corporate Social Responsiveness: An Introduction to the Corporate Social Policy Process," (BBS- CRM, BPP-17, 1986)

Jeffrey Pfeffer, "Bringing the Environment Back In: The Social Context of Business Strategy" (SBS, 1985)

LaRue T. Hosmer, "The Institutionalization of Unethical Behavior" (Univ. of Michigan BS, 1984)

William C. Frederick, "Toward CSR_3: The Normative Factor in Corporate Social Analysis" (SBA, Univ. of Pittsburgh, 1985)

_____, "From CSR_1 to CSR_2: The Maturing of Business and Society Thought" (SBA, Univ. of Pittsburgh, 1978)

University of Pennsylvania
The Wharton School
Fall 1988

BA 879

Management in the Regulatory Environment

Vance B5 M - W, 3:00 - 4:30 PM

Professor Faulhaber
3020 SH-DH
898-5544
Office Hours: Wed 1:30 - 3:00 PM and by appointment

Required readings for the course are:

1. *Business, Government, and the Public*, Murray Weidenbaum, Prentice-Hall, 3rd edition, 1986

2. *The Politics of Regulation*, James Q. Wilson, ed., Basic Books, Inc. 1980

3. *Regulation and Its Reform*, Stephen Breyer, Harvard University Press, 1982

4. *Telecommunications in Turmoil*, Gerald R. Faulhaber, Ballinger Press, 1987.

5. *The Political Economy of Deregulation: Interest Groups in the Regulatory Process*, Roger Noll and Bruce Owen, American Enterprise Institute, 1983.

A bulk pack of selected readings, available from Kinko's. The length of the article is noted in ().

Case: Commonwealth Edison. Harvard Case #9-384-190, 1984
Case: Allied Chemical. Harvard Case #379-137, 1979

Society and Regulation

    Weidenbaum, Ch. 1
    Wilson, Ch. 10
    Breyer, Ch. 1
    Stigler, "The Economists' Traditional... Functions of the
       State"(22)

Reich, "Warring Critiques of Regulation"(6)
Baumol, "Contestable Markets, Antitrust, and Regulation"(7)
Navarro, "Rent Control In Cambridge, Mass"(18)
Wolf, "A Theory of Nonmarket Failure: Framework for
   Implementation Analysis," (33)

Management and Regulation

   Weidenbaum, Ch. 16, 17, 18, 19

Regulation of Electric Power

   Wilson, Ch. 1
   Breyer, Ch. 2, 3
   Norton, "Regulation and Systematic Risk: The Case of
      Electric Utilities," (16)
   Joskow and Schmalensee, "Incentive Regulation for Electric
      Utilities," (51)
   Case: Commonwealth Edison

Regulation of the Drug Industry

   Wilson, Ch. 6
   Breyer, Ch 7
   Merrill, "FDA's Implementation of the Delaney Clause:
      Repudiation of Congressional Choice or Reasoned
      Adaptation to Scientific Progress?" (89)
   "Mismanaging Drug Research," *Economist* (1)
   "The U.S. Regulatory Patchwork," *Bio/Technology* (11)

Regulating the Macroeconomy

   Weidenbaum, Ch. 11, 12, 15

Regulation of Environmental Quality

   Weidenbaum, Ch. 5
   Wilson, Ch. 8
   Breyer, Ch. 14
   Noll and Owen, Ch. 5
   Bartel and Thomas, "Direct and Indirect Effects of
      Regulation: A New Look at OSHA's Impact," (26)

Bartel and Thomas, "Predation by Regulation: The Wage and Profit Effects of Occupational Safety and Health Administration and the Environmental Protection Agency," (26)

Case: Allied Chemical

Regulation and Deregulation I

Weidenbaum, Ch. 9, 10
Breyer, Ch. 16, 17
Noll and Owen, Ch. 2, 3
"A Comparison of Taxes, Regulation, and Liability Rules under Imperfect Information," (14)

Regulation and Deregulation II - Banking

Litan, "Evaluating and Controlling Risks of Financial Product Deregulation," (53)

DeMuth, "The Case Against Credit Card Interest Rate Regulation," (42)

Int'l Herald Tribune, "In London's Financial District, the Ax Begins to Fall," (2)

Regulation and Deregulation III - Airlines

Wilson, Ch. 3
Breyer, Ch. 11
Noll and Owen, Ch. 8
Wall Street Journal, "Airline Chaos: Looking for Solutions," (8)
Morrison and Winston, "Empirical Implications and Tests of the Contestability Hypothesis," (14)
Levine, "Airline Competition in Degegulated Markets: Theory, Firm Strategy, and Public Policy," (102)

Regulation and Deregulation IV - Telecommunications

Faulhaber, entire book.
Johnson, "Why Local Rates are Rising"(8)
Cornell, Pelcovits, and Brenner, "A Legacy of Regulatory Failure"(6)

Katz and Willig, "The Case for Freeing AT&T"(7)
Letters (on above three articles)(3)
Drucker, "Beyond the Bell Breakup" (25)
Noll, "'Let Them Make Toll Calls': A State Regulator's Lament"(5)
Perl, "Social Welfare and Distributional Consequences of Cost-Based Telephone Pricing"(25)

THE UNIVERSITY OF BRITISH COLUMBIA
FACULTY OF COMMERCE AND BUSINESS ADMINISTRATION
Winter Session 1989
Commerce 394   Sections 14 and 19

Instructor: Murray Frank

Office: H.A. 258

This course analyzes government policy to influence business. The behavior of business to affect policy decisions will also be considered. In order to evaluate future policy proposals it is helpful to be aware of the strengths and limitations of past policies. Both normative theory and descriptive (positive) analysis will be covered.

There has been a tremendous amount written concerning these matters. The readings package contains most of the material that will be used to complement the textbook. The readings differ both in length and in difficulty. In class guidance will be given concerning which should be read more carefully. Since there is roughly one article to be read per lecture it is important not to fall behind!!

Marks:

Midterm (February 14, 1989)	30%
Essay proposal (January 31, 1989)	5%
Essay (last class)	25%
Final Exam	40%
	100%

Required Texts:

Brander, J.A. (1988) <u>Government Policy Toward Business</u> Butterworths, Toronto. (denoted below as Brander)
Package of readings (denoted R below).

Tentative Reading List

1. Overview and Objectives
    Brander, chapter 1

2. Useful Economic Concepts
    Brander, chapter 2

    Sonnenschein, H. (1982) "The economics of incentives, an introductory account," R.

3. Normative analysis of Government
    Brander, chapter 3

    Arrow, K. (1973) "Social responsibility and economic efficiency," R.

    Friedman, M (1962) <u>Freedom and Capitalism</u>, excerpts, R.

Reich, R.B. (1982) "Why the U.S. needs an industrial policy," R.

Schelling, T. (1981) "Economic reasoning and the ethics of policy," R.

Watson, W.G. (1984) "It's still not time for an industrial strategy," R.

4. Positive Theory of Government
    Brander, chapter 4.

    Atkinson, M.M. and R.A. Powers (1987) "Inside the industrial policy garbage can: selective subsidies to business in Canada," R.

    Epstein, R. (1988) "The political economy of product liability reform," R.

    Frank, T. (1988) "The lobbyists," R.

    Phelps, E. (1985) "Problems of public choice," R.

    Weimer, D. and A. Vining (1989) "Thinking strategically about adoption and implementation," R.

5. Firms and Markets
    Brander, chapter 5.

6. Canadian Business Environment
    Brander, chapter 6.

    "Canada Survey" (October 8, 1988), R.

7. International Trade Policy
    Brander, chapters 7,8.

    Brander, J. (1986) "Rationales for strategic trade and industrial policy," R.

    Krugman, P. (1987) "Is free trade passé?" R.

    Smith, A. (1776) "On restraints upon the importation from foreign countries of such goods as can be produced at home," R.

8. Competition Policy
    Brander, chapter 9.

9. Anticompetitive Practices
    Brander, chapter 10

10. Theory of Price and Entry Regulation
    Brander, chapter 11

    Dawson, D.A. and L.P. Parent (1987) "Positive steps in transport deregulation - the prairies," R.

11. Regulation and Deregulation
    Brander, chapter 12

    Bailey, E. (1986) "Deregulation: causes and consequences," R.

    Kahn, A.E. (1988) "I would do it again," R.

    Sappington, D. and J. Stiglitz (1987) "Information and regulation," R.

12. Crown Corporations and Public Enterprise
    Brander, chapter 13

    Elford, E. and W.T. Stanbury (1986) "Mixed enterprises in Canada," R.

    Ledyard, J.O. (1986) "Incentive compatible space station pricing," R.

13. Externalities, Environmental Regulation, and Public Goods
    Brander, chapter 14

    Arrow, K. (1984) "Environmental preservation, uncertainty and irreversibility," R.

    D'Arge, R., W. Schulze and D. Brookshire (1982) "Carbon dioxide and intergenerational choice," R.

    Mitchell, R. and R. Carson (1986) "Property rights, protest, and the siting of hazardous waste facilities," R.

    Paté-Cornell, M.E. (1987) "Risk analysis and relevance of uncertainties in nuclear safety decision," R.

14. Stabilization Policy, Unemployment and the Public Debt
    Brander, chapter 15

    Lucas, R. (1976) "A review: Paul McCracken et. al. Towards full employment and price stability," R.

    Peterson, P. (1988) "The morning after," R.

15. Fairness, Ethics and Public Policy
    Brander, chapter 16

    Phelps, E. (1985) "Ideas of fairness," R.

CARNEGIE MELLON UNIVERSITY

GRADUATE SCHOOL OF INDUSTRIAL ADMINISTRATION

PROF. THOMAS M. KERR
Spring 1990 - 3rd Mini

45-740 - MANAGERIAL ENVIRONMENT I
"Crime in the Suites and Capitalist Punishment"

"A merchant shall hardly keep himself from doing wrong; and a huckster shall not be freed from sin...As a nail sticketh fast between the joinings of the stones, so doth sin stick close between buying and selling.

--Book of Ecclestiasticus, one of the
Later Books of Wisdom in the Apocrypha

COURSE OUTLINE

The external political, social and legal environment of the firm and its managers. Historical development as well as current and future economic and social implications will be analyzed. Problems dealing with legal and regulatory matters will be considered, including restrictive trade practices laws and regulations, acquisitions and mergers, licensing, officers' and directors' responsibilites and liabilities, manufacturers' responsibilites and liabilities, product liability, securities regulation, environmental protection, intellectual property, contracts, business associations; values in a business society; social implications of business policies, and corporate social responsibility. Particular consideration will be given to the role managers play in relations to governments.

REQUIRED TEXT:

Bill Shaw, Art Wolfe, *The Structure of the Legal Environment Law, Ethics and Business,* Kent Pub. Co., 1987.

COURSE REQUIREMENTS

A book report based upon a book included in a list of elective readings, which will be furnished, will be required. There will also be a Mid-Semester and a Final Written Examination.

Professor Thomas M. Kerr   Spring 1990

                        45-740 - ASSIGNMENTS

JAN 18, 1990   Shaw et al., text
                                pp. 34-48
                                pp. 85-91
                                pp. 106-120

JAN 23   PP. 210-237 - Corporate Governance

JAN 25   Shaw, et al., text
                                Chap 8, and
                                Chap 9

JAN 30   Text, Chs. 11-12

FEB 1   Ch. 13

FEB 6   Ch. 14

FEB 8   Ch. 15

FEB 13   Ch. 16, - Mid-Semester Written
                                      Examination, 1 hour

FEB 15   Ch. 17

FEB 20   Ch. 18

FEB 22   Ch. 19

FEB 27   Ch. 20

MAR 1   Chs. 21-23

MAR 6   Chs. 24-26

MY OFFICE HOURS:

Monday, Wednesday and Friday
    10:00 AM to 12:00 NOON

Tuesday, and Thursday, before and after evening class
    ROOM 204

ELECTIVE READINGS

45-740 - MANAGERIAL ENVIRONMENT I   70-332 - GOVERNMENT & BUSINESS

PROFESSOR THOMAS M. KERR

FALL 1989

	Abegglen, James C.; George Stalk, Jr., Kaisha: The Japanese Corporation. Basic Books. 1985.
338.644 A21b	Adams, Walter; James Brock, The Bigness Complex: Industry, Labor and Government in the American Economy, Pantheon. 1987.
917.61	Agee, James, Let Us Now Praise Famous Men. Houghton-Mifflin. 1960.
	Alger, Horatio, Brave and Bold, or The Fortunes of a Factory Boy, Aeonian Press, 1976.
	Alger, Horatio, Mark Manning's Mission, or The Story of A Shoe Factory Boy. Aeonian Press. 1976.
SPEC/FB A3946 c.1	Alger, Horatio, Jr., Bound To Rise or Up the Ladder. Hurst & Co. (Pref. 1873).
	Alger, Horatio, Jr., Struggling Upward: or, Luke Larkin's Luck. Coates. 1890.
973.91 A426	Allen, Frederick Lewis, The Big Change. Harper. 1952.
92 M8482	*Allen, Frederick Lewis, The Great Pierpont Morgan. Harper Row. 1949.
338.973 A45r	Alperovitz, Gar and Jeff Faux, Rebuilding America: A Blueprint for the New Economy. Pantheon. 1984.
	American Bar Association, Public Education Division. Law in the Workplace. You and the Law Series. American Bar Association. 1987.
A546h	Anderson, Edward. Hungry Men. Penguin Books. 1985.
92 R192a	*Anderson, Jervis, Who Killed Jim Crow: A Philip Randolph: A Biographical Portrait. Harcourt, Brace, Jovanovich. 1973.

Biographies and autobiographies are marked with an asterisk. Acquaintance with the experiences and decisions of others before us sometimes contributes to our using better judgment ourselves.

659.1125 A72t	Arlen, Michael J., *Thirty Seconds*. Farrar, Straus, & Giroux, 1980.
331.880973 A76w	Aronowitz, Stanley, *Working Class Hero*: A New Strategy for Labor. Pilgrim Press. 1984.
61.6 A 65	Arrow, Kenneth, et al., ed., *Applied Research for Social Policy*: The United States and the Federal Republic of West Germany Compared. ABT Assoc. 1979.
302.35 A77L	Arrow, Kenneth J., *The Limits of Organization*. W.W. Norton and Company. 1974. (paper).
	*Attali, Jacques, *A Man of Influence*. The Extraordinary Career of S.C. Warburg. Addler & Addler. 1987.
A898.HO	Auchincloss, Louis. *Honorable Men*. Houghton-Mifflin Co. 1985.
A898e	Auchinloss, Louis, *The Embezzler*. Houghton-Mifflin. 1966.
332.66 A92g	Auletta, Ken. *Greed and Glory on Wall Street*: The Fall of the House of Lehman. Random House, 1985.
	Auletta, Ken. *The Art of Corporate Success*: The Story of Schlumberger. G.P. Putman & Sons. 1984.
335.0973 A96h	Avrich, Paul. *The Haymarket Tragedy*. Anarchists and Trade Unionists in 19th-Century America. Princeton. 1984.
361.7 B16c	Bakal, Carl. *Charity USA*: An Investigation Into the Hidden World of the Multi-Billion Dollar Charity Industry. Times Books, 1979.
338.8 B215e	Bane, Charles A., *The Electrical Equipment Conspiracies: The Treble Damage Action*, Federal Legal Pub., Inc. Aberdeen Press.1973.
381.45 B25m	Barmash, Isadore, *More Than They Bargained For: The Rise and Fall of Korvettes*. Lebhar-Friedman Books. 1981.
92 A466b2	Barnard, Harry, *Eagle Forgotten*. The Life of John Peter Altgeld. Indianpolois. Bobbs-Merrill, 1938. Charter Books, paperback. 1962.
338.88 BC26g	Barnet, Richard J. and Ronald Miller, *Global Reach:* The Power of the Multi-National Corporations.N.Y.: Simon & Schuster, 1975.
	Barry, Vincent E., *Moral Issues in Business*, Wadsworth, 1979.

2

39

323.4 B28r		Barth, Alan (James Clayton, ed.) <u>The Rights of Free Men</u>, [See especially opp. 315 ff.], Knopf 1984. Distr. by Random House.
BE22V		Basso, Hamilton, <u>The View From Pompey's Head</u>, (Doubleday, 1954), Arbor House. 1985.
650.69 B348h		Baumhart, Raymond, S.J., <u>An Honest Profit</u>: What Businessmen Say About Ethics in Business. Holt, Rinehart, and Winston. 1968.
		Bazelon, David L., <u>Justice and Criminal Law</u>, Alfred A. Knopf.
951.03 B39c		Beeching, Jack, <u>The Chinese Opium Wars.</u> Harcourt, Brace, Jovanovich. 1976.
309.173 B43cu		Bell, Daniel, <u>The Cultural Contradictions of Capitalism.</u> Basic Books. 1976.
		Bell, Susan J. and 23 other members of the Young Lawyers Div. of the American Bar Association. <u>Full Disclosure:</u> Do You Really Want To Be A Lawyer? ABA. 1989.
		Bell, Thomas, <u>Out of This Furnace</u>, 1976.
306.0973 H116		Bellah, Robert N., Richard Madsen, William M. Sullivan, Ann Swidler and Steven M. Tipton, <u>Habits of the Heart.</u> Individualism and Commitment in American Life. Univ. of Calif. Press. 1985.
B435L		Bellamy, Edward, <u>Looking Backward. 2000-1887</u>, Ticknor, 1887.
		Bellush, Jewel and Bernard Bellush, <u>Union Power and New York.</u> Victor Gotbaum and District Counsel 37. Praeger, 1985.
387.7 B45c		Bender, Marylin, Selig Altschul, <u>The Chosen Instrument</u>. Juan Trippe Pan Am The Rise and Fall of An American Entrepreneur, Simon & Schuster, 1982.
338.973 H318g		Bennett, Harrison; Barry Bluestone, <u>The Great U-Turn: Corporate Restructuring and the Polarizing of America.</u> Basic. 1988.
330.97731 B47r		Bensman, David, Roberta Lynch, <u>Rusted Dreams</u>, McGraw-Hill. 1987.
305.42 B49e		Bergmann, Barbara R., <u>The Economic Emergence of Women</u> Basic Books, 1986.
338.7 B51a		Berle, Adolph A., Jr., & G.D. Means, <u>The Modern Corporation and Private Property</u>. Macmillan, 1983. (rev. ed. 1968).

3

40

621.3807 B53t	Bernstein, Jeremy, _Three Degrees Above Zero_. Bell Labs in the Information Age. Scribner's. 1984.
92 S2464b	Bilby, Kenneth, _The General: David Sarnoff & The Rise of the Communications Industry_. Harper & Row. 1986.
	Birmingham, Stephen, _Shades of Fortune._ Little, Brown. 1989.
330 B64h	Blinder, Alan S., _Hard Heads, Soft Hearts_, Addison-Wesley. 1987.
363.179 B65p	Block, Alan A. and Frank R. Scarpitti, _Poisoning for Profit_: The Mafia and Toxic Waste in America. Morrow. 1985.
361.973 M483	Block, Fred; R. Cloward, B. Ehrenreich, Francis Fox Piven, _The Mean Season:_ The Attack on the Welfare State. Pantheon Books. 1987.
	Blumenthal, Ralph, _Last Days of the Sicilians at War With the Mafia_: The FBI Assault on the Pizza Connection. Times Books.
	Bluestone, Barry; Bennett Harrrison, _The Great U-Turn:_ Corporate Restructuring and the Polarizing of America. Basic Books. 1988.
338.6 B65D	Bluestone, Barry, Bennet Harrison, _The De-Industrialization of America_. Basic Books. 1982.
	Blum, John Morton, _The Progressive Presidents._ Norton. (paperback). 1982.
338.74 134	Bock, Betty and Harvey J. Goldschmid, Ira M., Millstein, and F. M. Scherer, eds. _The Impact of the Modern Corporation_. Columbia Univ. Press. 1984.
305.8 B66L	Bodnar, John; Roger Simon & Michael P. Weber, _Lives of Their Own:_ Blacks, Italians, and Poles in Pittsburgh, 1900-1960. Univ. Illinois Press. 1982.
177. B68L	Bok, Sissela, _Lying_: Moral Choice in Public and Private Life. Pantheon. 1978.
177. B68s	Bok, Sissela, _Secrets_: On the Ethics of Concealment and Revelation. Pantheon. 1983.
882 B69M	*Bolt, Richard, _A Man for All Seasons._ Vintage, 1960, 1962.
338.766 b73C	Borkin, Joseph, _The Crime and Punishment of I. G. Farben._ The Free Press. 1978.
657.98	Bowe, Gerald G., _What Every Board and Staff Member of_

B78W	A Non-Profit Organization Should Know About Accounting and Budgeting. Charitable Fund. 1975.
92 C682b	*Bowen, Catherine Drinker, The Lion and the Throne, Little, Brown & Co. (Boston) 1956.
321.8 B78d	Bowles, A. and H. Gintis, Democracy and Capitalism: Property, Community, and the Contradictions of Modern Social Thought. Basic. 1986.
338.973	Bowles, Samuel, David M. Gordon, Thomas E. Weisskopf, Beyond The Waste Land: A Democratic Alternative to Economic Decline. N.Y: Anchor Press/Doubleday. 1983.
B7893d	Boyesan, H.H., A Daughter of the Philistines, Roberts. 1883.
B797m	Brackenridge, Hugh Henry, Modern Chivalry (1792-1815), College & Univ. Press Books, 1937.
658.408	Bradshaw, Thornton, David Vogel, eds., Corporations and Their Critics. Issues and Answers on the Problems of Corporate Social Responsibilities. McGraw Hill. 1981.
	Braitta, Louis, Jr. The Audit Director's Guide. How to Serve Effectively on the Corporate Audit Committee. Ronald Press. 1981.
332.1 B81o	Brandeis, Louis, Jr., Other Peoples Money: And How the Bankers Use It. Stokes. 1914. (Harper Torchbook. 1967).
308.1 B81	Brandeis, Louis, The Curse of Bigness. Edited by O. Fraenkel. Viking Press. 1934.
	Brandel, Fernand, The Wheels of Commerce: Civilization and Capitalism. 15th-18th Century. Harper. 1983.
331.09 B82L	Braverman, Harry. Labor and Monopoly Capital. Monthly Review Press. 1975.
B829t	Brecht, Berthold, Threepenny Novel, Grove Press. 1956.
361.3 B83d	Bremer, William W., Depression Winters. New York Social Workers and the New Deal. Temple Univ. Press. 1984.
338.8 A88a2	Brewster, Kingman. Antitrust and American Business Abroad. (New Edition). Arno Press. 1981.
353.008 B84r	Breyer, Stephen, Regulation and Its Reform, Harvard Univ. Press, 1982.
657.3	Briloff, Abraham, J., More Debits Than Credits: The Burnt

5

B85m	Investor's Guide to Financial Statements. Harper & Row. 1976.
657.3 B857M	Brilloff, Abraham, J., Unaccountable Accounting: Games Accountants Play. Harper & Row. 1972.
363.179 B860	Brodeur, Paul, Outrageous Misconduct. The Asbestos Industry. Pantheon Books. 1985.
613.6 B86e	Brodeur, Paul, Expendable Americans. N.Y., Viking Press. 1974.
364.14 B86M	Broehl, Wayne G., Jr., The Molly Maguires, Harvard, 1964.
338.8 B87t	Brooks, John, The Takeover Game. Dutton, 1987.
	Brooks, John, (ed.) The Autobiography of American Business. The Story Told by Those Who Made It. Anchor Doubleday Paperback. 1974.
332.09 B87g	Brooks, John, The Game Players: Tales of Men and Money. A Truman Talley Book. Times Books, 1980.
332.64 B87g	Brooks, John, The Go-Go Years. Weybright & Talley. 1973.
305.5 B87s	Brooks, John, Showing Off in America. From Conspicuous Consumption to Parody Display. Atlantic, Little, Brown. 1981.
338.8 B87t	Brooks, John M., Fate of the Edsel and Other Business Adventures, The, Harper & Row. 1963.
332.6 B87o	Brooks, John M., Once in Golconda: The True Drama of Wall Street, 1920-1938. Harper & Row. 1963.
394.6 B873t	Brooks, John, Telephone, The First Hundred Years: The Wondrous Invention That Changed the World and Spawned a Corporate Giant. Harper & Row. 1976.
391.8811 B87c	Brooks, Thomas R., Communications Workers of America: The Story of a Union. Mason/Charter Pub. 1977.
	Brown, Michael H., The Toxic Cloud. Harper & Row. 1987.
353.008 B87e	Brown, D. Clayton, Electricity for Rural America: The Fight for REA. Greenwood Press. 1980.
614.76 B78L	Brown, Michael, Laying Waste: The Poisoning of America by Toxic Chemicals. Pantheon. 1980.
332.632 B88p	Bruck, Connie, The Predator's Ball: The Junk Bond Raiders and the Man Who Staked Them. Simon & Schuster.

1988.

331.89 B95h	Burgoyne, Arthur G., with an afterword by David P. Demarest, Jr. The Homestead Strike of 1892. Univ. of Pittsburgh. 1979.
305.42 B93w	Buhle, Mari Jo, Women and American Socialism. 1870-1900. Univ. Illinois Press. 1981.
330.15B96 c.1 330.15B96 c.2	Burnham, James C., The Managerial Revolution: What is Happening in the World. John Day, 1941.
332.4 B97y	Burnstein, Daniel, Yen! Japan's New Financiasl Empire and Its Threat to America. Simon & Schuster.
658.85 M345	Buzzell, Robert, (ed.) Marketing in An Electronic Age. Harvard Business School Press. 1986.
791.45 B99f	Byron, Christopher, The Fanciest Dive: What Happened When the Media Empire of Time/Life Leaped Without Looking Into the Age of High-Tech. Norton. 1996.
338.8 M56	Cable, John, et al. Mergers and Economic Performance. Cambridge Univ. Press. 1980.
340 C132m	Cahn, Edmond, The Moral Decision: Right and Wrong in the Light of American Law. Bloomington, Indiana: Indiana Univ. Press. 1955.
	Caplan, S.L. and D. Callahan, (eds.),Ethics in Hard Times. Plenum Press. 1981.
	Carlzon, Jan. Moments of Truth. Ballinger Publ. 1988.
92 C289	*Carnegie, Andrew, Autobiography of Andrew Carnegie, Houghton-Mifflin. 1920.
304 C28	Carnegie, Andrew, The Empire of Business. Doubleday. 1902.
304 C28ga	Carnegie, Andrew, The Gospel of Wealth, and Other Timely Essays. Century. 1900
338.973 C28e	Carnoy, Martin, and Derek Shearer, Economic Democracy: The Challenge of the Eighties, M.E. Sharpe, 1980.
338.973 C29n	Carnoy, Martin, Derek Shearer, Russell Rumberger, A New Social Contract: The Economy and Government After Reagan. Harper & Row. 1983.
	Carpenter, D.C.; J. Feloni, The Fall of the House of Hutton. Henry Holt. 1989.

632.951 C32sl	Carson, Rachel, *Silent Spring*. Fawcett (paperback 1970.
92 Y74c	*Case, Josephine Young, Everett Needham Case, *Owen D. Young and American Enterprise*. A Biography. Godine, 1982.
C363m c.9 C363m c.10 (Spec/RB) c.1	Cather, Willa, *My Antonia*. Houghton Mifflin. 1918. (paperback).
C363d C.1 C363d C.2 C363d C.4	Cather, Willa, *Death Comes for the Archbishop*. Alfred Knopf Co.1927.
332.092 C44L	Caudill, Harry M., *Theirs Be the Power*: The Moguls of of Eastern Kentucky. Univ. of Illinois Press. 1984.
	Chafe, William H., *The American Woman:* Her Changing Social Economic, and Political Roles, 1972.
658.4 C44L	Chamberlain, Neil W., *The Limits of Corporate Responsibility*. Basic Books. 1973.
658.4 C456V	Chandler, Alfred D. Jr., *The Invisible Hand:* The Managerial Revolution in American Business (Pulitzer Prize in History, 1978).
	Chandler, Lester V., *America's Greatest Depression*. 1970.
	Cheape, Charles W., *Family Firm to Modern Multinational*: Norton Company, A New England Enterprise, Harvard Univ. Press. 1985.
92 T337c	*Cheney, Margaret, *Tesla: Man Out of Time*. Prentice-Hall 1981.
	Cherniak, Martin, *The Hawk's Nest Incident*: America's Worst Industrial (Occupational Health) Disaster. Yale Univ. Press. 1966.
C5261g	Cheuse, Alan *The Grandmother Club*, Peregrine Smith, 1986.
338.8 C51b	Chiet, Earl F., ed., *The Business Establishment*. John Wiley. 1964.
	Clairmonte, Frederick and John Cavanagh, *The World In Their Web*. The Dynamics of Textile Multinationals, ZED. 1983.
C617n	Clavell, James, *Noble House*. Delacorte, 1981.

363 C61r	Claybrook, Jean and the Staff of Public Citizen, <u>Retreat From Safety:</u> Reagan's Attack on America's Health. Pantheon. 1984.
323.4 B28r	Clayton, James (ed.), <u>Alan Barth The Rights of Free Men</u>. [See especially p. 315 ff] Knopf. 1984.
323.15 C67I	Cohen, Benjamin J., <u>In Whose Interest?</u>
	Cohen, Stephen S.; John Zysman, <u>Manufacturing Matters:</u> The Myth of the Post Industrial Economy. Basic Books. 1989.
92 D288C	Coleman, McAlister, <u>Eugene V. Debs - A Man Unafraid</u>. Greenberg Pub. 1930.
	Coll, Steve, <u>The Taking of Getty Oil</u>. Atheneum. 1987.
384.6 C69d	Coll, Steve, <u>The Deal of the Century</u>, The Breakup of A.T.&T. Atheneum. 1986.
338.76292 F69ZC	Collier, Peter and David Horowitz, <u>The Fords, An American Epic</u>, Summit. 1987.
J682te	Collins, Eliza G.C., <u>Dearest Amanda</u>. Harper & Row. 1984.
	Commons, Dorman L., <u>Tender Offer</u>, Univ. of Calif. Press. 1985.
331.886 C75b	Conlin, Joseph, <u>Bread and Roses Too:</u> Studies of the Wobblies, Greenwood. 1969.
331.886 A 86	Conlin, Joseph R., (edit). <u>At the Point of Production</u>: The Local History of the I.W.W., Greenwood Press. 1982.
	Conners, Tracy D., <u>The Nonprofit Organization Handbook,</u> McGraw-Hill, 1989.
C7542La	Conrad, Joseph, <u>Lord Jim</u>.
174 C77C	Cook, Fred J., <u>The Corrupted Land</u>: The Social Morality of Modern America. Macmillan, 1966.
338.2728 C771g	Cook, Fred J., <u>The Great Energy Scam</u>. Macmillan. 1983.
	Cook, James R., <u>The Start-Up Entrepreneur</u>: How You Can Succeed in Building Your Own Company Into a Major Enterprise Starting From Scratch. Harper & Row. 1987.
	Conran, Shirley, <u>Savages</u>. Simon & Schuster. 1987.

9

Corbin, David Alan, **Life, Work, and Rebellion in the Coal Fields:** The Southern West Virginia Miners, 1880-1922.

Cornwell, Rupert, **God's Banker.** Dodd, Mead. 1984.

C891c   Crane, Steven, **Maggie, A Girl of the Streets, 1893.**

320.973 C94A   Croly, Herbert, **The Promise of American Life.** 1909.
320.973 C94

Crossbey, William, **Politics and the Constitution in the History of the United States.** Univ. of Chicago Press. 1953.

Cunningham, Mary and Fran Schumer, **Powerplay:** What Really Happened at Bendix. Linden Press. 1984.

Dallos, Robert and Ronald Soble. **The Impossible Dream:** The Equity Funding Story: The Fraud of the Century. Signet, 1975.

Dalton, George (ed). **Essays of Karl Polanyi:** Primitive, Archaic and Modern Economics. Beacon Press. 1981.

338.065   Daughen, Joseph R., and Peter Binzen, **The Wreck of the**
D23W   **Penn Central,** Little, Brown & Co. 1972.

D247v   Davenport, Marcia, **Valley of Decision,** Bentley Reprint. 1979.

Davidson, Greg; Paul Davidson, **Economics for a Civilized Society.** W.W. Norton.

Davidson, Kenneth M., **Megamergers:** Corporate America's Billion Dollar Takeovers. Ballinger. 1985.

Davis, Glenn, Gary D. Helfand. **The Uncertain Balance:** Federal Regulators in a Changing Political Economy. Avery Pub. Group. 1985.

D2633L   Davis, Rebecca, **Life in The Iron Mills or The Korl Woman,** (First printed in Atlantic Monthly, April 1861. Feminist Press. 1972.

658.4   Deal, Terrence E., Allan A. Kennedy, **The Rites and Rituals**
D27c   **of Corporate Life.** Addison-Wesley. 1982.

331.88   DeCaux, Len, **Labor Radical:** From the Wobblies to CIO.
D29   Beacon Press. 1970.

338.4762138   DeLamarter, Richard Thomas. **Big Blue: IBM's Use and**
D33b   **Abuse of Power.** Dodd, Mead. 1987.

338.06	Dertouzos, Michael L., R. K. Lester, et al., Regaining the Productive Edge. MIT Press. (MIT Commission on Industrial Productivity. 1989.
342.72 T63a2	de Tocqueville, Alexis. Democracy in America. 1830.
	Dickens, Charles, Hard Times.
658.4 D56s	Dierkes, Meinolf, The Social Role of the Corporation and Corporate Social Accounting: Executive Summary and Selective Material - Systems Research Directorate Seminar, Westinghouse Research Laboratories, School of Urban and Public Affairs. Carnegie-Mellon Univ. 1973.
364.163 D59g	Dirks, Raymond and Leonard Gross. The Great Wall Street Scandal. McGraw-Hill. 1974.
	Disraeli, Benjamin, Sybil,
305.52	Domhoff, G. William. Who Rules America Now? A View for the 80's. Prentice Hall. 1984.
174.4 E842a2	Donaldson, Thomas and Patricia Werhane. Ethical Issues in Business: A Philosophical Approach. Prentice-Hall. 1983.
D723u	Dostoevsky, Fyodor, The Grant Inquisitor. From the Brothers Karamozov. Dutton. 1960.
D723u	Dos Passos, John, The Big Money. Signet Classics. 1969.1937.
D771f	Dreiser, Theodore, The Financier Vol. I. (Trilogy) Apollo, eds. 1974 (plaper).
D771s2	Dreiser, Theodore, Sister Carrie. Dell. 1960. (paper).
D771st	Dreiser, Theodore, The Stoic. Vol III (Trilogy), Apollo, ed. 1974.
D771t	Dreiser, Theodore, The Titan. II, (Trilogy) Apollo, eds., 1975. (paperback).
	Drucker, Peter F., The Practice of Management. 1954.
	Drucker, Peter F., Concept of the Corporation. 1946.
92 D814d	*Dubinsky, David, and A. H. Raskin. David Dubinsky: A Life with Labor. Simon & Schuster. 1977.
92 L674d	*Dubofsky, Melvin and Warren Van Tine, John L. Lewis A Biography. Quadrangle. 1977.

11

331.88 81w	Dubofsky, Melvyn, *We Shall Be All*. A History of the I.W.W. Quadrangle. 1969.
338.973 B9791	Dunlop, John T., (ed.), *Business and Public Policy*. Harvard Univ. Press. 1980.
361.6 D89c	Dunbar, Leslie W., *The Common Interest*. How Our Social Welfare Policies Don't Work and What We Can Do About Them.
330.122 E26C	Edwards, Richard C., Michael Reich, Thomas E. Weisskopf, *The Capitalist System*, Third Edit. 1986.
	Emerson, Steven, *The American House of Saud*. The Secret Petrodollar Connection. Franklin Watts. 1985.
	Engelmayer, Sheldon and Robert Wagman, *Lord's Justice*: One Judge's War Against the Infamous Dalkon Shield. Anchor Doubleday. 1985.
	Engler, Robert, *The Brotherhood of Oil*. Univ. of Chicago Press.
	Engler, Robert, *The Politics of Oil*. Univ. of Chicago Press.
	Engler, Rick, *A Job Safety and Health Bill of Rights*: Philadelphia Area Project on Occupational Safety and Health (3001 Walnut Street, Philadelphia, Pa., 19104).1984.
364.157 E64a	Epstein, Edward Jay, *Agency of Fear*: Opiates and Political Power in America. Putnam's. 1977.
380.13282 E64r	Epstein, Edward J., *The Rise and Fall of Diamonds* The Shattering of a Brilliant Illusion. Simon & Schuster. 1982.
353.008 A73e	Erickson, Don V., *Armstrong's Fight for FM Broadcasting*. One Man vs. Big Business and Bureaucracy. Univ. of Alabama Press. 1973.
	Erickson, Kai, *Everything in its path: The Destruction of Community in the Buffalo Creek Floor*. Touchtown Books,(Simon & Schuster), 1978.
	Etzioni, Amitai, *The Moral Dimension:* Toward a New Economics. Free Press. 1989.
658.3 E95d	Ewing, David W., *Do It My Way or You're Fired*: Employee Rights and the Changing Role of Management Perogatives. Wiley. 1982.

12

49

323.4 E95f	Ewing, David W., *Freedom Inside the Organization*. E.P. Dutton. 1977.
651.75 E95w2	Ewing, David W., *Writing for Results in Business, Government, The Sciences and the Professions*. 2nd. ed. Wiley. 1979.
92 O36f	*Fallon, Ivan and James Srodes, *Dream Maker*: The Rise and Fall of John Z. DeLorean. Putnam. 1983.
	Farley, Jennie, (ed.), *Women Working in Fifteen Countries: Essays in Honor of Alice Hanson Cook*. Cornell, ILR Press, 1985.
	Farrell, James, *Studs Lonigan*. 1932-35.
332.632	Fay, Stephen. *Beyond Greed*. Viking. 1983.
	Feiuchell, Stephen, *Other People's Money*, The Rise and Fall of OPM Leasing Services. Anchor. 1985.
385 F311	Fellmeth, R.C., *The Interstate Commerce Commission*. Grossman, 1980.
338.762904 F36e	Fernandez, Ronald, *Excess Profits*: The Rise of United Technologies. Addison-Wesley. 1983.
322.2 F49w	Fink, Leon, *Workingmen's Democracy: The Knights of Labor and American Politics*. Univ. Illinois Press. 1983.
343.73 F36e	Fisher, Franklin M., *Folded, Spindled and Mutilated:* Economic Analysis & U.S. v IBM. MIT Press, 1983.
158.2 F53g	Fisher, Roger and William Ury, *Getting to Yes*: Negotiating Agreement Without Giving In. Houghton-Mifflin. 1981.
510.78 F53c	Fishman, Katherine D., *Comupter Establishment, The*. Harper & Row. 1981.
F553g2	Fitzgerald, F. Scott. *The Great Gatsby*, Scribner's. (paperback). 1925.
	Fleisher, Arthur, Jr., G. C. Hazard, Mirian Z. Klipper, *Board Games*. Little, Brown, 1988.
955.054 F66o	Follett, Ken. *On Wings of Eagles*. Morrow. 1983. 1983.
331.69 F6702 C.1	Foner, Phillip. *Organized Labor and the Black Worker*. Praeger. 1974.
323/44 F32	Foner, Philip S., (ed.) *Fellow Workers asnd Friends*: I.W.W. Free-Speech Fights as Told by Participants. Greenwood Press. 1982.

13

	Foner, Philip S. *The Industrial Workers of the World, 1905-1917.* International Publishers, 1965
3331.88 F673w	Foner, Philip S., *Women and the American Labor Movement.* The Free Press. 1979.
659.109 F79m	Fox, Stephen, *The Mirror Makers*: A History of American Advertising and Its Creators. Morrow. 1984.
	Francis, David R., *Economics in the Real World*: How Political Decisions Affect the Economy. Simon & Schuster. 1985.
330 F82c	Frank, Robert H., *Choosing the Right Pond*: Human Behavior and the Quest for Status. Oxford Univ. Press. 1985.
	Frantz, Douglas. *Levine & Co.* Human Behavior and the Quest Scandal. Holt. 1987.
331.880973 F85w	Freeman, Richard B. and James Medoff. *What Do Unions Do?* Basic Books. 1984.
305.56 W926	Fresch, Michael H. & Daniel J. Walkowitz, *Working-Class America:* Essays on Labor, Community, and American Society. Univ. Illinois Press, 1983.
331 F91y	Friedman, Lawrence, *Your Time Will Come*: The Law of Age Discrimination and Mandatory Retirement. Russell Sage Foundations, 1984.
330.15 F91c	Friedman, Milton, *Capitalism and Freedom.* Univ. of Chicago Press. 1962.
323.44	Fromm, Erich, *Escape From Freedom.* 1941. Farrar & Reinhart, Inc.
330.1 M39zf	Fromm, Erich, *Marx' Concept of Man.*
338.47 F96g	Fuller, John G., *The Gentlemen Conspirators*: The Story of the Price-Fixers in the Electrical Industry. Grove Press. 1962.
330.973	Galbraith, John Kenneth, *The Affluent Society.* Houghton-Mifflin. 1958.
330.9 G14e	Galbraith, John Kenneth, *Economics in Perspective. A Critical History,* Houghton-Mifflin. 1987.
330.973 G14q2	Galbraith, J.K., *The Great Crash.* Houghton-Mifflin.

330.973 G14n2	Galbraith, J.K., The New Industrial State. Second ed. Revised. Houghton-Mifflin 1972. (paper).
303.3 G14a	Galbraith, John Kenneth, The Anatomy of Power. Houghton Mifflin. 1983.
	Gallese, Liz Roman, Women Like Us: A Milestone Study Drawn from Women of the Harvard Business School Class of '75. Morrow. 1985.
	Gans, Herbert, The Levit-Towers. 1967.
964 G22e	Gardner, Brian, The East India Company: A History. McCall. 1971.
	Gaskell, Elizabeth, Mary Barton
92 F699ge	*Gelderman, Carol. Henry Ford. The Wayward Capitalist. Dial. 1981.
658.04 G32m C.1 or C.2	*Geneen Harold, Managing. Doubleday. 1984.
	Gergacz, John William Attorney - Corporate Client Privilege. Garland Law Publishing. 1987.
361.973	Gilbert, Neil, Capitalism and the Welfare State: Dilemmas of Social Benevolence. Yale Univ. Press. 1983.
	Gilman, Charlotte Perkins, Her Land.
92 G288g	*Ginger, Ray, The Bending Cross, A Biography of Eugene Debs. Rutgers, 1949.
658.4 1985G496	Ginsberg, Eli, George Vojta, Beyond Human Scale. Basic Books, 1985.
353.009 G55w	Glazer, Myron Peretz, Penina M. Glazer, Whistle-Blowers. Exposing Corruption in Government & Industry, Basic Books, Inc.
629.1334 G584	Godson, John, The Rise and Fall of the DC-10. David McKay. 1974.
331.21 G61d	Gold, Michael Evan, A Dialogue on Comparable Worth. ILR Press. 1983.
973.8 G6r3	Goldman, Eric F., Rendezvous With Destiny. Vintage.
	Goldston, Robert. The Great Depression

338.74 G62f	Goldwasser, Thomas, *Family Pride.* Profiles of Five of America's Best-Run Family Businesses. Dodd, Mead. 1986.
92 G634ga	*Gompers, Samuel, *Seventy Years of Life and Labor*. Kelley. 1975.
	Goodman, Walter, *All Honorable Men.* Corruption and Compromise in American Life. Little, Brown & Co. 1963.
338.76 G6513	Goodwin, Jacob, *Brotherhood of Arms*: General Dynamics and The Business of Defending America. Times Books, 1985.
329.8 G65DA	Goodwyn, Lawrence, *The Populist Movement:* A Short History of the Agrarian Revolt in America. Oxford Univ. Press. 1978.
	Goodwyn, L. *Democratic Promise*: The populist Movement in America. 1986.
343.73 G65p	Goolrick, Robert M., *Public Policy Toward Corporate Growth*: The ITT Merger Cases. Kennikat. 1978.
332.642 G66s	Gordon, John Steele, *The Scarlet Woman of Wall Street.* Weindenfeld & Nicholson, 1988.
363.6	Gormley, Williasm T., Jr., *The Politics of Public Utility Regulation*, Univ. of Pittsburgh Press. 1983.
	*Gould, Jean & Hickok, Lorena, *Walter Reuther: Labor's Rugged Individualist*. Dodd, Mead & Co., 1971.
311.113	Gould, William B., *Black Workers in White Unions:* Job Discrimination in the U.S. Cornell Univ. Press.
92 M483g	*Goulden, Joseph, *Meany*. Antheneum, 1972.
92 W967g	Goulden, Joseph, *Jerry Wurf. Labor's Last Angry Man*. Antheneum. 1982.
	Goulden, Joseph. *Monopoly:* The Story of A.T.&T. Putnam. 1968.
92 B295g	*Grant, James, *Bernard M. Baruch*: The Adventures of A Wall Street Legend. Simon & Schuster. 1983.
658.155 G79c	Green, Mark and John F. Berry, *The Challenge of Hidden Profits*: Reducing Corporate Bureaucracy and Waste. William Morrow. 1985.

Green, Mark, and Norman Waitzman, <u>Business War on the Law.</u> The Corporate Accountability Research Group. 1979.

Greenwald (Grunwald) Carol, <u>Banks Are Dangerous To Your Health</u>.

332.11
G82s
Greider, William, <u>Secrets of the Temple</u>: How the Federal Reserve Runs the Country. Simon & Schuster. 1987. (Or see, <u>New Yorker Magazine</u> segments, 3 weeks in Nov.: Nov. 9, 16, & 23, 1987.)

Grenier, Guillermo J., <u>Inhuman Relations.</u> Quality Circles & AntiUnionism in American Industry. Temple U. Press. 1988.

Gross, Malvern J.; Steven F. Jablonsky, <u>Principles of Accounting and Financial Reporting for Nonprofit Corporations.</u>. John Wiley & Sons, 1979.

306.3
G98W
Gutman, Herbert G., <u>Work, Culture, and Society in Industrializing America</u>: Essays in America's Working Class and Social History. Knopf, 1987.

305.56
G984p
Gutman, Herbert, (Ira Berlin, ed.) <u>Power & Culture</u>: Essays on the American Working Class. Pantheon. 1988.

330.973
H11W
Hacker, Louis M., <u>The World of Andrew Carnegie, 1865-1981</u>. Lippincott. 1968.

Hall, Jacquelyn Dowd, James LeLoudis, Robert Korstad, Mary Murphy, Lu Ann Jones and Christopher B. Daly, <u>Like A Family</u>. The Making of a Southern Cotton Mill World. Univ. of North Carolina Press.

Hailey, Arthur, <u>Strong Medicine</u>, Doubleday, 1984.

H151m
Hailey, Arthur, <u>The Moneychangers</u>, Doubleday, 1975.

H151w
Hailey, Arthur, <u>Wheels</u>, Doubleday, 1971.

338.476292
H15R
Halberstam, David, <u>The Reckoning: The Challenge to America's Greatness</u>, (Detroit, Japan and the crisis in the Auto Industry. with Special Emphasis on Ford and Nissan.) Morrow, 1986.

Hamlin, David, <u>The Nazi/Skokie Conflict</u>, Beacon. 1980.

292.H217m c.4
292 H217m c.5
Hamilton, Edith, <u>Mythology</u>.

338.7677
H27a
Harevan, Tamara K., and Langenbach, R., <u>Amoskeag</u>: Life and Work in An American Factory City. Pantheon. 1979.

17

338.91 H311v	Harrington, Michael, *The Vast Majority*: A Journey to the World's Poor. Simon & Schuster. 1978.
309.173 H311d	Harrington, Michael, *Decade of Decision:* The Crisis of the American System. Simon & Schuster. 1981.
301.44 H31oA	Harrington, Michael, *The Other America*, Poverty in the United States. A Penguin Special (paperback) 1963.
305.56 H31n	Harrington, Michael, *The New American Poverty*. Holt, Rinehart & Winston. 1984.
305.569 Q6	Harris, Fred R.; Roger W. Wilkins (eds.) *Quiet Riots* Race & Poverty in the U.S. The Kerner Report Twenty Years Later. 1988.
331.6 H317h	Harris, William H., *The Harder We Run*: Black Workers Since the Civil War. Oxford Univ. Press. 1982.
	Harrison, Bennet; Barry Bluestone, *The Great U-Turn.*
070.44 M94	Harrison, John M. and Harry H. Stein, (eds.)*Muckraking Past, Present and Future*. Penn State Press. 1973.
	Hartrich, Edwin, *The Fourth and Richest Reich*. Macmillan. 1980.
	Hartz, Peter F., *Merger*: The Exclusive Inside Story of the Bendix-Martin-Marietta Takeover. Morrow. 1985.
92 F897h	*Harvey, George B., *Henry Clay Frick*. Scribner, 1928.
330.973 H39n	Hawken, Paul, *The Next Economy*. Holt, Rinehart & Winston. 1983.
H396c	Hawley, Cameron, *Cash McCall*. Houghton-Mifflin. 1955.
	Hawley, Cameron, *Executive Suite*.
	Hawley, Cameron, *The Lincoln Lords*. Little, Brown. 1960.
H399sc	Hawthorne, Nathaniel, *The Scarlet Letter (1850*. Garden City, Doubleday & Co., 1906. (paperback).
658.5 H41r	Hayes, Robert A., and Steven C. Wheelright. *Restoring Our Competitive Edge*: Competition Through Manufacturing. John Wiley. 1984.

338.8 F596b	Hazard, Jr., Fleischer, Arthur Jr., G.C., and M.Z. Klipper, <u>Board Games.</u> The Changing Shape of Corporate Power. Little, Brown. 1988.
332.12 H45b	Hector, Gary, <u>Breaking the Bank.</u> The Decline of Bank America. Little, Brown. 1988.
330.122 H 46 b	Heilbroner, Robert L., <u>Behind the Veil of Economics</u>. Essays in the Worldly Philosophy. Norton, 1988.
330.122 H46N	Heilbroner, Robert L., <u>The Nature and Logic of Capitalism</u>, Norton. 1985.
338.43 H46b	Heilbroner, Robert L., <u>Beyond Boom and Crash</u>. Norton 1970.
330.1 H466bu	Heilbroner, Robert L. <u>Business Civilization in Decline.</u> Norton. 1977.
335.4 H466M	Heilbroner, Robert L., <u>Marxism: For and Against</u>. Norton, 1980.
658.408 135	Heilbroner, Robert L., and Other, <u>In the Name of Profit:</u> Profiles in Corporate Irresponsibility. Doubleday & Co., 1972.
330.1 H466wa3	Heilbroner, Robert L., <u>The Worldly Philosophers.</u> The Lives, Times and Ideas of the Great Economic Thinkers. Simon & Schuster. 3rd rev. ed., 1967.
330.1 H466b	Heilbroner, Robert L., <u>Between Capitalism and Socialism</u>. Essays in Political Economics. Random House. 1970.
330.973 H46p	Heilbroner, Robertr and Lester Thurow, <u>Five Economic Challenges</u>. Prentice-Hall. 1981.
327.73 H46Gf	Heilbroner, Robert L. <u>The Future as History</u>. Harper & Co., 1960.
330.9 H46m4	Heilbroner, Robert L., <u>The Making of Economic Society</u>. Prentice Hall Co., 1972.
H477c	Heller, Joseph. <u>Catch-22</u>. Dell. 1963. (paper).
	Herling, J., <u>The Great Price Compiracy:</u> The Story of the Antitrust Violations in the Electrical Industry. (1962). Robert B. Luce., 1962.
338.7 H55c	Herman, Edward S., <u>Corporate Control, Corporate Power</u>. Cambridge Univ. Press. 1981.
92 5398h	*Hesson, Robert, <u>Steel Tital</u>: <u>The Life of Charles M. Schwab</u>. Oxford Univ. Press. 1975.

19

305.42 4612L	Hewlett, Sylvia Ann, *A Lesser Life: The Myth of Women's Liberation in America*. Morrow. 1986
	*Hickerson, J. Mell, *Ernie Breech:* The Story of Hs Remarkable Career at General Motors, Ford & TWA. Meredith. 1968.
382.0943 H63t	Higham, Charles, *Trading With the Enemy*. An Expose of the Nazi-American Money Plot. Delacorte. 1983.
305.56 H65i	Himmelfarb, Gertrude, *The Idea of Poverty*: England in Early Industrial Age. Knopf. 1984.
305.56 4512	Hoerder, Dirk, (ed.) *American Labor and Immigration History, 1877-1920's:* Recent European Research. Univ. Illinois Press, 1983.
338.476691. H69a	Hoerr, John P., *And the Wolf Finally Canme:* The Decline of the American Steel Industry, Univ. of Pittsburgh Press. 1988.
	Hodgson, Godfrey, *Lloyd's of London*. Viking. 1984.
917.3 H71a	Hofstadter, Richard, *Antiintellectualism in American* Knopf, 1763.
320.973 H71p	Hofstadter, Richard. *Paranoid Style in American Politics and Other Essays*, Knopf, 1966.
301H17 H17	Hofstadter, Richard, *Social Darwinism in American Thought*. Braziller, 1959.
973.91 H71a	Hofstadter, Richard, *The Age of Reform.* 1955.
923.3 H27a	Holbrook, Stewart H., *The Age of Moguls*, Doubleday, 1954. (paperback).
	Holland, Max, *When the Machine Stopped:* A Cautionary Tale From Industrial America. [The Story of Burg Tool Co., later renamed Burgmaster Corp.] Harvard Business School Press. 1989.
	Hoover, Kenneth & Raymond Plant, *Conservative Capitalism in Britain and the United States*. Routledge, Chapman & Ball.
	Hovenkamp, H. *Economics and Federal Antitrust Law*. 1985.
306.36H85B	Howard, Robert, *Brave New Workplace*. Viking. 1986.
	Howe, Irving, (ed.) *Alternative*: Proposals For America From the Democratic Left. Pantheon. 1984.

20

Call Number	Entry
301.444 H85W	Howe, Irving, *The World of the Blue Collar Worker*. Quadrangle, 1972.
331.4 H85p	Howe, Louis Kapp. *Pink Collar Workers*, Inside the World of Women's Work. G.P. Putnam's Sons. 1977.
H859ha	Howells, William Dean, *A Hazard of New Fortunes*. New American Library. 1965.
HL4 SPEC/RB X c.1	Howells, William Dean, *A Modern Instance (1882)*, Signet. 1882.
923.3 H89v	Hughes, Jonathan, *The Vital Few:* The Entrepreneur and American Economic Progress. Oxford Univ. Press. 1986.
	Hunt, James W., *The Law of the Workplace*. Bureau of National Affairs.
92 H9413h	Hurt, Harry, *Texas Rich:* The Hunt Dynasty. From the Early Oil Days. Norton. 1982.
364.168 H97o	Hutchison, Robert A., *Off the Books:* Citibank and the World's Biggest Money Game. Morrow. 1986.
W1342h	*Hutchmacher, Joseph J., *Senator Robert F. Wagner and the Rise of Urban Liberalism*. Atheneum. 1968.
H986BBRAV c.1 H986B c.9 H986BAZ c.1 H986 BA3 c.1	Huxley, Aldous, *Brave New World*. Harper & Row. 1969.
92 E17h	*Hyman, Sidney, *Marriner S. Eccles:* Private Entrepreneur and Public Servant. Stanford, Calif. 1977.
303.342 I11i	*Iacocca, Lee, *Iacocca:* An Autobiography. Bantam Books, 1984.
	Industrial Productivity, MIT Commission on, *Made in America:* Regaining the Productive Edge. 1989.
363.11 E96	Ives, Janes H., ed., *The Export of Hazard:* Transnational Corporations and Environmental Control Issues. Routledge & Kegan Paul. 1985.
	The Insight Team of the Sunday Times of London. *Suffer The Children*. The Story of Thalidomide. Viking. 1979.
338.09 J17e	Jacobs, Jane. *The Economy of Cities.* Random House, 1969.

21

711.4 J17d	Jacobs, Jane. <u>The Death and Life of Great American Cities</u>. Random House. 1961.
330.9 J17c	Jacobs, Jane, <u>Cities and the Wealth of Nations</u>. Principles of Economic Life. Random House. 1984.
338.768644 J17X	Jacobson, Gary; John Hillkirk, <u>Xerox: American Samurai</u>, Macmillan, 1986.
364.132 J17b	Jacoby, Neil H., Peter Nehemkis, Richard Eels, <u>Bribery and Extortion in the World of Business</u>. Macmillan, 1977.
330.952 J66M	Johnson, Chalmers, <u>MITI and the Japanese Miracle</u>: The Growth of Industrial Policy, 1915-75. Stanford Univ. Press. 1982.
	Johnson, Christopher, <u>Maurice Sugar:</u> Law, Labor and the Left in Detroit, 1912-1950. Wayne State Univ. 1988.
425 J83e C.1	Joseph, Albert, <u>Executive Guide to Grammar</u>. International Writing Institute. 1984.
92 H654j	*Joseph, Matthew, <u>Sidney Hillman</u>: Stateman of Labor. Doubleday. 1952.
92 L232	*Josephson, Matthew, <u>Edison, a biography</u>. McGraw-Hill. 1959.
332.0973	Josephson, Matthew. <u>The Great Finance Capitalists. 1919-1950</u>. Bergenfield, New American Library. 1973.
923.3 J83	Josephson, Matthew. <u>The Robber Barons</u>. Harcourt, Brace, 1934.
K11a C.1	Kafka, Franz, <u>Amerika</u>, A New Directions Paperbook. 1946.
K11c C.3	Kafka, Franz, <u>The Castle</u>. Alfred A. Knopf Co. 1954.
342.73 K15M	Kammen, Michael, <u>A Machine That Would Go Of Itself</u>: The <u>Constitution in American Culture</u>. Knopf. 1986.
302.35 K16M	Kanter, Rosabeth Moss, <u>Men and Women of the Corporation.</u> (Winner of the 1977 C. Wright Mills Award for the year's best book on social issues). Basic Books. 1977.
658.314 K16c	Kanter, Rosabeth Moss, <u>The Change Masters</u>: Innovations for Productivity in the American Corporation. Simon & Schuster. 1983.

381.45 K19b	Katz, Donald R., *The Big Store:* Inside the Crisis and the
	Katz, Leo, *Bad Acts and Guilty Minds:* Conundrums of the Criminal Law, Univ. of Chicago Press. 1987.
331.88 K21s	*Kaufmann, Stuart Bruce, *Samuel Gompers and the Origin of the AFL.* Greenwood, 1973.
338.8 K23u	Kaysen, Carl, *United States v. United Shoe Machinery Co.* Harvard Economic Studies, 99, Harvard, 1956.
	Kazen, Michael, *Barons of Labor*: The San Francisco Building Trades and Union Power in the Progressive Era.
658.304 K29g	Kelley, Robert E., *The Gold Collar Worker*, Harnessing the Brainpower of the New Workforce. Addison-Wesley, 1985.
K3621	Kennedy, William, *Ironweek*, Viking Press. 1983.
	Kerner, Otto & the National Advisory Commission, *The Kerner Report:* The 1968 Report of the National Advisory Commission on Civil Disorders, (paperbound). 1988.
331.4 K420	Kessler-Harris, *Alice. Out to Work*: A History of the Wage-Earning Women in the United States. Oxford. 1982.
	Kessler, Ronald. *The Life Insurance Game*. Holt, Rinehart. 1985.
330.1 K44	Keynes, John J., *The General Theory of Employment, Interest and Money.* Harcourt, Brace & World. 1936.
621.381952 K46s	Kidder, Tracy, *The Soul of a New Machine.* Atlantic Monthly Press. Little, Brown. 1982.
92 G697K	*Klein, Maury, *The Life and Legend of Jay Gould.* Johns Hopkins Univ. Press. 1986.
384.6 K64b	Kleinfield, Sonny, *The Biggest Company on Earth*: A Profile of AT&T. Holt, Rinehart & Winston. 1980.
	Kleinfield, Sonny. *The Traders.* Holt, Rinehart & Winston. 1984.
	Kohn, Harold, *Who Killed Karen Silkwood?* Summit Books. 1981.
	Kolko, G., *Railroads and Regulation.* Princeton, 1965.
	Kolko, G., *The Triumph of Conservatism*. Glencoe, 1963.

339.4 K81w (LL Storage)	Kolko, Gabriel, <u>Wealth and Power in America.</u> Praeger, 1962.
	Kolko, Joyce, <u>America and the Crisis of World Capitalism</u>. Beacon Press. 1981.
305.56 K84w c.1	Korpi, Walter, <u>The Working Class in Welfare Capitalism</u> Routledge and Kegan Paul. 1978.
	*Koskoff, David E., <u>The Mellons</u>: The Chronical of Richest Family. Thomas Y. Crowell. 1978.
4G1242 B6K87 c.2 (SEI.BK)	Kotz, Nick, <u>Wild Blue Yonder:</u> Money, Politics, and the B-1 Bomber, Princeton Univ. Press. 1989.
92 W676k	Kotz, Nick and Mary L. Kotz, <u>A Passion for Equality</u>: George Wiley and the Movement. W.W. Norton. 1977.
381.0973 K88m C.1	Kowinski, William. <u>The Malling of America</u>. An Inside Look at the Great Consumer Paradise. William Morrow. 1985.
	Kurzman, Dan, <u>A Killing Wind</u>: Inside Union Carbide & the Bhopal Catastrophe. McGraw Hill. 1987.
387.73 K97g	Kuter, Lawrence S., <u>The Great Gamble: The Boeing 747</u>. Univ. of Alabama Press. 1973.
330 K97e	Kuttner, Robert, <u>The Economic Illusion:</u> False Choices Between Prosperity and Social Justice. Houghton Mifflin. 1984.
338.76292 F69ZL	Lacey, Robert, <u>FORD:</u> The Men and the Machine. Little, Brown, & Co. 1986.
8.8 L237t	Lampert, Hope. <u>Till Death Do Us Part:</u> Bendix vs. Martin Marietta. San Diego: Harcourt Brace Jovanovich. 1983.
92 B85146	Larrowe, Charles F., <u>Harry Bridges:</u> The Rise and Fall of Radical Labor in the United States. Lawrence Hill. 1972.
301.42 L341h	Lasch, Christopher, <u>Haven in a Heartless World.</u> Basic Books. 1977.
363.7 L34s	Lash, Jonathan, <u>Season of Spoils</u>. The Story of the Reagan Administration's Attack on the Environment. Pantheon. 1984.
973.917 L34d	Lash, Joseph P., <u>Dealers and Dreamers</u>: A New Look at The New Deal. Doubleday.

24

92 F6991L	*Lasky, Victor, Never Complain. Never Explain: The Story of Henry Ford II. Richard Marek. 1981.
338.973 L39s	Lave, Lester B., The Strategy of Social Regulation. Brookings Institution. Wash. D.C., 1981.
368.973 L41b	Law, Sylvia A., Blue Cross: What Went Wrong? New Haven. Yale Univ. Press. 1974.
338.973 L53e	Lekachman, Robert. Economist at Bay: Why the Experts Will Never Solve Your Problems. McGraw-Hill. 1976.
338.973 L53g	Lekachman, Robert, Greed is Not Enough. Reaganomics. Pantheon. 1982.
	Lekachman, Robert, The Age of Keynes, 1966.
301.44 L54f	LeMaster, E.E. Blue Collar Aristocrats: Life Styles at a Working Class Tavern. Wisconsin Univ.Press. 1975.
92G3 94L C.1	*Lenzner, Robert, The Great Getty, The Life and Loves of J. Paul Getty. Crown. 1986.
338.973 L58w	Leone, Robert A., Who Profits: Winners, Losers, and Government Regulation. Basic, 1986.
330.1 V24pa	Lerner, Max, ed., Portable Veblen. Viking. 1948.
332.1 L61i	Lernoux, Penny. In Banks We Trust: Bankers and Their Class Associates: The CIA, The Mafia, Drug Traders, Dictators, Politicians and the Vatican. Anchor/Doubleday. 1984.
92 K43L	*Leslie, Stuart W., Boss Kettering. Columbia Univ. Press. 1983.
	Leuchtenberg, William E., The Perils of Prosperity. 1958.
973.917 L65f2	Leuchtenberg, William E., Franklin D. Roosevelt and the New Deal. Harper & Row. 1963.
	Levin, Doron P., Irreconcilable Differences: Ross Perot versus General Motors, Little, Brown, 1989.
92 D362L	Levin, Hillel, Grand Delusions: The Cosmic Career of John DeLorean. Viking Press, Inc. 1983.
	Levine, Marc V. Charles Noble, Carol Mac Lennan and John J. Kushma, Jeff Faux and Marcus Baskin, The State and Democracy: Revitalizing America's Government. Routledge, Chapman & Hall.

25

658.4 L66c	Levinson, Harry and Stuart Rosenthal, _CEO Corporate Leadership in Action_. Basic Books, 1984.
	Levison, Andrew, _The Full Employment Alternative_. Coward-McCann. 1985.
658.8 L66m	Levitt, Theodore, _The Marketing Imagination_. Free Press. 1984.
92 C512c	Levy, Jacques E., _Cesar Chavez_: Autobiography of La Causa. Norton.
	Levy, Leonard W., _Origin of the Fifth Amendment._
323.42 L67g	Lewis, Anthony, _Gideon's Trumpet_. Vintage Books, 1966.
309.173 L67v	Lewis, Oscar, _La Vida_. A Puerto Rican Family in the Culture of Poverty. San Juan and New York. Random House. 1966.
L675d	Lewis, Sinclair, _Dodsworth_. Harcourt, Brace & Co. 1929.
L675b	Lewis, Sinclair. _Babbitt_. Harcourt, Brace. 1922.
L675a c.5,c.7,c.10	Lewis, Sinclair, _Arrowsmith_,
	Lieberstein, Stanley H., _Who Owns What Is In Your Head?_ Trade Secrets and the Mobile Employee. Hawthorn. 1979.
338.8 L27b	Lilienthal, David E., _Big Business: A New Era_. Harper. 1953.
330 L74p	Lindblom, Charles E., _Politics and Markets_, The World's Political-Economic Systems. Basic. 1979.
331.892 L57p	Lindsey, Almont, _The Pullman Strike_. Univ. of Chicago, 1943. (paper).
	*Linowitz, Sol M., _The Making of a Public Man_. Little, Brown. 1986.
	Linowes (or Linones?), David P., _Privacy in America_: Is Your Private Life in the Public Eye? Univ. of Illinois Press, 1989.
331.88 U58	Lipset, Seymour Market, (ed.) _Unions in Transition:_ Entering the Second Century. ICS Press. 1986.

92 C289L	Livesay, Harold, <u>Andrew Carnegie and the Rise of Big Business</u>, Little, Brown, 1975.
	Lodge, David, <u>Nice Work</u>, Viking.
	Lodge, George Cabot, <u>The New American Ideology</u>. Knopf. 1976.
L847i	London, Jack, <u>The Iron Heel</u>. Daily Worker. 1937.
L847bu	London, Jack, <u>Burning Daylight</u>., London, Arco. 1968.
813 L84ZL	London, Jack, <u>The Call of the Wild</u>. Nelson-Hall, 1980.
973.917 M235	Louchheim, Katie, <u>The Making of the New Deal</u>. The Insiders Speak. Cambridge, Mass.: Harvard Univ. Press. 1983.
92 N855L	Lowitt, Richard, <u>George Norris</u>. <u>The Making of a Progressive. 1861. 1912.</u> Syracuse Univ. Pres. 1963.
328.73 N85zL	Lowitt, Richard, <u>George W. Norris</u>. <u>The Persistance of a Progressive. 1913-1933</u>. Univ. of Illinois. 1971.
303.483 L92m	Lowrance, William W., <u>Modern Science and Human Values</u>. Oxford Univ. Press. 1985.
92 436L	Lundberg, Ferdinand, <u>Imperial Hearst - A Social Biography</u>. Equinox Cooperative Press. 1936.
301.44 L96r	Lundberg, Ferdinand, <u>The Rich and the Super-Rich</u>. Stuart. 1968.
	Lutz, Mark A., Kenneth Lux. <u>Humanistic Economics:</u> The New Challenge. The Bootstrap Press. 1989.
331.8809 R 198	Lynd, Alice, and Staughton Lynd, Eds. <u>Rank and File</u>: Personal Histories by Working-Class Organizers. Beacon. 1973.
973.91 L98m 16975m	Lynd, Robert Staughton and Helen M. Lynd, <u>Middletown</u>. Harvest, 1956. and Lewis, Sinclair, <u>Main Street</u>, The Story of Carol Kennicott, Harcourt Brace, 1959.
338.74 L87r	Lydenberg, Steven, Alice Tepper Marlin, Sean O'Brien Strub & the Council on Economic Priorities, <u>Rating America's Corporate Conscience</u>. Addison-Wesley, 1986.

658.87 L97r C.1	Luxenberg, Stan. Roadside Empires: How the Chains Franchised America. Viking. 1985.
658.4 M12g	Maccoby, Michael. The Gamesman. Simon & Schuster. 1977.
658.4 M12L	Maccoby, Michael. The Leader. Simon & Schuster. 1982.
658.42. M14d	Mace, Myles, Directors: Myth and Reality. Harvard Business School. 1971.
305.5 M16h	MacLeod, Celeste, Horatio Alger. The End of the American Dream. Seaview. 1980.
342.73 F29a	Madison, James, The Federalist. Number Ten. 1987.
338.0973 M18M	Magaziner, Ira C., Robert B. Reich, Minding America's Business: The Decline and Rise of the American Economy. Harcourt, Brace. 1982.
338.8 M18t	Madrick, Jeff, Taking America. How We Get From the First Hostile Takeover to Megamergers, Corporate Raiding, and Scandal. Bantam, 1987.
812 M264g	Mamet, David, Glengarry Glen Ross. Grove Press. 1984.
812 M264a	Mamet, David, American Buffalo. A Play. Grove Press. 1975.
	Mann, ERic, Taking on General Motors: A Case Study of the UAW Campaign to Keep GM Van Nuys Open, Instit. of Ind. Rel., Univ. of Cal., Los Angeles, 1988.
M357p	Marquand, John Phillips, Point of No Return. Little, Brown. 1949.
92 P448M	Martin, George, Madam Secretary: Frances Perkins. Houghton-Mifflin. 1976.
335.4 M39c	Marx, Karl. Das Capital. The Modern Library.
	Mason, Alpheus T., The Brandeis Way: A Case Study in the Workings of Democracy. Princeton. 1938.
	Mason, A.T.; Gordon E. Baker, Free Government in the Making 4th Division. Oxford Univ. Press. 1985.
338.7 M39c	Mason, Edward S., ed. The Corporation in Modern Society. Cambridge: Harvard. 1959.

658.3152 M41p	Mason, Ronald M., _Participatory and Workplace Democracy_. So. Illinois Univ. Press. 1982.
331.881 M43t	*Matles, James M. and James Higgins. _Them and Us_. Struggles of a Rank-and-file Union. Prentice-Hall. 1974.
305.43 M43e	Mattaei, Julie A., _An Economic History of Women in America_. Women's Work, the Sexual Division of Labor, and tdhe Development of Capitalism. Schocken Books. 1982.
332.1 M46b	Mayer, Martin, _The Bankers_. Weybright and Rally. 1975.
332.632 M46m	Mayer, Martin, _Markets:_ Who Plays,..Who Risks..Who Gains..Who Loses..? W.W. Norton & Co., 1988.
301.36 M468b	Mayer, Martin, _The Builders_: Houses, People, Neighborhoods, Governments, Money. W.W. Norton & Co. 1978.
	McCaig, Donald _The Butte Polka_, Rawson, Wade. 1980.
	McCartney, Laton, _Friends in High Places:_ _The Bechtel Story:_ The Most Secret Corporation and How It Engineered the World. Simon & Schuster. 1988.
364.163 M12s	McClintick, David, _Stealing from the Rich_: The Homestake Oil Swindle. Evans. 1977.
364.162 M12	McClintick, David, _Indecent Exposure_. William Morrow. 1982.
320.973 M12a	McCloskey, Robert G., _American Conservatism in the Age of Enterprise_: A Study of William Graham Summer. Stephan J. Field and Andrew Carnegie. Harvard, 1951.
	McCoy, Drew R., _The Last of the Fathers._ James Madison and the Republican Legacy. Cambridge Univ. Press.
	McCraw, Thomas M., _The Tennessee Valley and the Power Fight_.
338.973 R34	McCraw, Thomas, ed., _Regulation in Perspective_. Harvard Univ. 1981.
338.973 M13p	McCraw, Thomas M. _Prophets of Regulation:_ Charles Francis Adams, Louis D. Brandeis, James M. Landis, Alfred E. Kahn. Harvard Univ. Press. 1984.
973.916 M14g	McElvaine, Robert, _The Great Depression_: America, 1929-1941. Holt, Rinehart & Winston. 1984.

331.892 M14g	McGovern, George. *The Great Coalfield War*. Houghton-Mifflin. 1971.
92H7943m	McJimsey, George, *Harry Hopkins:* Ally of the Poor and Defender of Democracy. Harvard Univ. Press.
344.73 M15s	McKinnon, Catharine A., *Sexual Harrassment of Working Women*. Yale. 1979.
	McKibben, Bill, *Reflections: (The End of Nature)*. The New Yorker, Sept. 11, 1989.
335.4 M164M	McLelland, David, *Marxism Ater Marx*: An Introduction. Harper & Row. 1980.
557.9 M17f	McPhee, John. *Basin and Range*. Farrar, Straus, & Giroux. 1981.
331.763 M17 S814G	*McWilliam, Carey, *Factories in the Field*. Little, Brown, 1939. TOGETHER WITH Steinbeck, John, *The Grapes of Wrath*. Viking. 1939.
331.88 M51b	Meier, August and Elliott Rudwick, *Black Detroit and Rise of the UAW*. . Oxford, 1979.
301.M57a c.7 301.M57a3 c.1, c.2	Merton, Robert, *Social Theory and Social Structure*. 1949.
	Metcalf, Lee and Vic Reinemer, *Overcharge*. David McKay Co. 1967.
	Metz, Tim, *Black Money:* The Catastrophe of October 19, 1987...and Beyond. William Morrow, 1988.
331.4 S51	Meyer, Oestreich, Collins and Berchtold, *Sexual Harrassment*. Petrocelli. 1981.
	Michel, Allen and Israel Shaked, *Takeover Madness, Corporate America Fights Back*. John Wiley. 1986.
812 M64d	Miller, Arthur, *Death of a Salesman*. Viking. 1949.
	Miller, Arthur, *All My Sons.*
	Miller, Russell, *The House of Getty*. Henry Holt. 1986.
338.973 M65r	Miller, S.M. Donald Tomaskovic-Devey, *Recapitalizing America*: Alternatives to the Corporate Distortion of National Policy. Routledge & Kegan Paul. 1983.
917.3 M65p	Mills, C. Wright. *Power Elite*. Oxford Univ. Press. 1959.

332.1	Mintz, Beth, Michael Schwartz. _The Power Structure of American Business_. Univ. of Chicago Press. 1985.
338.761 M66a	Mintz, Morton, _At Any Cost_: Corporate Greed, Women and the Dalkon Shield. Pantheon. 1985.
330.1 V24W	Mitchell, Welsey C., ed. _What Veblen Taught_. Kelley (rep. 1936). 1964.
	MIT's Commission on Industrial Productivity, _Made in America: Regaining the Productive Edge._, MIT press.
364.168 M71c	Mokhiber, Russell, _Corporate Crime and Violence:_ Big Business Power and the Abuse of the Public Trust. Sierra Club, 1988.
301.424 P82h	Montagu, Ashley, _The Natural Superiority of Women_. Macmillan. 1968.
331.8 M78W	Montgomery, David, _Workers' Control in America_: Studies in the History of Work: Technology and Labor Struggles. Cambridge. 1980.
331.88 M78f	Montgomery, David, _The Fall of the House of Labor_: The Workplace, The State, and American Labor Activism, 1865-1925. Cambridge Univ. Press. 1987.
	Moore, George S., _The Banker's Life_. Norton. 1987.
	Moore, Kathleen Dean, _Pardons._ 1989.
331.4 N899	Moore, Lynda L. (ed.). _Not As Far As You Think_. The Realities of Working Women. Lexington Books. 1986.
382.41 M84M	Morgan, Dan. _Merchants of Grain._ Viking. 1979.
338.7621 M86m	Morita, Akio. _Made in Japan._ Dutton. 1986.
92 D9381M	*Mosley, Leonard, _Blood Relations_: The Rise and Fall of the duPonts of Delaware. Atheneum. 1980.
973.927 M938s	Moyers Bill, _The Secret Government._ The Constitution in Crisis, Seven Locks Press, 1988.
	Mukherjee, Santosh, _Through No Fault of Their Own_: Systems for Handling Redundancy in Britain, France, and Germany. A PEP Report. London: Macdonald, 1974.
	Munson, Richard. _The Power Makers_. Rodale Press. 1985.

31

Call #	Reference
353.09 M98u	Musolf, Lloyd D., *Uncle Sam's Private, Profit Seeking Corporations*: Comsat, Fannie Mae, Amtrak, and Conrail. Lexington Books. 1983.
326 M99	Myrdal, Gunnar, *An American Dilemma*: Univ. of Michigan Microfilms. 1971.
338.7 M99ha	Myers, Gustavus, *History of the American Fortunes*, Modern Library. 1936.
338.644 N13b	*Nader, Ralph, and William Taylor. *The Big Boys: Styles Corporate Power*. Pantheon. 1986.
629.1 N13u	Nader, Ralph. *Unsafe at Any Speed*. The Designed-in Dangers of the American Automobile. Grossman. 1965.
658.4	Nader, Ralph, and Mark Green, *Corporate Power in America*. Grossman. 1973.
346.73 N13t	Nader, Ralph, Mark Green and Joel Seligman. *Taming the Giant Corporation*. W.W. Norton & Co. 1976.
614.7 W62	Nader, R., R. Brownstein, J. Richard, *Who's Poisoning America?* Sierra Club. 1981.
387.7 N175S C.1	Nance, John J., *Splash of Colors*: The Self-Destruction of Braniff International. William Morrow. 1984.
338.8 N34a2	Neale, A.D. and D. G. Goyder, *The Antitrust Laws of the U.S.A.* A Study of Competition Enforced by Law. Cambridge. 1980.
	Neuharth, Allen H. *Confessions of an S.O.B.* 1989.
92 R682n	Nevins, Allan, *John D. Rockefeller*. Scribner. 1959.
971.2 N55c	Newman, Peter C., *Company of Adventurers*. Viking. 1985.
158.5 N67a C.1	Nierenberg, Gerard. *The Art of Negotiating*. Simon & Schuster. 1983.
	Nixon, Richard M., *White House Conversations*, 1972-73, (June 23, 1972, Sept 15, 1972, 3/13/73, 3/21/73), Hearings Before the Committee on the Judiciary, House of Representatives, 93rd Congress, 2nd Session, (U.S. Government Printing Office, 1974).
303.483 N74f	Noble, David F., *Forces of Production*: A Social History of Industrial Automation. Knopf. 1984.
	Noonan, John T. Jr., *Usury*.

364.132 N816	Noonan, John T., Jr. <u>Bribes</u>, Macmillan, 1984.
	Nordhaus, Willioam <u>Invention, Growth & Welfare:</u> A Theoretical Treatment of Technological Change. MIT Press, 1969.
N855p	Norris, Frank <u>The Pit</u>. Random House. 1934.
813 N852dqv C.1	Norris, Frank. <u>The Octopus</u>.
331.892 N93g	Novak, Michael. <u>The Guns of Lattimer</u>: The True Story of a Massacre and a Trial. August 1897-March 1898. Basic Books. 1978.
	Nussbaum, Karen, <u>9 to 5: The Working Woman's Guide to Office Survival.</u>
	O'Connell, Brian, <u>The Board Member's Book (Making A Difference in Voluntary Organizations)</u>, The Foundation Center, 1985.
	O'Connor, Jessie Lloyd, Harvey O'Connor and Susan N. Bowler, <u>Harvey & Jessie</u>, A Couple of Radicals, Temple Univ. Press.
	O'Connor, Edwin. <u>The Last Hurrah</u>. Little. 1985.
92M5270	O'Connor, Harvey, <u>Mellon's Millions.</u>
92 G9420	O'Connor, Harvey, <u>The Guggenheims:</u> The Making of an American Dynasty, Covici, Friede, 1937.
	O'Connor, Harvey, <u>History of the Oil Workers International Union</u>
	O'Connor, Harvey, <u>The Empire of Oil.</u>
331.880979 018r	O'Connor, Harvey, <u>Revolution in Seattle, A Memoir</u>, Monthly Review Press. 1964.
178.5 O23	Odegard, Peter. <u>Pressure Politics</u>: The Story of the Anti-Saloon League. Columbia Univ. Press. 1928.
	OECD Publications, <u>Annual Report on Competition Policy in OECD Member Countries</u>. [current year] OECD. Wash. D.C.
335.43 O51c	Ollman, Bertell, <u>Class Struggle is the Name of the Game</u>: True Confessions of a Marxist Business Man. William Morrow. 1983.

33

70

353.0082 O52s	Olson, James S., Saving Capitalism: The Reconstruction Finance Corporations and the New Deal. 1933-1940. Princeton Univ. Press.
901 O 77r	Ortega y Gassett, Jose, The Revolt of the Masses. W.W. Norton. 1957.
079nL	Orwell, George. Nineteen Eight-Four. New American Library. 1961.
	O'Toole, Patricia, Corporate Messiah: The Hiring and Firing of Million Dollar Managers. Morrow. 1984.
658.3219 O93t	Ouchi, William G., Theory Z: How American Business Can Meet the Japanese Challenge. Addison-Wesley. 1981.
659.1 P11h	Packard, Vance, The Hidden Persuaders. McKay. 1957.
307.32973 P11n	Packard, Vance, A Nation of Strangers. McKay. 1972.
658.31 P11p	Packard, Vance. The Pyramid Climbers. McGraw-Hill. 1962.
	Paine, Thomas, Common Sense. (edited by Isaac KramRuck), Penguin, 1980.
P3462c	Payne, David, Confessions of a Taoist on Wall Street. Houghton-Mifflin, 1984.
328.73 P46g	Pertschuk, Michael. Giant Killers. Norton. 1986.
339.47 P46r	Pertschuk, Michael, Revolt Against Regulation: The Rise and Pause of the Consumer Movement.
	Petzinger, Thomas Jr., Oil and Honor: The Texaco-Penzoil Wars: Inside the $11 Billion Battle for Getty Oil. Putnam. 1987.
338.761 P46n	Perry, Susan and Jim Dawson, Nightmare, Women and the Dalkon shield. Macmillan. 1985.
338.06 P66s	Piore, Michael J. and Charles F. Sabel. The Second Industrial Divide: Possibilities for Prosperity. Basic Books. 1984.
322.4 P69p	Piven, Frances Fox and Cloward, Richard A., Poor People's Movements: Studies from the Contemporary United States. Pantheon. 1977.

361.6 P69n	Piven, Frances Fox, Richard A. Cloward, The New Class War: Reagan's Attack on the Welfare State and Its Consequences. Pantheon Books. 1982.
324.973 p69w	Piven, Frances Fox; Richard A. Cloward. Why Americans Don't Vote.
330.9 P76gl	Polanyi, Karl, The Great Transformation. The Political and Economic Origins of our Time. Beacon. 1944.
	Posner, Richard A., Law and Literature. A Misunderstood Relation. Harvard, 1988.
338.8 Q7g	*Quinn, T.K., Giant Business. Threat to Democracy: The Autobiography of an Insider. Exposition Press. 1953.
302.3 R14a	Raiffa, Howard. The Art and Science of Negotiation: How to Resolve Conflicts and Get the Best Out of Bargaining. Harvard Univ. Press. 1982.
179.9 R26t	Rawls, John. A Theory of Justice. Harvard. 1971.
92 R2871r	Reagan, Ronald, Richard G. Hubler, Where's the Rest of Me? Duell, Sloan and Pearce. 1965.
973.92 R33a C.1	Reeves, Richard, Article on deToqueville. The New Yorker, April 5 and April 12. 1982.
174.4 J96	Regan, Tom (edited by), Just Business. Philadelphia. Pa., Temple Univ. Press. 1983.
92 M6122r	Reich, Gary, Financier: The Biography of Andre Meyer. Morrow. 1983.
338.76292 R34n	Reich, Robert B. and John D. Donahue, New Deals. The Chrysler Revival and the American System. Times Books. 1985.
	Reich, Robert B., Tales of a New America.
322.3 R34n	Reich, Robert B., The Next American Frontier. Times Books. 1983.
621.3817 R35c	Reid, T.R., The Chip: How Two Americans Invented The Microchip and Launched a Revolution. S & S. 1984.
155.8973 R56Laa	Reisman, David, The Lonely Crowd: A Study of the Changing American Character. Yale Univ. Press. (paper). 1976.
331.88 R42w	Renshaw, Patrick, The Wobblies. Doubleday, 1967.

658.408 U58c	U.S. Department of Commerce, Report of the Task Force On Corporate and Social Performance. Corporate Social Reporting in the United States and Western Europe.1979.
923.31 R446	Reuther, Victor G., The Brothers Reuther and the Story of the UAW: A Memoir. Houghton-Mifflin. 1977.
338.76691 R44s	Reutter, Mark, Sparrows Point: Making Steel - The Rise and Ruin of American Industrial Might. Summit Books, 1989.
331.880973 R56N	Rifkin, Jeremy and Randy Barber, et al. The North Will Rise Again. Pensions, Politics, and Power in the 1980's. Beacon Press. 1981.
	Robertson, James Oliver, America's Business. Hill and Wang. 1985.
R643g	Roberts, Elizabeth Madox, The Great Meadow. Signet. 1961.
	Robin, Donald, P.; R. Eric Reidenbach. Business Ethics - Where Profits Meet Value Systems. Prentice-Hall.
330.1 R662ec	Robinson, Joan. Economic Philosophy. Aldine Pub. Co. 1962.
338.91	Robinson, Joan. Aspects of Development and Underdevelopment. Cambridge Univ. Press. 1979.
	Robinson, Jo Ann Ooiman, Abraham Went Out. A Biography of A. J. Muste. Temple U. Press.
R755g	Rolvaag, Ole, Giants in the Earth (1927). Perennial. 1929.
330.9172 R81h	Rosenberg, Nathan and L. E. Birdzell, Jr. How the West Grew Rich. The Economic Transformation of the Industrial World. Basic Books. 1985.
	Rosencrance, Richard. The Rise of the Trading State: Commerce and Conquest in the Modern World. Basic. 1986.
	Roszak, Theodore, The Cult of Information. Pantheon. 1986.
658.409 R89	Ruch, Richard S. and Ronald Goodman. Image at the Top: The Crisis and Renaissance in American Corporate Leadership. The Free Press. 1984.
92 M182ru	Rutland, Robert Allen, James Madison. The Founding Father. Macmillan. 1987.

	Ryckman, W.C., *What Do You Mean By That?* The Art of Speaking and Writing Clearly.
385.065 S17n	Salsbury, Stephen, *No Way to Run a Railroad*. The Story of the Penn-Central Crisis. McGraw-Hill. 1982.
92 D288s	Salvatore, Nick, *Eugene V. Debs*: Citizen and Socialist. Univ. of Illinois Press. 1982.
387.7 S19e C1	Sampson, Anthony, *Empires of the Sky*: The Politics, Contests and Cartels of World Airlines. Random House. 1985.
332.15 S19M	Sampson, Anthony. *The Money Lenders*. Bankers and a World in Turmoil. Viking. 1982.
338.27282 S19	Sampson, Anthony. *The Seven Sisters*. The Great Oil Companies and the World They Made. The Viking Press. 1975.
384.065 S193	Sampson, Anthony, *The Sovereign State of ITT*: Stein & Day. 1973.
341.3 S19a	Sampson, Anthony. *The Arms Bazaar:* From Lebanon to Lockheed. Viking. 1977.
331.88 S31e	Schatz, Ronald W. , *The Electrical Workers*: A History of Labor at General Electric and Westinghouse, 1923-1960. Univ. of Illinois Press. 1984.
331.4 S38a	Schroedel, Jean Reith, *Alone in a Crowd*. Women in the Trades Tell Their Stories. Temple Univ. Press. 1985.
659.1 384a	Schudson, Michael. *Advertising. The Uneasy Persuasion*: Its Dubious Impact on American Society. Basic. 1984.
S386w2	Schulberg, Budd, *What Makes Sammy Run?* Random House. 1941.
338.91 S39s	Schumacher, E.F., *Small is Beautiful*: Economics as If People Mattered. Harper/Torchbooks. 1975.
335 S39	Schumpeter, Joseph A., *Capitalism, Socialism and Democracy*. Harper & Row. 1950.
330.122 S39c	Schumpeter, Joseph A., *Can Capitalism Survive?* With an Intro. by Robert Lekachman. Harper Coloplion Books. 1978.

658.1 C734	Schwartz, Donald E., (ed.), <u>Commentaries</u> <u>on</u> <u>Corporate</u> <u>Structure</u> <u>and</u> <u>Governance</u>. The ALI/ABA Symposiums 1977-1978. American Bar Assoc. 1980.
92B5142s	Schwartz, Jordan A., <u>Liberal</u>: Adolph A. Berle and the Vision of An American Era. The Free Press/ Macmillan. 1988.
92B295s	*Schwartz, Jordan, A., <u>The</u> <u>Speculator.</u> <u>Bernard</u> <u>M.</u> <u>Baruch</u> <u>in</u> <u>Washington.</u> <u>1917-1965.</u> Chapel Hill, N.C., Univ. of No. Carolina. 1981.
	Schwartz, Flynn & First, <u>Government</u> <u>Regulation.</u> <u>6th</u> <u>ed.</u> Foundation Press, Inc. 1985.
320.973 s41a	Schwarz, John E., <u>America's</u> <u>Hidden</u> <u>Success</u>: A Reassessment of Twenty Years of Public Policy. W.W. Norton & Co., 1983.
	Sen, Amartya, <u>On</u> <u>Ethics</u> <u>and</u> <u>Economics.</u> Basil Blackwell.
301.424 S55c	Seidenberg, Robert, <u>Corporate</u> <u>Wives.</u> <u>Corporate</u> <u>Casualties</u>. Anchor Press-Doubleday. 1975.
301.55 S49u4	Sethi, S. Prakash, <u>Up</u> <u>Against</u> <u>the</u> <u>Corporate</u> <u>Wall</u>, (4th ed. 1982.) Prentice-Hall.
S4955s	Settle, Mary Lee, <u>Scapegoat</u>, Random House. 1980.
330.973 S528g	Shannan, David A., <u>The</u> <u>Great</u> <u>Depression</u>: A Spectrum Book. Englewood Cliffs, N.J. Prentice-Hall. 1960.
364.168 S52w	Shapiro, Susan P., <u>Wayward</u> <u>Capitalists</u>: Targets of the Securities and Exchange Commission. Yale, 1984.
	Shaplen, Robert, "Annals of Crime: Lockheed in Japan". <u>The</u> <u>New</u> <u>Yorker</u>. Jan 23, Jan 30, 1978.
822 S534maj4	Shaw, G.B., <u>Major</u> <u>Barbara</u>.
822 S534saab	Shaw, Bernard, <u>Saint</u> <u>Joan.</u> Modern Library. 1956.
338.973 C28e	Shearer and Derek, <u>Economic</u> <u>Democracy</u>: The Challenge of the 1980's. M.E. Sharpe. 1980.
338.27282 S55o	Sherrill, Robert, <u>The</u> <u>Oil</u> <u>Follies</u> <u>of</u> <u>1970-1980</u>. How the Petroleum Industry Stole the Show (And Much More Besides). Garden City, N.Y.: Anchor Press/ Doubleday. 1983.
330 S58e	Silk, Leonard, <u>Economics</u> <u>in</u> <u>the</u> <u>Real</u> <u>World</u>. Simon & Schuster, 1984.

650.69 S58e	Silk, Leonard. **Ethics and Profits:** The Crisis of Confidence in American Business. New York. Simon & Schuster. 1976.
338.4761519 S58p	Silverman, Milton Morris, Philip R. Lee, and Mia Lydecker. **Prescription for Death**: The Drugging of the Third World. Univ. of Calif. Press. 1982.
658.018 S59s	Simon, H., **The Shape of Automation for Men and Management**. Harper & Row. 1970.
	Simon, James F., **The Antagonists.** Hugo Black, Felix Frankfurter, and Civil Liberties in Modern America. Simon & Schuster, 1989.
92 M848si	*Sinclair, Andreew, **Corsair: The Life of J. Pierpont Morgan**. Little, Brown, and Co., 1981.
	Sinclair, Lister; Probst, George, **Democracy in America**, Scripts of 14 Dramatizations based on Alexis De Tocqueville), National Educational TV and Radio Center.
S6162j	Sinclair, Upton, **The Jungle**, Signet, (paperback). 1986.
332.12 S61f	Singer, Mark, **Funny Money**. Knopf. 1985.
92K445s	Skidelsky, Robert, **John Meynard Keynes. Volume One: Hopes Betrayed, 1863-1920.** Viking. 1986.
338.8S62c and on order	Sklar, Martin J., **The Corporate Reconstruction of America Capitalism:** 1890-1916.
338.4 S63t	*Sloan, Allen, **Three Plus One Equals Billions**. The Bendix Martin Marietta War. Arbor House. 1983
338.4 S63M	*Sloan, Alfred P., Jr. **My Years With General Motors**. Doubleday. 1970.
332.67 G65M	Smith, Adam, (pseudonym for Goodman, George J.) **The Money Game**. Random House. 1968.
332.4 S642p	Smith, Adam, (pseud. for Goodman, George J.), **Paper Money**. Summitt. 1981.
332.67 G65s	Smith, Adam, (pseud. for Goodman George J.), **Supermoney**. Random House. 1972.
330 S64a	Smith, Adam, **The Wealth of Nations**. 1776.

	Smith, Donald L., *Zachariah Chaffee, Jr. Defender of Liberty and Law*. Harvard Univ. Press. 1987.
882 S71an	Sophocles, *Antigone*. Oxford Univ. Press. 1973.
332.12 S766	Sprague, Irvine H., *Bailout. An Insider's Account of Bank Failures and Rescues*. Basic. 1986.
338.4761519 S87f	Stage, Sarah, *Female Complaints*: Lydia Pinkham and the Business of Women's Medicine. Norton. 1979.
	Stansell, Christine, *City of Women*.
338.6 D324	Staudohar, Paul D., and Holly E. Brown. *Deindustrialization and Plant Closure*. D.C. Heath & Co., 1987.
92 S817s2	*Steffins, Lincoln, *The Autobiography of Lincoln Steffins*. Harcourt, Brace & World. 1931.
S818p	Stegner, Wallace. *Preacher and the Slave*. Univ. of Nebraska Press. 1980.
974.71 S81t	Stein, Leon. *The Triangle Fire*. Philadelphia.
331.881 094	Stein, Leon, (ed.).*Out of the Sweatshop*: The Struggle of Industrial Democracy. N.Y.Times Books Co.1977.
S819i	Steinbeck, John, *In Dubious Battle*. Viking Press. 1974. (orig. 1936).
S819.ga	Steinbeck, John. *The Grapes of Wrath*. Viking Press. 1939.
621.4835 S83t	Stephens, Mark. *Three Mile Island*. Random House. 1981.
345.73 S83b	Stern, Gerald M., *The Buffalo Creek Disaster*. The Story of the Survivors' Unprecented Lawsuit. Random House. 1976.
	Stevens, Mark, *Sudden Death. The Rise and Fall of E. F. Hutton*.
338.761 S94b	Stevens, Mark, *The Big Eight*. Macmillan 1981.
340.09753 S84p	Stewart, James B. *The Prosecutors: Inside the Offices of the Government's Most Powerful Lawyers*. Touchstone/Simon & Schuster. 1988.

330 S855e	Stigler, George, <u>The Intellectual and the Marketplace.</u> Harvard. 1984.
330 S855e	Stigler, George, <u>The Economist As Preacher and Other Essays</u>. Univ. of Chicago. 1982.
346.73 S67s	Stone, Christopher, <u>Should Trees Have Standing</u>? Toward Legal Rights for Natural Objects. Harper & Row. 1974.
338.7 S87w	Stone, Christopher D., <u>Where the Law Ends</u>: The Social Control of Corporate Behavior. Harper & Row. 1975.
S877a	Stone, Irvin, <u>Adversary in the House</u>, Doubleday. 1947.
	Stover, Robert V. <u>Making It and Breaking It.</u> The Fate of Public Interest Commitment During Law School. Univ. of Illinois Press. 1989.
	Strohmeyer, John. <u>Crisis in Bethlehem</u>. Big Steel's Struggle to Survive. Adler & Adler. 1987.
364.38 S96a	Sutherland, Edwin H., <u>White Collar Crime</u>: The Uncut Version. Yale Univ. Press. 1983.
92 T459sw	*Swanberg, W.A., <u>Norman Thomas</u> - <u>The Last Idealist</u>. Charles Scribner's Sons. 1976.
	Sweeney, John J.; Karen Nussbaum, <u>Services for the New Work Force: Politics for a New Social Contract.</u> Seven Locks Press, 1989.
	Sweeney, John J., Karen Nussbaum, <u>Solutions for the New Workforce.</u> Policies for a New Social Contract. Seven Locks Press. 1988.
330.15 S97a	Sweezy, Paul, <u>The Theory of Capitalist Development</u>. Monthly Review. 1968.
	Tamari, Meir, <u>With All Your Possessions:</u> Jewish Ethics and Economic Life.
332.644 T15n 338.2 T17	Tamarkin, Bob., <u>The New Gatsbys</u>, Fortunes and Misfortunes: Commodity Traders. Morrow. 1985. Tarbell, Ida M.,Edited by David Chalmers, <u>History of The Standard Oil Company</u>, Harvard Torchbooks, T.B., 307. (paperback), 1966.
92 Y74t	*Tarbell, Ida M., <u>Owen D. Young:</u> A New Type of Industrial Leader. Macmillan. 1932.
330.1 T23	Tawney, R. H., <u>The Acquisitive Society.</u> Harvest Books. 1950.

41

Tax, Meredith, <u>Union Square.</u>

Taylor, John, <u>Storming the Magic Kingdom</u>: Wall Street, the Raiders, and the Battle for Disney. Knopf. 1987.

658.7
T24p2
Taylor, Frederick Winslow. <u>The Principles of Scientific Management</u>. Harper. 1923.

338.476797
T24s.
Taylor, Peter, <u>The Smoke Ring</u>: Tobacco, Money and Multinational Politics. Pantheon. 1984.

309.173
T31h
Terkel, Studs, (Compiled and edited by) <u>Hard Times:</u> An Oral History of the Great Depression in America. Pantheon. 1970.

331.2
T31W
Terkel, Studs, <u>Working</u>. Pantheon. 1972.

973.927
T31g
Terkel, Studs, <u>The Great Divide.</u> Second Thoughts on The American Dream.

Todd, A.L. <u>Justice on Trial:</u> The Case of Louis D. Brandeis. McGraw-Hill, 1964.

Tolchin, Susan; Martin Tolchin, <u>Buying Into America</u>: How <u>Foreign Money Is Changing the Face of our Nation.</u> Times Books. 1988.

338.973
T36r
Thayer, Frederick C., <u>Rebuilding America.</u> The Case for Economic Regulation. Praeger, 1984.

T459s C.1
Thomas, Michael M., <u>Someone Else's Money</u>. Simon & Schuster. 1982.

Thomas, Michael J.M., <u>Ropespinner Conspiracy</u>. Warner.1987.

T459h
Thomas, Michael M., <u>Hard Money</u>. Viking. 1985.

Thomas, Michael M., <u>Green Money</u>.

Thurow, Lester, <u>World Class</u>. S&S. 1985.

330.973
T54Z
Thurow, Lester C., <u>The Zero-Sum Society:</u> Distribution and Possibilities for Economic Change. Basic Books. 1985.

338.973
T54d
Thurow, Lester, <u>Dangerous Currents</u>: The State of Economics. Random House. 1983.

338.76797
T57r
Tilley, Nannie M., <u>The R.J. Reynolds Tobacco Co.,</u> Univ. of North Carolina Press. 1985.

363.3 T62i	Tobias, Andrew, *The Invisible Bankers*. Everything the Insurance Industry Never Wanted You to Know. Linden/Simon & Schuster. 1982.
352 T64d	Tolchin, Susan J. and Martin Tolchin. *Dismantling America*. The Rush to Deregulate. Boston: Houghton-Mifflin. 1983.
	Tolstoy, Leo. *Death of Ivan Ilych.*
658 T74u	Townsend, Robert, *Up the Organization*. Knopf, 1970.
658 T74u	Townsend, Robert, *Further Up the Organization*. Knopf. 1970.
332.09 T76f C.1	Train, John, *Famous Financial Fiascos*. Clarkson N. Potter. 1985.
363.7384 T85e	Trost, Cathy, *Elements of Risk*: The Chemical Industry and Its Threat to America.. Times Books. 1984.
	Tuleja, Tad, *Beyond the Bottom Line*: How America's Top Corporations Are Proving that Sound Business Ethics Means Good Business Practice. Penguin Books, 1987.
C625h2	Twain, Mark, *The Adventures of Huckleberry Finn*.
818c62ma	Twain, Mark, *A Connecticut Yankee in King Arthur's Court.*
796.357 T97b	Tygiel, Jules, *Baseball's Great Experiment*: Jackie Robinson and His Legacy. Oxford. 1983.
338.76 T98r	Tyler, Patrick, *Running Critical*: The Silent War, Rickover and General Dynamics. Harper & Row, 1988.
	U.S. Department of Commerce Task Force on Corporate Social Performance. *Business and Society*: Strategies for the 1980's. 1980.
658.408 U58c	U.S. Dept. of Commerce. *Corporate Social Reporting in U.S. and Western Europe*. U.S. Dept. of Commerce, Task Force on Corp. Social Performance. 1979.
Y4.Ed 8/1	U.S. House Rep. 96th Congress. 1st Session, Hearings, *Pressures in Today's Workplace*. Oversight Hearings Before the Subcommittee on Labor Management Relations of the Committee on Education Management Relations of the Committee on Education and Labor. Vol. 1. U.S. Govt. Printing Office. 1979.
363.17 V286	Van Strum, Carol. *A Bitter Fog:* Herbicides and Human Rights. San Francisco: Sierra Club. 1983.

43

Call #	Reference
364.106 V36c	Vaughan, Diane, **Controlling Unlawful Organizational Behavior**. Social Structure and Corporate Misconduct. Univ. of Chicago Press. 1983.
330.1 V24.ta	Veblen, Thorstein, **The Theory of the Business Enterprise**. Transaction Books, 1978.
330 V39	Veblen, Thorstein, **Absentee Ownership**. Kelly 1923. (rep).
330.9 V39	Veblen, Thorstein, **Engineers and the Price System** Lelly, (rep. 1921).
338.4 V24	Veblen, Thorstein, **The Instinct of Workmanship and the State of the Industrial Arts**. Kelly, (1918 rep.)
330.1 V24	Veblen, Thorstein, **The Theory of the Leisure Class**. Macmillan. 1899.
322.3 V87f	Vogel, David, **Fluctuating Fortunes:** The Political Power of Business in Americaz. Basic Books. 1989.
	von Hirsch, Andrew, **Doing Justice**. 1976.
V946p	Vonnegut, Kurt, **Player Piano**. 1952.
V946j	Vonnegut, Kurt, **Jailbird**. Delacorte. 1979.
	Voorhis, Jerry, **American Cooperatives**. Harper & Row. 1961.
W149h	Wakeman, Frederick, **Hucksters**. Rinehart & Co. 1946.
	Waldo, Charles M., **Boards of Directors**. Quorum Books, 1985.
301.444 W18w	Walkowitz, Daniel J., **Worker City, Company Town:** Iron & Cotton Worker Protest in Troy and Cohoes. New York, 1855-84. Univ. Illinois Press. 1978.
92 C 289WaL C.1	*Wall, Joseph Frazier, **Andrew Carnegie**. Oxford. 1970.
309.17481 W18r	Wallace, Anthony, F.C. **Rockdale**: The Growth of an American Village in the Early Industrial Revolution. Knopf, 1978.
307.766 W18s	Wallace, Anthony F.C. **St. Clair. A Nineteenth-Century Coal Town's Experience with a Disaster-Prone Industry**. Knopf. 1987.
338.8 W23c	Walton, Clarence C., and Fred Cleveland Jr., **Corporations on Trial**: The Electrical Cases. Wadsworth. 1964.

222.12 W24s	Walzer, Michael, Exodus and Revolution. Basic. 1985.
320.011 W46s	Walzer, Michael, Spheres of Justice: A Defense of Pluralism and Equality. Basic Books. 1983.
92 W2464w	Wang, An, (with Eugene Linden). Lessons: An Autobiography, (A once one-person firm in Boston called Wang Labor Laboratories). Addison-Wesley. 1986.
321 W25f	Ward, Barbara, Five Ideas That Changed The World. Norton. 1959.
301.31 W25h	Ward, Barbara, The Home of Man. 1976.
330.9 W25p	Ward, Barbara, Progress for a Small Planet. Norton. 1969.
338.91 W25r	Ward, Barbara, The Rich Nations and the Small Nations. 1962.
327 N25s	Ward, Barbara, Spaceship Earth. Columbia. 1966
301.31 W25o	Ward, Barbara and Rene Dubos, Only One Earth. W.W.Norton & Co., 1972.
W26221	Ward, Robert, Red Baker. Dial Press. 1985
812 W29a	Warren, Robert Penn, All the King's Men. Dramatists Play Service. 1960. Harcourt, 1946.
	Warren, Robert Penn, Night Rider.
810.9 W346	Watts, Emily Stipes, The Businessman in American Literature. Univ. of Georgia Press. 1982.
338.74 W36s	Weaver, Paul H, The Suicidal Corporation: How Big Business Fails America. Simon & Schuster. 1988.
261 W37a	Weber, Max. The Protestant Ethic and the Spirit of Capitalism. Scribners. 1958.
782.8 R76i	Weidman, Jerome, I Can Get It For You Wholesale. Random House. 1962.
172.2 W42r	Weisband, Edward and Thomas M. Franck, Resignation in Protest. Grossman. 1975.
51W464p	Welty, Eudora, The Ponder Heart, Harcourt Brace. 1954.

914.97 W51a	West, Rebecca, <u>Black Lamb and Grey Falcon: A Journey Through Yugoslavia</u>. Penguin, 1982.
331.01	Westin, Alan F., (ed.) <u>Whistle Blowing</u>. McGraw-Hill. 1980.
323.4 I39	Westin, Alan F., Stephan Salisbury (eds.), <u>Individual Rights in the Corporation</u>: A Reader on Employee Rights. Pantheon. 1980.
323.4 W55L	Whalen, Barbara, Charles Whalen, <u>The Longest Debate.</u> The Legislative History of the 1964 Civil Rights Act. Seven Locks Press. 1985.
338.2 W55r	Wheatcroft, Geoffrey, <u>The Randlords</u>, Antheneum. 1986.
	White, Larry C., <u>Merchants of Death</u>, The American Tobacco Industry. Beech Tree/Morrow. 1988.
353.09 W581	White, Lawrence J., <u>Reforming Regulations</u>: Processes and Problems. Prentice-Hall. 1981.
W5889c	White, William Allen, <u>A Certain Rich Man</u>. Macmillan. 1923.
01.15 W6201	Whyte, William H.,Jr., <u>The Organization Man</u>. Simon & Schuster. 1956.
323.352 W62a2	Whyte, William F., <u>Street Corner Society</u>, 2nd ed., 1955.
	Wideman, John Edgar, <u>Reuben</u>. Henry Holt, 1987.
338.91 W66p5	Wilcox, Clair, <u>Public Policies Toward Business</u>. R.D. Irwin, Inc. 1975.
	Wilentz, Sean, <u>Chants Democratic.</u>
331.29 W69c	Willborn, Steven L., <u>A Comparable Worth Primer</u>. Lexington Books, 1986.
W7281w	Williams, William Carlos, <u>White Mule</u>. New Directions Pub. Co., 1967.
338.973 P76	Wilson, James Q., ed., <u>The Politics of Regulation</u>, Basic Books, 1980.
W753m	Wilson, Sloan, <u>The Man in the Gray Flannel Suit.</u> Simon & Schuster, 1955.
	Wilson, Sloan, <u>The Man in the Gray Flannel Suit II.</u> Simon & Schuster, 1955.

362.5 W75t	Wilson, William Julius, *The Truly Disadvantaged*. The Inner City, The Underclass, and Public Policy. Univ. of Chicago Press. 1987.
364.168 W75f	Winans, R. Foster, *Trading Secrets: Seduction and Scandal at the Wall Street Journal*. St. Martins. 1986.
	Wolf, Thomas, *The Nonprofit Corporation. An Operating Manual*, Prentice-Hall, 1984.
338.4 W951o	Wright, J. Patrick. *On A Clear Day You Can See General Motors*. Gross Martin, Wright Enterprises. 1979.
	Wright, Richard, *Native Son*, 1940.
	Yates, Richasrd, *Revolution Road*. 1961.
	Yolton, John W., (ed.) *The Locke Reader*. Cambridge. 1977.
	Zilg, Gerald Colby, *Du Pont: Behind the Nylon Curtain* Prentice-Hall. 1974.
8432866	Zola, Emile, *Germinal*.
HD45.2 Z93(SEI-BK) 338.06z93	Zukoff, Shoshana, *In the Age of the Smart Machine*, The Future of Work and Power. Basic. 1988.
658.315 Z97w	Zwerdling, D., *Workplace Democracy*. A Guide to Workplace Ownership, Participation, and Self-Management Experiments in the United States and Europe. Harper & Row. 1980.

*Biography

Please Note: Unnumbered are on order.

11/1/89

COMPARATIVE BUSINESS-GOVERNMENT RELATIONS

Professor George C. Lodge

Course Syllabus

Spring 1990

Harvard University

Graduate School of Business Administration

COMPARATIVE BUSINESS-GOVERNMENT RELATIONS
COURSE OBJECTIVES AND ORGANIZATION

I. Course Objectives

Our purpose will be to discover a realistic way of thinking effectively about the roles and relationships of government and business in the world today. We shall endeavor to perceive what those roles are in different countries, how they fit with one another, how and why governmental policies affecting business are adopted, and what their impact is on firms. The stakes are high. The global fortunes of companies depend to a great extent on how effectively they manage their relations with governments. We shall see this played out in a number of cases; for example: telecommunications in Japan and France, computers in Brazil, semiconductors and electronics in the United States and Europe, health equipment in the United States, and earth imaging from satellites around the world.

We shall seek the ingredients of effective management of government-business relations. The comparative approach will help us keep an open mind. It will help us to recognize and respect how the history of different countries has shaped these relations. It will expand our field of choice as we look for what works best. It will remind us that increasingly the relationships of government and business in one country affect those in others and that as a consequence new forms of transnational government such as the IMF and the European Community, seem inevitable.

We shall try to strengthen our capacity to think systemically. The institutions of government and business are in themselves complex systems. Each is fraught with internal divisions reflecting the interests of different constituencies. Together they are part of larger systems which are at once political, social, economic, and cultural. Effective management requires perception and understanding of how these systems work and interact.

Finally, we shall refine our moral understanding. Government-business relationships and the purposes which drive them lie at the heart of the public spirit in different communities: they are intimately tied to that community's definition of morality. Both sets of institutions depend for their legitimacy on a framework of ideas, an ideology. Effective managers are sensitive to what those ideas are and how they may be changing.

II. Course Focus

We shall focus on a few countries, principally, although not exclusively, Japan, the United States, Brazil, France, and Europe as a region; and on only a few industries, satellites, computers, semiconductors, telecommunications, and biotechnology. It is also necessary to concentrate on only selected issues, those which are most controversial and politically charged, affecting the lifeblood of nations, and stability of regimes, as well as the fortunes of great corporations. Some concern substance, such as industrial policy and government targeting to promote a predetermined definition of the national interest. Other issues relate to processes: how that interest is determined, how influence is exerted, how decisions are made, and how control is exerted. Still others concern behavior. Who are the actors in government, for example, what motivates them, what is their relationship to one another and to business?

This course takes you a step beyond the first-year course **Business, Government and the International Economy**. There you became familiar with the idea of national strategy in which governments, such as those of Japan and Korea take an active role in managing economic development, allocating resources, protecting their domestic markets, and regulating the entry of foreigners. In CBGR we move down to look inside government at how and by whom those strategies are implemented and to examine in some detail how they affect industry. We look also at the response of the United States and Europe to the Asian strategies and at how those responses are changing the relationships of government and business. We shall evaluate the effectiveness of the responses as well as the attempts of other countries, such as Brazil, to follow the Asian example.

III. Organization

The course is divided into four segments following an introductory class comparing the influence of government policy on the earth-imaging industry in France and the United States.

The first segment, **Government Targeting and U.S. and European Response**, examines industrial policies in Japan and Brazil, the challenges the policies pose to government and industry in the United States and Europe, and the responses taken. It is designed to reveal different purposes and structures of business- government relations, to allow analysis of how they came to be and discussion of which way they are likely to go.

The second segment, **Managing the Government Affairs Function**, begins with an overview of the subject and provides an opportunity to discuss the design, organization, and management of the government affairs function in multinational corporations, as well as the role of industry associations.

The third segment, **Managing at the Interface**, combines the first two. Focused on telecommunications in Japan and France, three classes explore the nature of the governmental decision-making apparatus--bureaucrats and the like--and the relationship of firms to that apparatus. AT&T's management of the government interface in France and the United States is studied. This segment ends with an analysis of the public policy implications of corporate restructuring.

A fourth segment, **Insuring Economic Justice**, compares how four countries save ailing industrial giants who are too important to die. We also examine how the United States approaches the problem of minorities in business.

IV. Grading and Paper Assignment

Instead of a final exam you will be required to write a 2,500-word paper, due in Baker 233 before May 1, which analyzes the governmental relations aspects of the job which you intend to take upon graduation, your judgment of how those aspects are evolving, and your recommendation for change. Alternatively, you may direct this analysis at the governmental relations of a company where you have worked or with which you are familiar. Your grade will be based 50% on classroom participation and 50% on the paper.

Cases, Readings, and Study Questions

Date   Class No.

I. Introduction

1/22   1

Required Reading: Sensing the Earth From Space (N9-389-154) Rev. 6/89

A U.S. government contractor wonders about its role in maintaining or perhaps recovering the United States' lead in commercial imaging of the earth from rocket-launched satellites.

Study Questions:

1. How did Williams get into this mess?
2. What's his problem?
3. What would you recommend?

II. Government Targeting and the U.S. Response

1/23   2

Required Reading: Mastering the Market: Japanese Government Targeting of the Computer Industry (1-389-016)

This case reveals a model of government-business relations, variations of which we shall see in France, Brazil and even the United States: government being not a referee but a coach and perhaps a quarterback.

Study Questions:

1. What were the objectives of the Japanese government? Why were they selected?
2. Do you regard this as a success story? If so, what makes it work?
3. Would it work in the United States?
4. Was it "fair?"

Date	Class No.	
1/29	3	**Required Reading:** <u>Cooperation for Competition: U.S. and Japan</u> (9-386-181) Rev. 7/88

The U.S. microelectronics industry responds to the Japanese challenge, combining for cooperative endeavor. Here we see how the VLSI project in Japan was actually organized and managed; we can evaluate the likely effect of the U.S. response.

Study Questions:

1. Should AMD join MCC?

2. Would Bobby Inman make a good CEO of MCC? (He was appointed in December 1982.)

3. What were his problems?

4. What can he learn from the VLSI/TRA project? |
| 1/30 | 4 | **Required Reading:** <u>Sources and Implications of Strategic Decline: The Case of Japanese-American Competition in Microelectronics</u> (8-388-105)

Optional Background Reading: <u>Semiconductor Statistical Supplement</u> (8-389-079) Rev. 5/89 provides updated data.

Charles Ferguson's description of this high-tech failure raises profound questions about the American system, including the role of government and its relationship to business.

Study Questions:

1. Are you persuaded? Is Ferguson right?

2. Identify the components of the "two sectoral systems" to which the author refers on page 1.

3. Should the United States change? Can it change? |
| 2/5 | 5 | **Required Reading:** <u>Sematech</u> (9-389-057) Rev. 7/89

Optional Background Reading: <u>Note on the Structure of the U.S. Government Decision-Making Process</u> (9-381-022) Rev. 4/81; <u>Semiconductor Statistical Supplement</u>. |

Date	Class No.	
2/5	5 (cont.)	Although the United States has tried industrial policy throughout its history to fight wars, go to the moon, and such, this initiative stands out as in many ways a first. The semiconductor industry suppressed its individualistic tendencies and joined forces to seek $500 million of government subsidies to get back in the game. Many believe Sematech marks a permanent shift in U.S. thinking. We want to know what is the shift? Why did it occur? And how was the decision made? (Note: This case gives us our first look at decision making in the U.S. government.)

Study Questions:

1. How do you account for the success of Sematech to date?

2. Will it work?

3. What are Robert Noyce's problems?

4. What should he do?

| 2/6 | 6 | **Required Reading:** JESSI (N9-389-135) Rev. 7/89 |

JESSI is the European version of Sematech. Although potentially larger and more extensive, it is still in its infancy. There are many decisions which must be made before it takes off.

The chief protagonist is Robert Hamersma of Philips. He has to think through his own objectives and figure out a formula for aligning them with the interests of the other players in the JESSI game: Jans Huijbregts of the Dutch Ministry of Economic Affairs; Professor Anton Heuberger, FhG Institute, Berlin; Julio Grata, Division Head of the European Commission's DG-XIII Microelectronics Area; Sir Leon Brittan, head of the European Commission's Directorate for Competition, DG-IV; and Dr. Melvyn Larkin of Plessey of the United Kingdom.

Study Questions:

I have divided the class into six groups, one representing each of these characters (see below). Please study the case from the point of view of your character. What are your interests? What do

91

Date	Class No.	
2/6	6 (cont.)	you want from JESSI? How should JESSI be funded and governed? Be as specific as possible.

Please see Exhibits 7, 8, 10, 11, 12, 15, 27, 28, and 29 in the Semiconductor Statistical Supplement which you have.

Group 1 - Larkin
Group 2 - Huijbregts
Group 3 - Grata
Group 4 - Brittan
Group 5 - Hamersma
Group 6 - Heuberger

2/19	7	**Required Reading:** Brazil's Informatics Policy: 1970-1984 (1-389-044) Rev. 4/89

Supplement: (2-389-045) Rev. 11/88 (To be handed out in class.)

Brazil became the first non-Asian country to try targeting. The case invites an evaluation of Brazil's computer strategy as of 1984 and whether it is time to change course. To do that we must understand why the policy was adopted in the first place. Who were the "guerrillas" who fostered it? What were they after?

Study Questions:

1. How did CAPRE do what it did between 1972 and 1979?

2. What should SEI do?

3. Evaluate the Brazilian strategy from the point of view of: the president of Brazil, IBM, the USTR, and Data General.

2/20	8	**Required Reading:** The USTR and Brazil: 1985-1988 (9-389-046) Rev. 2/89

Supplement: (9-389-047) Rev. 11/88 (To be handed out in class.)

Again, we examine the response of the United States to a foreign challenge, and consider what that response tells us about government-business relations. This case allows us also to consider

Date	Class No.	
2/20	8 (cont.)	the difficulties confronting a multinational corporation trying to manage those relations across national boundaries, and thus provides a transition to the next segment.

Study Questions:

1. Who are the stakeholders in this case? What are their interests?

2. What action would you recommend that Clayton Yeutter take?

III. Managing the Government Affairs Function

2/26	9	**Required Reading:** Roles and Relationships of Business and Government (9-388-159), Parts I and II, pages 1-26.

Optional Background Reading: Thomas K. McCraw, "American Society: Public and Private Responsibilities" (Division of Research Reprint)

Lecture in class on ideology as a framework for comparative analysis.

The Roles and Relationships note is a general overview of the subject. It is designed to allow us to focus in the next class on what the function of managing government-business relations in a large corporation entails.

Study Questions:

1. What are the major forces affecting government-business relations in the world today?

2/27	10	**Required Reading:** Roles and Relationships of Business and Government (9-388-159) Parts III and IV, pages 26-40.

In this class we will discuss both the note and the lecture.

Study Questions:

1. How would you design and organize the governmental affairs office of a large multinational?

Date	Class No.		
2/27	10 (cont.)	2.	What would be its functions?
		3.	What sort of people would you recruit?
		4.	What problems would you imagine that it would encounter?

3/5   11   **Required Reading:** <u>Governmental Programs at IBM</u> (8-389-109) Rev. 5/89

Charles McKittrick, vice president, governmental programs, IBM, here describes the origins and functions of his office. He also touches on some of his problems.

Study Questions:

1. What are McKittrick's objectives?
2. What does it take to achieve them?
3. How does he get there?
4. What are the dangers or obstacles in his path?
5. How does he avoid them?
6. What does "issue management" mean (see p. 3)?
7. What issue areas would you select to focus on?
8. What should an issue manager do?
9. How would you evaluate an issue manager?
10. How would you evaluate the international coordinator in the Governmental Programs office?

3/6   12   **Required Reading:** <u>The Health Industry Manufacturers' Association</u> (N9-389-085) Rev. 6/89

HIMA is an innovative industry association in Washington with some 300 member companies which make products ranging from bedpans to brainscans. Its president, Frank Samuel, has sought to develop more cooperative relationships between the industry and government. HIMA's incoming board chairman wonders whether the disparate interests of the membership and institutional traditions will allow such an approach to work.

Date	Class No.		
3/6	12 (cont.)	Study Questions:	
		1. What are Mr. Dole's problems?	
		2. What should he do?	
3/19	13	**Required Reading:** Monsanto: Government Relations and Biotechnology	
		Study Questions: To be announced.	

IV. Managing at the Interface

3/20	14	**Required Reading:** MITI, MPT, and the Telecom Wars: How Japan Makes Policy for High Technology (8-388-167) Rev. 10/88

This is an inside look at the Japanese decision-making system, at who governs, and how they do it. It invites comparison with the Sematech case above. The bitter rivalry between MITI and MPT over power and influence turns out to be an important determinant of policy. Strategy in this sense comes from structure. How do you lobby in this setting? What is the job of a corporate governmental affairs office in Japan?

Study Questions:

1. Identify the key players in the Telecom Wars. What were their interests? Where did they get their power and authority?

2. What are the prerequisites for effective lobbying by an American multinational in Japan? In any foreign country?

3/26	15	**Required Reading:** French Telecommunications in the 1980s (A) (9-388-160) Rev. 9/88

This describes the French government's policies aimed at creating the world's preeminent telecommunications system, second to none. The new Finance Minister Edouard Balladur must decide which foreign company will be permitted to enter the lucrative French digital switch market. AT&T clearly appears to be the favorite.

Date	Class No.	
3/26	15 (cont.)	**Study Questions:**

1. What factors must Balladur consider as he makes his decision?

2. What do you predict he will do? Why?

3. How well has AT&T done so far?

3/27	16	**Required Reading:** <u>French Telecommunications in the 1980s (B)</u> (9-389-037) Rev. 1/89 (To be handed out in class the previous day.)

Balladur's decision is announced. Observers differ as to the reasons for his actions.

Study Questions: To be announced.

4/2	17	**Required Reading:** <u>Senator Riegle and U.S. Corporate Restructuring</u> (N9-390-031) Rev. 10/89

Senator Riegle is the new head of the Senate Banking Committee confronting the issues surrounding LBOs, restructuring, and debt. We want to use comparative analysis to get to the bottom of the matter.

Study Questions:

1. What are the issues before Senator Riegle?

2. What, if anything, should he do?

3. What, if anything, is the problem?

V. **Insuring Economic Justice**

4/3	18	**Required Reading:** <u>Bailout</u> (8-389-031) Rev. 3/89

This is a comparative study of how Japan, Germany, the U.K. and the United States dealt with the failure of a major company which none of the countries were willing to let die. The issue for analysis is what makes for an effective bailout.

Study Questions:

1. Which bailouts do you regard as most successful?

Date	Class No.		
4/3	18 (cont.)	2.	Why?
		3.	What do the different approaches reveal about each country's business-government relations?

4/9	19

Required Reading: <u>Government Redress of Market Imperfections: Procurement from Minority Firms</u> (9-388-108)

For many years the U.S. government has sought to protect and promote small business. In the last 20 years special efforts have been made to encourage the growth of minority-owned small business.

Study Questions:

1. Evaluate the "minority set-aside" program.

4/10	20

Required Reading: To be announced.

4/5/89

BOOKS RECOMMENDED FOR FURTHER STUDY
for
Comparative Business-Government Relations
Professor George C. Lodge

I.   GENERAL COMPARISONS: Europe, Asia, the United States

The following are among the best studies of comparative business-government relations by historians, political scientists, and political economists:

Aberbach, Joel D., Putnam, Robert D., and Rockman, Bert A., Bureaucrats and Politicians in Western Democracies (Cambridge: Harvard University Press, 1981). See especially Chapter 1 for a summary of the authors' findings from a survey of roles and relationships of bureaucrats and politicians in seven western countries.

Badaracco, Joseph L., Loading the Dice: A Five-Country Study of Vinyl Chloride Regulation (Boston: HBS Press, 1985). In 1974, the industrial world discovered that vinyl chloride, a gas widely used in the production of plastic, was a deadly carcinogen. This is a study of how business and government in five countries--the United States, Japan, Britain, France and Germany--responded to the regulatory challenge. It raises the questions of when a cooperative approach to governmental relations is more effective than an adversarial one, and of what some of the prerequisites to cooperation are.

Berhman, Jack N., Industrial Policies: International Restructuring and Transnationals (Lexington: D.C. Heath & Co., 1984). Berhman is Luther Hodges Distinguished Professor at the University of North Carolina Graduate School of Business Administration. From 1961 to 1964 he served as assistant secretary of commerce for domestic and international business in the Kennedy and Johnson administrations. He has written over 20 books on comparative business-government relations, of which this is the most recent. It has three parts: the first is a handy primer on industrial policies of government in Japan, France, Germany, Brazil, South Korea,

98

Taiwan, and the United States. Part II examines pressures toward international industrial integration, and Part III focuses on various international organizations, like the OECD, which play a role in industrial restructuring and cooperation.

Chandler, Alfred D., Jr. and Herman Daems, eds., Managerial Hierarchies: Comparative Perspectives on the Rise of the Modern Industrial Enterprise (Cambridge: Harvard University Press, 1980). This is a short (237 pages), up-to-date (1970s) description and analysis of the rise of managerial hierarchies in the four leading Western economies-- the United States, Britain, Germany, and France. Chandler's chapter on the United States is a particularly useful summary of his work. Although the book does not focus directly on government relations, it reveals how the historical evolution of corporations was affected by the particular roles and policies of different governments.

Katzenstein, Peter J., ed., Between Power and Plenty: Foreign Economic Policies of Advanced Industrial States (Madison: The University of Wisconsin Press, 1978). This is a collection of essays by eminent professors of history, government, and political economy analyzing and comparing the foreign economic policies of the United States, four European countries, and Japan. The authors argue that the domestic structure of a country--its business and government bureaucracies and their relationships to each other--is a critical variable shaping the country's political strategy as well as its international relationships. The book has a theoretical orientation, focusing in part on how and why nations gain or lose control in the international economy.

Lindblom, Charles E., Politics and Markets: The World's Political-Economic Systems (New York: Basic Books, 1977). This remains a useful analysis of the logic of the market as a device for controlling communities and of its opposite--state planning. It also contains an interesting contrast between government planning of industrial activity in the USSR (pre-perestroika) and China (pre-Deng).

Lodge, George C. and Ezra F. Vogel, eds., Ideology and National Competitiveness: An Analysis of Nine Countries (Boston: HBS Press, 1987). Seven authors from different academic disciplines demonstrate the use of ideology as a way of comparing national systems. The authors find that national competitiveness requires that certain ideological characteristics be present, and that there appears to be a convergence of ideologies toward some version of communitarianism.

Wilks, Stephen and Maurice Wright, eds., <u>Comparative Government-Industry Relations: Western Europe, the United States, and Japan</u> (New York City: Clarendon Press, Oxford, 1987). This collection of essays by European and American social scientists focuses on such industries as chemicals, pharmaceuticals, and telecommunications. It compares legal cultures, methods of coping with industrial decline, industrial policy formulation, and cost containment.

Zysman, John, <u>Governments, Markets, and Growth: Financial Systems and the Politics of Industrial Change</u> (Ithaca: Cornell University Press, 1983). A political economist assesses what makes different governments more or less capable of exercising industrial leadership. He looks at the role of the state in the marketplace, comparing the major industrial countries during the late 1970s and early 1980s.

II. THE UNITED STATES:

The following deal specifically with government-business relations in the United States.

Bower, Joseph L., <u>Two Faces of Management: An American Approach to Leadership in Business and Politics</u> (Boston: Houghton Mifflin Company, 1983). An analysis of the peculiar forces that keep business and government apart in the United States, Bower concludes that both "technocratic" and "political" managers can work more closely together if they understand how differently they view their tasks.

Chandler, Alfred D., Jr., "Business and Public Policy," <u>Harvard Business Review</u>, Nov.-Dec., 1979. A brief but most useful historical review of the relationship between business and public policy in the United States and how different it is from other countries. See also Thomas K. McCraw, ed., <u>The Essential Alfred Chandler</u> (Boston: Harvard Business School Press, 1988) for a useful collection of Chandler's work describing and analyzing the evolution of "managerial capitalism" in America, and comparing it to business development in other countries.

Choate, Pat and Jayne Linger, "Tailored Trade: Dealing with the World as It Is," <u>Harvard Business Review</u>, Jan.-Feb., 1988, p. 86. A brief discussion of how and why America differs from her competitors in international trade. Contains some useful figures and maps.

Fritschler, A. Lee and Bernard H. Ross, <u>How Washington Works: The Executive's Guide to Washington</u> (Cambridge: Ballinger Publishing Co., 1987). The best of many how-to-do-it handbooks on Washington lobbying. It describes how the system works in clear and simple terms.

Huntington, Samuel P., American Politics: The Promise of Disharmony (Cambridge: Harvard University Press, 1981). A classic review of American political history exploring the roots of the adversarial relationship between government and business.

Kelman, Steven, Regulating America, Regulating Sweden: A Comparative Study of Occupational Safety and Health Policy (Cambridge: The MIT Press, 1981). Similar to Badaracco's broader comparative study of governmental responses to vinyl chloride pollution, this is a two-country study of government policies toward business.

Krugman, Paul R., "Is Free Trade Passe?" Economic Perspectives (Fall 1987): I: 2:136. A landmark admission by a distinguished economist that traditional American economics may need to adjust to the fact that Japanese industrial targeting works--at least for them.

Lodge, George C., The American Disease (New York: New York University Press, 1986) and The New American Ideology (New York: Alfred A. Knopf, 1980). The concept of ideology is defined and used to describe the evolution of government and business in the United States. Ideology is also seen as a restraint on behavior by both sets of institutions. The author calls for ideological renovation in order to cope more effectively with the problems of the 1980s.

Lowi, Theodore, J., The End of Liberalism: The Second Republic of the United States, 2nd edition (NY: W.W. Norton & Co.). A classic analysis of how interest group pluralism shapes governmental policies and priorities in the United States.

Scott, Bruce R. and George C. **Lodge**, eds., U.S. Competitiveness in the World Economy (Boston: HBS Press, 1984). A collection of essays in which the roles and policies of government and the relationship between government and business are seen as a major cause of the competitive decline of the United States in the world economy. Industries studied include microelectronics, automobiles, and textiles.

Smith, Hedrick, The Power Game: How Washington Works (New York: Random House, 1988). This is a view of Washington in 1987 by a veteran reporter for the New York Times. It is filled with fascinating anecdotes as well as a good many useful facts and figures.

Vietor, Richard H.K., <u>Energy Policy in America Since 1945: A Study of Business-Government Relations</u> (Cambridge University Press, 1984). A profound and insightful historical analysis of business-government relations in industries associated with energy, especially oil and coal.

Vogel, David, <u>National Styles of Regulation: Environmental Policy in Great Britain and the United States</u> (Ithaca: Cornell University Press, 1986). Vogel compares the patterns of government regulation in Great Britain and the United States and explains why these two nations have adopted such "divergent approaches to controlling the externalities associated with industrial growth."

Weinberg, Martha Wagner, "The Political Education of Bob Malott, CEO," <u>Harvard Business Review</u>, May-June, 1988. This is an insightful study of the efforts of Malott, CEO of FMC Corporation, to obtain legislation to provide federal product liability standards.

Yoffie, David B., "How an Industry Builds Political Advantage," <u>Harvard Business Review</u>, May-June 1988. Yoffie describes how the Semiconductor Industry Association successfully obtained quotas against Japan as a means of opening the Japanese market and preventing Japanese chip dumping.

Zysman, John and Laura Tyson, <u>American Industry in International Competition</u> (Ithaca: Cornell University Press, 1983). A political scientist and an economist team up to provide one of the first and clearest assessments of how and why United States government policies toward business have contributed to erosion of the nation's competitiveness. They argue that the concept of comparative advantage among nations is no longer static. It can be created by government and business acting together.

III. JAPAN:

The following focus on Japanese government-business relations:

Hirschmier, J. and T. Yui, <u>The Development of Japanese Business, 1600-1980</u> (London: George Allen and Unwin, Ltd., 2nd edition). A good history of Japanese business, including its relationships to government.

Johnson, Chalmers, <u>MITI and the Japanese Miracle: The Growth of Industrial Policy, 1925-1975</u> (Stanford: Stanford University Press, 1982). A Berkeley political scientist provides a classic analysis of the working of Japanese government and business over a 50-year time span. It is indispensable to an understanding of modern Japan.

McCraw, Thomas K., ed., <u>America Versus Japan</u> (Boston: Harvard Business School Press, 1986). This is a comparative analysis of government-business relations in the United States and Japan by a team of Harvard professors, headed by Professor McCraw. Industries examined include agriculture, energy and banking; policy areas analyzed include trade, competition, investment, disinvestment, environmental regulation, and government finance.

Prestowitz, Clyde, V., Jr., <u>Trading Places</u> (New York: Basic Books, Inc., 1988). After serving five years as the United States government's chief negotiator with Japan, Prestowitz, a former Department of Commerce official, tells what it was really like. He exposes the incoherence and conflict of interest among Washington executive departments, the confused nature of American goals, and the continuing failure of U.S. negotiations against better prepared, better organized and more unified Japanese rivals.

Yoshino, Michael Y. and Thomas B. **Lifson**, <u>The Invisible Link: Japan's Sogo Shosha and the Organization of Trade</u> (Cambridge: MIT Press, 1986). A useful description and analysis of how Japan's trading companies work, including an exploration of their relations to the Japanese government.

IV. THE CORPORATE VIEWPOINT:

The following approach government-business relations more explicitly from the corporate viewpoint.

Bower, Joseph L., <u>When Markets Quake</u> (Boston: HBS Press, 1987). Bower examines the restructuring of the world chemical industry during the early 1980s in response to worldwide overcapacity. He considers also the general problem of coping with overcapacity in other industries, such as automobiles, steel, and semiconductors. In many countries, government is a major player in reshaping markets as well as suppliers to those markets.

Encarnation, Dennis and Louis T. **Wells**, Jr., "Sovereignty En Garde: Negotiating with Foreign Investors," <u>International Organization</u> (Winter 1985): I: 47. This article reports on the authors' research concerning government policies in a variety of countries concerning foreign investment. They examine both constraints on such investment as well as incentives to do more of it.

Gomes-Casseres, Benjamin, "MNC Ownership Preferences and Host Government Regulations: An Integrated Approach" (Boston: HBS Working Paper #89-023, August 1988). Gomes-Casseres reviews government policies in a variety of countries concerning the ownership of multinational corporations operating in those countries.

Porter, Michael E., ed., <u>Competition in Global Industries</u> (Boston: Harvard Business School Press, 1986). A collection of essays about the strategies of global industries. Of special interest are Porter's "Introduction and Summary" and Chapter 1 which sets forth his conceptual framework; and Chapters 7-9: "Government Policies and Global Industries" by Yves L. Doz, "Competitive Strategies in Global Industries: A View from Host Governments" by Dennis J. Encarnation and Louis T. Wells, Jr., and "Government Relations in the Global Firm" by Amir Mahini and Louis T. Wells, Jr.

Vernon, Raymond, <u>Sovereignty at Bay: The Multinational Spread of U.S. Enterprises</u> (New York: Basic Books, Inc., 1971). Vernon's classic explores the tension between the policies and interests of governments, especially in developing countries, and multinational corporations operating in their domain.

UNIVERSITY OF MINNESOTA

MBA 8055 and 8055E

BUSINESS, GOVERNMENT, AND MACROECONOMICS
Fall, 1989

Sec.3: 10:00 A.M.Bleg.425.T.TH
Sec.4: 1:00 P.M.Bleg.435.T.Th
Sec.91: 5:30 P.M.Bleg.425.Th

Instructor:
Alfred Marcus
854 Mgmnt & Econ
624-2812

Office Hours:
Tues. & Thurs.
4:45 - 5:30

Teaching Assistants: Doug Schuler 625-0304
Reena Mittal 333-1033

In a free enterprise, private property system, a corporate executive is an employee of the owners of the business. He has direct responsibility to his employers. The responsibility is to conduct the business in accordance with their desires which generally means to make as much money as possible while conforming to the basic rules of society and those embodied in ethical custom.

-- Milton Friedman
Capitalism and Freedom, 1962

Increased awareness of social involvement is simply a reality. The general and underlying mechanism for this involvement is not some vague and moralistic doctrine of social responsibility but the public policy process which is a framework for and supplement to the operation of firms and markets. Based on this analysis we propose the principle of public responsibility as a thesis or guideline.

-- Lee Preston & James Post
Private Management and Public Policy, 1975

OBJECTIVES

1. To develop managerial skills and knowledge on how to deal with the ethical constraints and imperatives of modern business.

2. To identify and explore the relationships between business and key constituencies such as investors, consumers, and employees.

3. To engender an awareness of the technological and legal forces affecting the firm.

4. To acquaint students with the nature of government and government regulation in the United States and in other countries.

5. To understand how the macroeconomy works.

CLASS SCHEDULE (Cases are in parentheses)

		Thurs.	Tues.
Intro.	Ethics: What is right/wrong, good/bad?	9/21	9/26
Business	Social Responsibility: Who is affected by the firm's decisions? (Dayton Hudson/Mobil)	9/28(memo)*	10/03
	The Impact of Technology: Who might be harmed? (Proposition II/Carbide)	10/05	10/10
	The Law: What are the firm's obligations to those who might be harmed? (Pinto/Manville)	10/12(memo)*	10/17
Gov't.	The Purpose of the State: What role should gov't. play? (World Auto Industry/in-class case analysis)	10/19	10/24
	Internat. Competition: What role does the gov't play in other countries? (Competition in Manufacturing/Zenith)	10/26(memo)*	10/31
	Regulation: How can the firm can take advantage & avoid harm? (IT Corporation/mid-term)	11/02	11/07
Macroec.	Federal Spending & Taxation: Does the federal deficit harm the economy?	11/09	11/14
	Stabilization Policy: Can economists predict the future?	11/16	11/21
	Monetary Policy and Foreign Exchange: Why is there so much instability?	11/30(paper)*	11/28
		FINAL	

*See separate handout, Position Paper Assignment

FORMAT

In the first seven weeks we will discuss cases that deal with ethics, social responsibility, technology, law, government, international competition, and government regulation. Each of the cases has associated readings that will enhance your understanding of the cases. Professor Marcus will introduce the associated readings and lead the discussion of the cases. In the final three weeks we will discuss issues having to do with macroeconomics -- federal spending and taxation, stabilization policy, monetary policy, and foreign exchange rates. The main readings are from a textbook by Gwartney and Stroup. Again, Professor Marcus will introduce the concepts and lead the discussion.

Be prepared. The quality of the discussion ultimately depends on your participation. Read the material carefully. Scan the questions provided with the list of weekly readings and plan how you would answer them. If called upon, you should be ready to open the discussion. Once the discussion has started you will want to make intelligent contributions. Listen intently to what others are saying, and time your remarks accordingly. Effective participation should

* add to the class' understanding of a situation;

* show evidence of thoughtful analysis;

* be relevant to the discussion by being linked to the comments of others; and

* show a willingness to test new ideas rather than being a mere repetition of what has already been said and is known.

Don't talk merely for the sake of talking, but realize that it pays to contribute. Inevitably, in the discussion, there will be some rambling. It can play a positive role as we get our bearings on an issue. Help us get back on track if we stray too far. The size of our class is large. Therefore, for some purposes we will divide into smaller groups. These groups will be established on the first week of class and part of your contribution to the classroom discussion will come from your participation in these groups. Seating also will be fixed on the first week of class. Each of you will have your name displayed on a folded index card. Treat your folded index card as your ticket of admission: please remember to bring it to every class.

REQUIREMENTS AND GRADES

Classroom Participation

Participation in classroom discussion will count for 15% of your grade.

Position Paper

You will draft a position paper on a vital public issue facing business. The position paper will count for 30% of your grade. More details are available in a separate handout.

ii

In-Class Case Analysis

On 10/24 (10/19, the last 1 hr. and 45 minutes for the evening class), you will be given a case, which is not part of the reading package you purchase at Kinkos, to analyze in class. You will be asked to write a short memo about the business problem that the case poses. You will need to establish criteria, evaluate the alternative solutions to the problem based on these criteria, and choose the solution that you consider most appropriate. The case analysis will count 10% toward your final grade.

Midterm and Final

The midterm and final will be multiple choice tests. The midterm will cover the material introduced during the first seven weeks. The schedule is for the day students (in Sections 3 and 4) to have the midterm on 11/7, and for the night students (in Section 99) to have it on 11/2, the last part of class. The midterm will count 20% toward your grade.

The final exam, which will be given sometime during finals week -- Dec. 4-9, will cover the macroeconomic material. It will count 25% toward your grade.

REQUIRED MATERIAL

A reading packages is available at Kinkos. It is a collection of material that includes associated readings, cases, and recommended additional readings. You should also purchase at the University Bookstore on the West Bank James Gwartney and Richard L. Stroup, Understanding the Macroeconomy, Harcourt, Brace, Javonich, 4th ed., 1987.

WEEKLY READINGS

Week 1

Introduction

Ethics: What is Right & Wrong/ Good & Bad?

Class Handouts: Larue Tone Hosmer, "Seven Ethical Problems for Moral Reasoning;" from L.T. Hosmer, The Ethics of Management, Irwin, 1987: pp. 109-113; and Richard P. Nielsen, "Changing Unethical Organizational Behavior," The Academy of Management Executive, May 1989: pp. 123-130.

BUSINESS

Week 2

Social Responsibility: Who is Affected by the Firm's Decisions?

Milton Friedman, "The Social Responsibility of Business Is to Increase Its Profits," reprinted in Charles S. McCoy, The Management of Values, Pitman, 1985: pp. 253-260.

Alfred Marcus, "Managing the Political and Social Environment," 1988, pp. 1-47.

iii

Alfred Marcus, "Ethics and Political Philosophy: Selections From the Major Sources in Western Culture," 1989 pp. 1-12;

Ronald Henkoff, "Is Greed Dead?" *Fortune*, August 14, 1989: pp. 40-49.

Case #1: Terry Cauthorn, "Dayton Hudson Corporation," Harvard Business School, 1976: pp. 1-23.

Study Questions:

1) What types of questions might the Board raise about Dayton Hudson's program? What types of answers should be given if these questions are raised?

2) In light of the questions that might be raised, and other concerns that might exist, how, if at all, should Dayton Hudson revise its program?

Case #2: Judith Esterquest, "Mobil Oil and Advocacy Advertising," Harvard Business School, 1980: pp. 1-30.

Study Questions:

1) How would you evaluate Mobil's public affairs programs? Is it worth the expenditure of $21 million annually?

2) Should it be revised? In what way?

Week 3

The Impact of Technology; Who Might Be Harmed?

Alfred A. Marcus, "Risk, Uncertainty, and Scientific Judgement," *Minerva*, Summer 1988: 138-152.

Stephen Schneider, "The Changing Climate," *Scientific American*, September 1989: pp. 70-79; S.Fred Singer, "Fact and Fancy on Greenhouse Earth," *WSJ*, August 30, 1988; John Gibbons, Peter Blair, and Holly Gwin, "Strategies for Energy Use," *Scientific American*, September 1989: pp. 136-43; and Edmund Faltermayer, "Taking Fear Out of Nuclear Power," *Fortune*, Aug. 1, 1988: pp. 105-114.

David E. Whiteside, "Note on the Export of Pesticides from the United States to Developing Countries," from Kenneth E. Goodpaster, *Ethics in Management*, Harvard Business School, 1984: pp. 121-136; Marlise Simons, "A Battle Over the Causes of Pesticide Misuse in Third World," *International Herald Tribune*, June 1, 1989.

Case #3: Joseph Badaracco, "Proposition II (A), (B), (C)" Harvard Business School, 1981: pp. 1-26, 1-2, 1-2. Appendices: Yasushi Matsuda, "Nuclear Power in Japan: Present and Future, Journal of Japanese Trade and Industry, 1984: pp. 12-16; Birgitta Dahl, "Dismantling Sweden's Nuclear Power Stations," Inside Sweden, July 1989, p. 12; and Alfred Marcus, "French Leadership in Nuclear Power: Another Case of Lagging American Development," 1989: pp. 1-4.

Study Questions:

1) What is your appraisal of Union Electric's Campaign against Proposition II?

2) In light of public opinion about nuclear power and the world energy situation, make suggestions about how Union Electric should plan for providing for the energy needs of its customers in the future?

Case #4 Thomas Gladwin, "A Case Study of the Bhopal Tragedy," and Will Lepkowski, "Chemical Safety in the Third World," from Charles S. Pearson (ed.) Multinational Corporations, Environment, and the Third World, Duke University Press, 1987: pp. 223-255.

Study Questions:

1) What caused the Bhopal tragedy? What were its consequences? What steps should American chemical manufacturers take to prevent such accidents from occurring?

2) What lessons should American companies learn from Bhopal about the use of chemicals in so-called Third World Countries?

Week 4

The Law: What Are the Firm's Obligations to those Who Might Be Harmed?

Alfred Marcus, "Notes for Class Use: The Law of Harm," based on Robert Cooter and Thomas Ulen, "An Economic Theory of Torts," Law and Economics, Scott, Forseman, 1988.

J. Mark Ramseyer, "Reluctant Litigant Revisited: Rationality and Disputes in Japan," Journal of Japanese Studies, 14,1, 1988.

Alfred Marcus, "Compensating Victims for Harms Caused by Pollution and Other Hazardous Substances," Law and Policy, 8, 2, 1986: pp. 189-211.

Walker F. Todd, "Aggressive Uses of Chapter 11 of the Federal Bankruptcy Code," Quarterly Economic Review, Federal Reserve Bank of Cleveland, 1986: pp. 20-26.

Case #5: Dekkers Davidson & Kenneth E.Goodpaster, "Managing Product Safety: The Ford Pinto," from Kenneth E. Goodpaster, Ethics in Management, Harvard Business School, 1984: pp. 111-119.

Study Questions:

1) Was Ford "negligent" in the Pinto case? By what standard?

2) What are the costs of producing defective vehicles? What, if anything, should Ford do to prevent future product recalls?

Case #6: George A. Steiner and John F. Steiner, "Asbestos Litigation Bankrupts Manville," from George A. Steiner and John F. Steiner, Business, Government, and Society: A Managerial Perspective, Random House, 1988: pp. 44-53. Appendices: "Manville News;" Steiner and Steiner, "A.H. Robins Co. and the Dalkon Shield."

Study Questions:

1) Did Manville make responsible use of the bankruptcy laws? Is the Manville reorganization and settlement plan fair?

2) Is current product liability law in need of reform? What type of legislation, if any, should the business community support?

Recommended Additional Readings: Laurie P. Cohen & Alix M. Freedman, "Cracks Seen in Tobacco's Liability Dam," WSJ, June 15, 1988; Glenn Warchol, "Hit'em and Hit'em Hard," TCR, Aug. 24-30, 1988; Peter Huber, "The Legal Revolution in Product Liability," Center for the Study of American Business, 1989: pp. 1-18; Richard Schmitt, "California High Court Makes Mark on Law by Limiting Damages," WSJ, July 11, 1989.

GOVERNMENT

Week 5

The Purpose of the State: What Role Should Government Play?

Milton Friedman, "The Role of Government in a Free Society," from Paul Peretz (ed.), The Politics of American Economic Policy Making, M.E. Sharpe, 1987: pp. 30-40; Alfred Marcus, "Note on Liberal and Neo-Conservative Views on the Rationale for Government," 1989.

Gwartney and Stroup, "Supply and Demand for the Public Sector," pp.79-99.

Gwartney and Stroup, "Understanding Government and Government Failure," pp.491-515.

James C. Miller III, Thomas F. Walton, William E. Kovacic, and Jeremy A. Rabkin, "Industrial Policy: Reindustrialization Through Competition or Coordinated Action;" Stuart Eizenstat, "Reindustrialization Through Coordination or Chaos," Yale Journal on Regulation, 2, 1, 1984: pp. 1-51.

Case #7: Mark Fuller, "Note on The World Auto Industry in Transition," and "Note on Auto Sector Policies," Harvard Business School, 1982: pp. 1-43 and 1-31; Appendix: Doron P. Levin, "Auto Makers' Plea on Pollution," NYT, July 21, 1989.

Study Questions:

1) What is the long-term future of the American automobile industry? What does the industry have to do to assure its future?

2) What, if anything, should the auto industry ask or expect the government to do to enhance its competitiveness?

Week 6

Global Competition: What Role Does the Government Play in Other Countries?

Gwartney and Stroup, "Comparative Economic Systems," pp. 437-64.

Gwartney and Stroup, "Gaining from International Trade," pp. 369-90.

Mary Sutherland and Erica Liederman, "Japan in the Mid-1980s: Miracle at Risk," Harvard Business School, 1983: pp. 1-18

William Ouchi, "Elements of the M-Form," from William Ouchi, The M-Form Society, Addison-Wesley, 1984: pp. 62-90

Case #8: Constantinos Markides, "U.S. Competitiveness in Manufacturing," Harvard Business School, 1986: pp. 1-27;

Study Questions:

1) What are some of the competitive challenges that American firms face in world market places? What positions should the business community take on these issues?

2) To counter the role played by other governments should the business community encourage a more activist role by the American government?

Recommended Additional Readings: Lester Thurow, "Technology Leadership and Industrial Competitiveness," Center for the Development of Technological Leadership, 1988: pp. 1-16; Bruce Stokes, "High Tech Tussling," National Journal, 5/13/89: pp. 1180-1184; W.J. Moore, "Sprouting in Brussels," National Journal, 5/13/89: pp. 1185-1188; Bruce Stokes, "Off and Running," National Journal, 6/17/89: pp. 1562-66; Louis Richman, "How Capital Costs Cripple America," Fortune, August 14, 1989: pp. 50-56.

Case #9: David Yoffie, "Zenith and the Color Television Fight," Harvard Business School, 1982: pp. 1-17; and David Yoffie, "Note on Free Trade and Protectionism," Harvard Business School, 1983: pp. 1-7.

Study Questions:

1) What position should Zenith take on the free-trade protectionist debate? How can it prepare for an adverse position from public officials? What is the likelihood of an adverse position?

2) How can Zenith best advance its position in the political market place?

Week 7

Government Regulation: How Can the Firm Take Advantage and Avoid Harm?

George Stigler, "The Theory of Economic Regulation," from Robert Rabin, Perspectives on the Administrative Process, Little Brown, 1979: pp. 81-90.

Robert Leone, "Note on the Regulatory Process," Harvard Business School, 1980: pp. 1-6.

Alfred Marcus, "Measuring and Analyzing Regulatory Changes," from The Adversary Economy, Quorum, 1984: pp. 33-52; "Regulation Rises Again," and "A Breath of Fresh Air From the White House," Business Week, June 26, 1989: pp. 58-60.

Gwartney and Stroup, "Problem Area for the Market," pp. 467-90.

Case #10: Gale D. Merseth, "IT Corporation (A)," Harvard Business School, 1982: pp. 1-13 and Bruce L. Krag, "Note on the Hazardous Waste Management Industry," Harvard Business School, 1982: pp. 1-29. Appendix: Stratford P. Sherman, "Trashing a $150 Billion Business," Fortune, Aug. 28, 1989: pp. 90-101.

Study Questions:

1) What competitive strategy should IT pursue to achieve its growth objectives?

2) What role do government policies play in determining its future growth? To what extent will it be constrained by its competitors?

MACROECONOMICS

Week 8

Federal Spending & Taxation: Does the Federal Deficit Harm the Economy?

Gwartney and Stroup, "Government Spending and Taxation," pp.99-127.

Gwartney and Stroup, "Modern Macroeconomics: Fiscal Policy," pp. 243-268; Lawrence Haas, "Stand but Don't Deliver," National Journal, 6/24/89: pp. 1636-1639.

Gwartney and Stroup, "Economic Development and the Growth of Income," pp. 415-437.

Richard Rose, "How Exceptional Is the American Political Economy?" *Political Science Quarterly*, Spring 1989: pp. 91-117.

Issue #1: The National Debt

Study Question:

1) "The national debt is a mortgage against the future of our children and grandchildren. We are forcing them to pay for our irresponsible and unrestrained spending." Evaluate.

Issue #2: Marginal Tax Rates

Study Question:

1) Why doe we have marginal (i.e. progressive) tax rates? What effects do marginal tax rates have on economic growth?

Week 9

Stabilization Policy: Can Economists Predict the Future?

Gwartney and Stroup, "Taking the Nation's Economic Pulse," pp. 127-151.

Gwartney and Stroup, "Economic Fluctuations, Unemployment, and Inflation," pp. 151-175.

Gwartney and Stroup, "Expectations, Inflation, and Unemployment," pp. 321-345; Alfred A. Marcus and Baruch Mevorach, "Planning for the U.S. Political Cycle, *Long Range Planning*, 1988: pp. 50-56.

Gwartney and Stroup, "Stabilization Policy, Output, and Unemployment," pp. 345-369; John Erceg, "Inflation and Soft Landing Prospects," Federal Reserve Bank of Cleveland, July 1989.

Issue #3: Predicting the Economic Future

Study Question:

1) What factors stand in the way of more accurate economic predictions? When are economists more likely to be right about future economic conditions? When are they more likely to be wrong?

Week 10

Monetary Policy and Foreign Exchange: Why is There So Much Instability?

Gwartney and Stroup, "Money and the Banking System," pp. 269-293.

Gwartney and Stroup, "Modern Macroeconomics: Monetary Policy," pp. 293-321; "Greenspan's Moment of Truth," *Business Week*, July 31, 1989: pp. 58-66.

Gwartney and Stroup, "International Finance and the Foreign Exchange Market, pp. 391-415.

C.R. Henning and I.M. Destler, "From Neglect to Activism: American Politics and the 1985 Plaza Accord," *Journal of Public Policy*, 3/4, 1989: pp. 317-333; Jonathan Rauch, "Up and Away Again," *National Journal*, 6/24/89: 1625-1629.

Issue #4: The Instability of the Dollar

Study Question:

1) What factors account for the recent instability of the dollar? What effect does the dollar's instability have on a company's operations in the U.S. and abroad?

ALFRED A. MARCUS

Associate Professor of Business, Government, and Society, Carlson School of Management; formerly on the faculty of the universities of Pittsburgh and Washington

Among other works he is the author of <u>The Adversary Economy: Business Responses to Changing Government Requirements</u>, Greenwood Press, 1984.

Education

PH.D. Harvard University, 1977 -- Public policy and administration
M.A.   University of Chicago, 1973 -- Political philosophy
B.A.   University of Chicago, 1971 -- Modern history

Professional Experience

Researcher, energy and environmental policy, Battelle, Seattle, 1979-84.

Current Projects

Organizational Learning in High Risk Technologies: The Organization and Management of Nuclear Power Plants

Awards

Fourth Annual Theodore Lowi Award for the outstanding <u>Policy Studies Journal</u> article published in 1986.

Foreign Experience

Fullbright Scholar in France Spring 1989

MBA 8055/EMBA 8055

Fall 1989

Position Paper Assignment

Businesses compete not only in selling and manufacturing goods and services but also in the marketplace of ideas and public issues. In the marketplace for public policy the competition is stiff and challenging. In this case you are selling an intangible -- ideas. To be effective, you must believe in your "product" and be knowledgeable about it. Your expertise and logic must be superior to that of your competitors.

Your assignment is to develop a position paper for the Business Roundtable. The Business Roundtable is the country's premier business organization. Run by chief executive officers of the major *Fortune* 500 companies, its stated purpose is "to examine public issues that affect the economy, develop positions that reflect sound economic and social principles, and make these positions known to the public and its representatives in government." The Roundtable selects issues that are in the public interest as well as in the interest of the business community, develops carefully reasoned positions concerning these issues, and communicates them to government officials and members of the corporate community.

Topics

You must define a specific proposal that comes under the rubric of one of the broad topics covered in this course (see the reading list). Choose a topic that is of personal interest to you, something that you care about, are curious about, or want to know more about for compelling career or personal reasons. If you are currently working, have had interesting job experience, or aim to work for a specific company or in a particular industry try to connect the topic you choose to your work interests.

A number of the general areas that you might want to pursue are listed below:

1. the budget deficit
2. the FSLIC crisis
3. 3rd world debt
4. international trade
5. productivity
6. global competitiveness
7. education
8. energy and the environment
9. corporate takeovers
10. innovation and technology
11. safety and health
12. business ethics

Remember that these are just general areas. When choosing your topic be very specific. For example, if choosing the crisis in American education do not cover the entire spectrum of issues, but pin it down to the need for better mathematical education or more language instruction at the high school level. If dealing with international trade and competitiveness, limit it to something manageable like steel import quotas or the problems of the semiconductor industry. A final example would be to focus on cuts in specific defense programs or a special innovative idea to raise revenues when dealing with the budget deficit.

Working in a Group

In developing the position paper, group work is encouraged but it is not mandatory. Group size can be as large as five or six or as small as two or three. If you decide to work in a group a common grade will be assigned to all group members.

Format

After a few statements that introduce the topic, the position paper should read as follows: "The Business Roundtable would like the government of the United States to do (or not to do) X, Y, or Z for the following reasons." You should then:

    (1) develop some of the details about your proposal, what form it would take, and how it would be implemented

    (2) provide a list of the three to five reasons why the U.S. should (or should not) engage in the actions you propose,

    (3) develop these reasons, and

    (4) explain why alternatives were rejected.

Remember to:

    *Put the call for action first, or summarize the important findings and conclusions immediately.

    *Conclude with a brief repetition of the main points, reminding the audience of the recommendations.

    *Emphasize the main points via headings, lists, and enumeration.

    *Make use of figures, diagrams, and charts when necessary.

Logically connect your arguments and try to anticipate and then answer the objections that a hostile critic might have. Your aim is to convince and your grade will be based on how persuasive you are.

Interviews and Library Research

To be convincing you will need to rely on appropriate (1) theories (2) statistical evidence, and (3) anecdotal evidence. The theories and statistical evidence will appeal to the rational side of your audience. The anecdotes are designed to bring to life the theories and statistics and to appeal to your audience emotionally.

Ideally, to access theories, statistics, and anecdotes you would want a key informant or a number of them, a group of people active in the area whom you could informally interview. Lacking such a person or group of people you will have to rely on library research. To locate the appropriate journals, books, and government documents, start by contacting the Business Reference Service on the 2nd floor of Wilson Library. There are numerous business and management, general interest, technical, and specialized industry data bases that the librarians can show you. Also check out the Government Documents Room on the top floor of Wilson Library as well as the Periodicals Room in the basement. Depending on your area of interest, you may also want to use the Law Library.

Research Tasks and Deadlines

I.   Identify the specific controversy that interests you. To do so, examine recent issues of <u>the Wall Street Journal</u>, <u>the New York Times</u>, <u>Fortune</u>, <u>Forbes</u>, <u>Business Week</u>, the <u>Economist</u>, the <u>National Journal</u>, <u>the Harvard Business Review</u>, <u>the Academy of Management Executive</u>, <u>Long Range Planning</u>, the New

Republic, or other newspapers or magazines. Do not rely solely on such sources as Time, Newsweek, or U.S. News and World Report. Briefly discuss the controversy you have chosen in a one-page memo listing at least three sources you have consulted. This memo is due the second week of the quarter on the date noted in the reading list. On time satisfactory completion of the memo will provide you with two points toward your final grade.

I. Try to refine and sharpen your definition of the controversy. To do so, consult at least three scholarly publications in journals such as the Public Interest, the Journal of Public Policy Analysis and Management, the American Economic Review, the Journal of Law and Economics, the California Management Review, the Journal of Legal Studies, the Academy of Management Journal, the Academy of Management Review, the Strategic Management Journal, Administrative Sciences Quarterly, the Rand Journal of Economics, Policy Studies Journal, Policy Studies Review, Law and Policy, Journal of Public Policy, Harvard Law Review, Harvard Environmental Law Review, Yale Journal of Regulation, Journal of Political Economy, Rand Journal of Economics, Political Science Quarterly, etc. Summarize what you learned from the three articles in a brief (no more than two pages) memo. This memo is due the fourth week of the quarter on the date noted in the reading list. On time satisfactory completion of the memo will provide you with four points toward your final grade.

III. Gain additional familiarity with the issue's history and current context, why and how it became a public issue, and the major policy issues that are involved in its resolution. For this purpose you should consult

    a. congressional testimony and other government documents that can be found in the top floor of Wilson Library and/or

    b. recent books published by Washington think tanks such as the Brookings Institution and the American Enterprise Institution or reputable independent scholars and publishing houses.

Summarize what you learned from at least two such sources in a brief (no more than 2 page) memo. This memo is due the sixth week of the quarter on the date noted in the reading list. On time satisfactory completion of the memo will provide you with four points toward your final grade.

V. Draw on the research that went into the three earlier tasks, plus other research you have done, to write your position paper. Follow the guidelines listed earlier. The position paper is due the tenth week of the quarter on the date noted in the reading list. It will count 20 points toward your final grade.

Length and References

The text of the position paper must be at least 12 double-spaced typed pages excluding figures, diagrams, and charts. Sources should be properly cited and footnoted -- numerical footnotes in the text with full citations at the end of the document. The footnotes do not count toward the 12 page limit. Appendices can be used to amplify or explicate the main points. The total length of the paper with footnotes and appendices should be no more than 20 pages. You may work with the people in the Communications Office (Candy Kummerfeld and Donna McCarthy) in editing your paper.

UNIVERSITY OF MINNESOTA

8203

Winter 1990

SOCIAL ISSUES IN MANAGEMENT
Energy Policy

10-11:30 T, Th
Social Sciences 660

Alfred Marcus
624-2812

The purpose of this course is to develop a model for research in the social issues area and to illustrate this model by closely investigating recent changes in American energy policy. The model consists of two realms. First, there is the "macrocosm" where broad societal change takes place. Then there is the "microcosm," the process by which corporations adjust to such change. In both realms, there is relevant theory, descriptions, and/or empirical work. Almost withouut exception these two realms are not joined in the existing literature, where the macrocosm is studied without close scrutiny of the microcosm and the microcosm is studied without close scrutiny of the macrocosm. The premise of this course, therefore, is that a deeper understanding can be attained only if investigation of both realms is pursued.

As an experiment, we will attempt to investigate the two realms simultaneously. Our purpose is to see what insights such an investigation will yield. Thus, the structure of the course is as follows. Each Tuesday for the next 10 weeks we will delve into the macrocosm of energy policy changes, and each Thursday we will take up the microcosm of corporate adjustment. In a sense, two reading lists will be pursued simultaneously, the first being related to the macrocosm of broad social change and the second to the microcosm of corporate adjustment.

You are expected to do enough reading and __skimming__ of the material (you cannot possibly read all of it) to hold your own in the class discussions (10% of your grade), and to take a take-home final at the end of the quarter (90% of your grade).

The "two" reading lists follow.

Reading List 1: Tuesday

week 1

I. THE MACROCOSM

BACKGROUND

Various figures and graphs from Energy Information Administration, "Annual Energy Review: 1988."

week 2

A. ENERGY ECONOMICS AND POLICIES

1. Natural Resource Scarcity in Economic Theory

Smith & Krutilla, "The Economics of Natural Resource Scarcity: An Interpretive Introduction," in Smith (ed.) Scarcity and Growth Reconsidered, 1979: 1-36.

Stiglitz, "A Neoclassical Analysis of the Economics of Natural Resources," in Smith (ed.) Scarcity and Growth Reconsidered, 1979: 36-67.

Daly, "Entropy, Growth, and the Political Economy of Scarcity," in Smith (ed.) Scarcity and Growth Reconsidered, 1979: 67-95.

Williams & Larson, "Materials, Affluence, and Industrial Energy Use," ARE, 1987: 99-144.

Solo, "Developing An Energy Alternative," in Ender & Kim, Energy Resources Development, 1987: 141-155.

weeks 3-4

2. Energy and the Economy

a. Energy Shocks

Tsai, "Energy Shocks and Economic Stability," in Tsai, The Energy Illusion and Economic Stability, 1989: 27-45.

Pindyck & Rotemberg, "Energy Shocks and the Marcroeconomy," in Alm & Weiner (eds.), Oil Shock, 1984: 97-121.

Huntington, "Oil Prices and Inflation," ARE, 1985: 317-339.

b. Economic Growth

Tsai, "Energy and Economic Growth," in Tsai, The Energy Illusion and Economic Stability, 1989: 99-117.

Yu & Choi, "The Causal Relationship Between Energy and GNP: An International Comparison," JED, 1985: 249-272.

Erol & Yu, "On the Causal Relationship Between Energy and Income for Industrialized Countries," JED, 1988: 113-139.

Wang & Latham, "Energy and State Economic Growth: Some New Evidence," JED, 1989: 197-221.

c. Productivity

Berndt & Wood, "Energy Price Shocks and Productivity Growth," in Gordon et. al., Energy, 1987: 305-343.

Schurr, "Energy Use, Technological Change, and Productive Efficiency," ARE, 1984: 409-425.

weeks 5-6

3. U.S. Government Policies

Levine, "A Decade of United States Energy Policy," ARE, 1985: 557-87.

McKie, "Federal Energy Regulation," ARE, 1984: 321-349.

Wilson, "The Petro-Political Cycle," in Ender & Kim, Energy Resources Development, 1987: 1-21.

Carmichael, "Energy Policy and the Economy," in Ender & Kim, Energy Resources Development, 1987: 21-33.

Hoole & Hart, "U.S. Petroleum Dependency and Oil Price Decontrol," in Ender & Kim, Energy Resources Development, 1987: 69-81.

Tugwell, The Energy Crisis and American Political Economy, 1988: 139-212.

Geller, "The Role of Federal Research and Development in Advancing Energy Efficiency: A $50 Billion Contribution to the U.S. Economy," ARE, 1987: 357-395.

weeks 7-8

4. Cartel Theory and OPEC

Tsai, "Economic Theory and Cartel," in Tsai, The Energy Illusion and Economic Stability, 1989: 45-65.

Gately, "Lessons from the 1986 Oil Price Collapse," Brookings Papers on Economic Activity, 1986: 237-284.

Samii, "The Organization of the Petroleum Exporting Countries and the Oil Market: Different Views," JED, 1985: 159-173.

Shaaf, "Strong Dollar, Low Inflation, and OPEC'S Terms of Trade," JED, 1985: 121-128.

Mead, "The OPEC Cartel Thesis Reexamined: Price Constraints from Oil Substitutes," JED, 1986: 213-242.

Lowinger, Wihlborg, & Willman, "An Empirical Analysis of OPEC and Non-OPEC Behavior," JED, 1986: 119-141.

Gately, "The Prospects for Oil Prices Revisited," ARE, 1986: 513-588.

Tanner, "OPEC Adds Capacity, Easing Risk That Cost of Oil Will Soar in 90s," WSJ, 11/22/89: 1.

weeks 9-10

5. International Comparisons

a. Japan

Sakisaka, "Japan's Energy Supply/Demand Structure and Its Trade Relationship with the United States and the Middle East," JED, 1985: 1-11.

Ramstetter, "Interaction Between Japanese Policy Priorities: Energy and Trade in the 1980s," JED, 1986: 285-301.

Mossavar-Rahmani, "Japan's Oil Sector Outlook," ARE, 1988: 185-213.

b. France

Giraud, "Energy in France," ARE, 1983: 165-191.

Jestin-Fleury, "Energy Conservation in France," ARE, 1988: 159-183.

c. The U.K. & Europe

Carter, "The Changing Structure of Energy Industries in the United Kingdom," ARE, 1986: 451-69.

Bending, Cattell, and Eden, "Energy and Structural Change in the United Kingdom and Western Europe," ARE, 1987: 185-222.

Jochem & Morovic, "Energy Use Patterns in Common Market Countries Since 1979," ARE, 1988: 131-157.

Lonnroth, "The European Transition from Oil," ARE, 1983: 1-25.

d. Soviet Union & Developing Countries

Hewett, *Energy Economics and Foreign Policy in the Soviet Union*, 1984: 1-24, 144-193.

Sathaye, Ghirardi & Schipper, "Energy Demand in Developing Countries," ARE, 1987: 253-281.

Reading List 2: Thursday

week 1

I. THE MICROCOSM

A. ENVIRONMENT, STRATEGY, & PERFORMANCE

1. Organizational Environments

Lenz & Engledow, "Environmental Analysis: The Applicability of Current Theory, SMJ, 1986: 329-346.

Milliken, "Three Types of Perceived Uncertainty About the Environment: State, Effect, and Response Uncertainty," AMR, 1987: 133-143.

Wholey & Brittain, "Characterizing Environmental Variation," AMJ, 1989: 867-882.

Jauch & Kraft, "Strategic Management of Uncertainty," AMR, 1986: 777-790.

Butler & Carney, "Strategy and Strategic Choice: The Case of Telecommunications," SMJ, 1986: 161-177.

Ireland, Hitt, Bettis, & De Porras, "Strategy Formulation Processes: Differences in Perceptions of Strength and Weaknesses Indicators and Environmental Uncertainty by Managerial Level," SMJ, 1987: 469-485.

week 2

2. Organizational Performance

a. Economic Performance

Venkatraman & Ramanujam, "Measurement of Business Performance in Strategy Research: A Comparison of Approaches," AMR, 1986: 801-814.

Chakravarthy, "Measuring Strategic Performance," SMJ, 1986: 437-458.

b. Social Performance

Ullmann, "Data in Search of a Theory: A Critical Examination of the Relationship Among Social Performance, Social Disclosure, and Economic Performance," AMJ, 1985: 540-557.

McGuire, "Corporate Social Responsibility and Firm Financial Performance," AMJ, 1988: 854-872.

Szwajkowski, "Organizational Illegality: Theoretical Integration and Illustrative Application," AMR, 1985: 558-567.

Yeager, "Analyzing Corporate Offenses: Progress and Prospects," Corporate Social Performance and Policy, 1986: 93-120.

weeks 3-4

3. Linking the Environment, Performance, & Strategy

a. Institutional Theory, Organizational Ecology & Adaptation

Scott, "The Adolesence of Institutional Theory," ASQ, 1987: 493-511.

Wholey & Brittain, "Organizational Ecology: Findings & Implications," AMR, 1986: 513-533.

Betton & Dess, "Application of Population Ecology Models to the Study of Organizations," AMR, 1985: 750-57.

Hrebiniak & Joyce, "Organizational Adaptation: Strategic Choice and Environmental Determinism," ASQ, 1985: 335-348.

Lawless, "Choice and Determinism: A Test of Hrebiniak and Joyce's Framework on Strategy-Environment Fit," SMJ, 1989: 351-365.

Marcus, "Responses to Externally Induced Innovation: Their Effects on Organizational Performance," SMJ, 1988: 387-402.

b. Contingency Theory

Venkatraman, "The Concept of Fit in Strategy Research: Toward Verbal and Statistical Correspondence," AMR, 1989: 423-444.

Van de Ven & Drazin, "The Concept of Fit in Contingency Theory," Reserach in Organizational Behavior, 1985: 333-365.

Fry & Smith, "Congruence, Contingency, and Theory Building," AMR, 1987: 117-132.

Ginsberg & Venkatraman, "Contingency Perspectives of Organizational Strategy: A Critical Review of the Empirical Research," AMR, 1985: 421-434.

Hambrick & Lei, "Toward An Empirical Prioritization of Contingency Variables for Business Strategy," AMJ, 1985: 763-788.

weeks 5-6

4. Defining Strategy

Ginsberg, "Measuring and Modeling Changes in Strategy: Theoretical Foundations and Empirical Directions," SMJ, 1988: 559-575.

Segev, "A Systematic Comparative Analyis and Synthesis of Two Business Level Strategic Typologies," SMJ, 1989: 487-505.

Herbert and Deresky, "Generic Strategies: An Empirical Investigation of Typology Validity and Strategy Content," SMJ, 1987: 135-147.

Kotha & Orne, "Generic Manufacturing Strategies: A Conceptual Synthesis," SMJ, 1989: 211-231.

Venkatraman and Grant, "Construct Measurement in Organizational Strategy Research," AMR, 1986: 71-87.

a. Porter's Framework

Hill, "Differentiation Versus Low Cost or Differentiation and Low Cost: A Contingency Framework," AMR, 1988: 401-412.

Murray, "A Contingency View of Porter's 'Generic Strategies,'" AMR, 1988: 390-400.

Wright, "A Refinement of Porter's Strategies," SMJ, 1987: 93-101.

b. Strategic Groups

McGee & Thomas, "Strategic Groups: Theory, Research, and Taxonomy," SMJ, 1986: 141-160.

Hatten & Hatten, "Strategic Groups, Asymmetrical Mobility Barriers, and Contestability," SMJ, 1987: 329-342.

c. Diversification

Ramanujam & Varadarajan, "Research on Corporate Diversification: A Synthesis," SMJ, 1989: 523-551.

Grant & Jammine, "Performance Differences Between the Wrigley/Rumelt Strategic Categories," SMJ, 1988: 333-346.

week 7

5. Empirical Studies

Miller, "The Structural and Environmental Correlates of Business Strategy," SMJ, 1987: 55-76.

Bourgeois, "Strategic Goals, Perceived Uncertainty, and Economic Performance," AMJ, 1985: 548-73.

Kim & Lim, "Environment, Generic Strategies, & Performance In a Rapidly Developing Country: A Taxonomic Approach," AMJ, 1988: 802-827.

Romanelli, "Environments and Strategies of Organization Start-Up: Effects on Early Survival," ASQ, 1989: 369-387.

Prescott, "Environments As Moderators of the Relationship Between Strategy and Performance," AMJ, 1986: 329-346.

Daft, Sormunen, & Parks, "Chief Executive Scanning, Environmental Characteristics, and Company Performance," SMJ, 1988: 123-139.

Smith, "Environmental Variation, Strategic Change, and Firm Performance," *SMJ*, 1987: 363-376.

weeks 8-10

6. The Electric Utility Industry In Transition

    a. General Trends

Fenn, *America's Electric Utilities Under Seige and In Transition*, 1983: 1-99.

Russo, "The Electric Utility Industry in the United States," in Russo, *Generating Strategy: A Dynamic Analysis of Regulation and Diversification in the Electric Utility Industry*, 1989: 90-116.

McCormick, "Inflation, Regulation, and Financial Adequacy," in Moorhouse, *Electric Power*, 1986: 135-163.

    b. Nuclear Power

Thomas, *The Realities of Nuclear Power*, 1988: 1-117.

Campbell, "Financial Crisis," in Campbell, *Collapse of an Industry*, 1988: 92-110.

    c. Regulatory Politics

Navarro, *The Dimming of America*, 1985: 1-93.

Anderson, "Regulatory Tasks and Structural Change," in Anderson, *Regulatory Politics and Electric Utilities*, 1981: 61-89.

Hyman & Habicht, "State Electric Utility Regulation: Financial Issues, Influences, and Trends," *ARE*, 1986: 163-185.

    d. Competition

Zardkoohi, "Competition in the Production of Electricity," in Moorhouse, *Electric Power*, 1986: 63-97.

Joskow, "The Evolution of Competition in the Electric Power Industry," *ARE*, 1988: 215-238.

Monroe, "Electric Utility Competition: Lessons from Others," *JED*, 1987: 203-214.

INDIANA UNIVERSITY

SYLLABUS
G406 Sec. 4950 &
G503 Sec. 5241
MW 11:15 a.m.-12:30 p.m.
BU 406

Professor David D. Martin
BU 438
Office Hours: MW 9:30-11:00 a.m.
Tel. 855-9219

OBJECTIVES OF THE COURSE: To give the student a better understanding of the role of governments in the world economy; to provide an historical perspective on the evolution of that economy; and to encourage students to think, interpret, analyse, and communicate.

Required Textbooks:

Baldwin, William L., *Market Power, Competition, and Antitrust Policy*, (Irwon, 1987).
Brown, Lester R., *State of the World, 1989*, (Worldwatch Institute, 1989).
Leonard, Dick, *Pocket Guide to the European Community*, (The Economist Publications, 1988).

Grading Policies:

Class attendance is expected and required. Assignments must be read on schedule so that each student is prepared to participate in discussion at each class period. To encourage such behavior there will be several short quizzes at unannounced times instead of a single mid-term exam. These quizzes, taken together will count one-third of the semester grade.

The final exam will cover the whole course and it will count one-third.

A term paper will count one-third. For G406 students the paper must be no more than seven pages (typewritten, double spaced) not counting footnotes and bibliography. For G503 students there is no restriction on length. The topic must be approved in advance. It should be related to the changing structure of the European Community but it can deal with any policy area such as antitrust, environment or trade restriction.

Short oral reports on the term paper before a video camera will be required.

Reading Assignments:

INTRODUCTION

Aug. 30 Find in the library and read The Declaration of Independence, The Articles of Confederation, and the Constitution of the United States.

Spt. 4 Leonard: Contents, Notes, Foreward, Introduction (pp. i-xiii) and Chapter 1, "The Origins," (pp. 3-7), and Index (pp. 203-210).

Baldwon: Preface, Contents, (pp. v-xvi), Chapter 1 "The Business Firm and Economic Activity in the United States," (pp. 3-11) and Indices (pp. 517-533).

Brown: Acknowledgements, Contents, Foreward, (pp. vii-xvi), and Chapter 1, "A World at Risk," (pp. 4-20).

U.S. ANTITRUST POLICIES

Spt. 6 Baldwin, Chapters 2 and 3, pp. 12-51.

Spt. 11 Baldwin, Chapters 4 and 5, pp. 52-104.

Spt. 13 Baldwin, Chapters 6 and 7, pp. 107-148.

Spt. 18 Baldwin, Chapters 15 and 16, pp. 345-393.

Spt. 20 Baldwin, Chapters 17 and 18, pp. 394-443.

Spt. 25 Baldwin, Chapters 19, pp. 444-473, and court opinions in one antitrust case.

Spt. 27 Baldwin, Chapters 20 and 21, pp. 474-515.

THE EUROPEAN COMMUNITY

Oct. 2 Leonard, Part I, "The Background" and Part II, "The Institutions," pp. 3-56.

Oct. 4 Leonard, Part III, "The Competences," Chapters 1-7, pp. 58-99.

Oct. 9 Leonard, Part III, Chapters 8-16, pp. 100-141.

Oct. 11 Leonard, Part III, Chapters 17-23, pp. 142-170.

Oct. 16 Leonard, Part IV, "Special Problems" and "Appendices," pp. 172-202.

ECOLOGICAL CONSEQUENCES OF ECONOMIC ACTIVITY

Oct. 18 Brown, Chapter 2, "Halting Land Degradation," pp. 21-40 and Chapter 3, "Reexamining the World Food Prospect," pp. 41-58.

Oct. 23 Brown, Chapter 4, "Abandoning Homelands," pp. 59-76, and Chapter 5, "Protecting the Ozone Layer," pp. 77-96.

Oct. 25 (NOTE: Last day for automatic withdrawal with grade of W). Brown, Chapter 6, "Reghinking Transportation," pp. 97-112, and Chapter 7, "Responding to AIDS," pp. 113-131.

Oct. 30 Brown, Chapter 8, "Enhancing Global Security," pp. 132-153, and Chapter 9, "Mobilizing at the Grassroots," pp. 154-173.

Nov. 1 Brown, Chapter 10, "Outlining a Global Action Plan," pp. 174-194.

CLASS REPORTS ON TERM PAPER TOPICS:

Nov. 6 - Dec. 6

DEC. 15, FINAL EXAM, 5:00 - 7:00 p.m.

University of British Columbia

Commerce 588-001-MBA
Public Policy Analysis
Th 6.30-9.30, HA 415

Professor D. Nickerson
Office: HA268 224-8475
Office Hours: WTh 5-6

Course Description

This course broadly examines the design of public policies, the assessment of public welfare and the relation between government and the economy in Canada. Emphasis will be placed on understanding the economic approach to the design of public policy in a market economy and developing concepts relevant to the application of economics to policy design and public choice. The course will include an exposition of the neoclassical model of consumer and producer behavior, an examination of circumstances under which private markets fail to allocate goods and services efficiently, an analysis of the criteria by which social welfare may be measured, a description of the technique of benefit-cost analysis, and applications of economic theory to the design and analysis of policies intended to remedy actual problems in the Canadian economy.

Required Materials

Primary sources for readings will include articles from professional journals and selections from the following texts:

J. Brander, Government and Business, UBC Commerce mimeo, 1988.

L. Friedman, Microeconomic Policy Analysis, McGraw-Hill-Ryerson, 1984.

R. Haveman and J. Margolis, Public Expenditures and Policy Analysis, Markham, 1970.

J. Hirshleifer, Price Theory and Applications, Prentice-Hall, 1980.

R. Just, D. Hueth and A. Schmitz, Applied Welfare Economics and Public Policy, Prentice-Hall, 1982.

P. Ordeshook, Game Theory and Political Theory, Cambridge, 1986.

R. Russell and M. Wilkinson, Microeconomics, Wiley, 1979.

E. Silberberg, The Structure of Economics, McGraw-Hill-Ryerson, 1978.

R. Sugden and A. Williams, The Principles of Practical Cost-Benefit Analysis, Oxford, 1978.

A package containing all required readings will be made available through the copy centre. Additional readings will be provided in class or placed on reserve in the Lam Library.

Grading

The primary basis of evaluation will be an essay applying the principles of economics and public choice from the course to a current or historical problem in public policy. Details about the requirements of this essay, which will be due no later than 5 April 1988, are provided on an appended page. Secondary sources of evaluation will be class participation and occasional problem sets. The relative weights of the primary and secondary requirments will be respectively eighty and twenty percent of the final course score.

Course Outline and Readings

I. Policy Analysis, Economics and Public Choice

    A. Policy Analysis: an Overview

        Brander, Ch. 1
        Friedman, Ch.1*
        JHS, Ch. 1
        Silberberg, Ch.1
        Steiner, "The Public Sector and the Public Interest," in Haveman and Margolis
        Nelson, "The Economics Profession and the Making of Public Policy," JEL, March 1987, 49-91

    B. Four Economic Concepts

        Brander, Ch. 2*
        Rhoads, Chs. 1-4

    C. Philosophical Foundations of Policy Analysis

        Brander, Ch. 3*
        Schultze, "The Public Use of Private Interest," mimeo, 1977*
        Tribe, "Policy Science: Analysis or Ideology," Philosophy and Public Affairs, Fall 1972, 66-110.
        Bromley, "Econonomics and Public Decisions," JEI, December 1976

II. Basic Microeconomic Theory

    A. Individual Preferences and Consumer Demand

        Friedman, Ch.2, part 1*
        Hirshleifer, Chs. 3,4
        Russell and Wilkinson, Chs. 2,3,4
        Silberberg, Ch.8
        Bator, "The Simple Analytics of Welfare Maximization," AER, March 1957, 22-59.

B. Preference Aggregation and Social Welfare

> Friedman, Ch.2, part 2*
> JHS, Ch. 2,3
> Ordeshook, Chs. 1,2
> Russell and Wilkinson, Chs. 19,20

C. Equilibrium, Efficiency and the Gains from Exchange

> Nickerson, Handout*
> Hirshleifer, Ch. 7
> Friedman, Ch. 10
> JHS 4,5
> Russell and Wilkinson, Chs. 11, 12

D. Market Organization

> Brander, Ch. 4*
> Hirshleifer, 10-13
> Russell and Wilkinson, 13, 14

IV. The Normative Role for Government Policy

A. Efficiency and Market Failures

> Brander, Ch. 5*
> Friedman, Ch. 11*
> Arrow, "The Organization of Economic Activity: Issues Pertinent to the Choice of Market vs. Nonmarket Allocation," in Haveman and Margolis*
> Ledyard, "Market Failures," mimeo, 1987
> Bator, "The Anatomy of Market Failure," QJE, 72, 1958, 351-379

B. Equity and other Rationales for Policy Intervention

> Brander, Ch. 5*
> Friedman, Chs. 3,4

C. Cost-Benefit Analysis

> V. Kerry Smith, "A Conceptual Overview of the Foundations of Benefit-Cost Analysis," in Bentkover, et al. (eds), _Benefits Assessment: State of the Art_, Reidel, 1985*
> Weimer and Vining, _Policy Analysis_, Chs 6,7*
> Sugden and Williams, Chs. 7-11, 13, 16
> Prest and Turvey, "Cost-Benefit Analysis: A Survey," EJ, 75, 1965, 683-735
> Azzi and Cox, "Equity and Efficiency in the Evaluation of Public Programs," QJE, 87, 1973, 495-502

V. The Positive Theory of Government

        Brander, Ch. 6*
        Weimer and Vining, Ch. 4*
        Tullock, "Transitional Gains Traps," <u>Bell Journal of Economics</u>, 1976, 671-8
        Litvak, "Lobbying Strategies and Business Interest Groups," <u>Business Quarterly</u>, Summer 1983, 42-50
        Buchanan, "Rent-Seeking and Profit-Seeking," in Buchanan and Tullock, <u>The Calculus of Consent</u>, U of Michigan, 1965
        Ordeshook, Ch 5
        Stanbury, "Grappling with Leviathan," UBC Commerce mimeo

VI. Applications and Major Policy Areas

    A. Welfare, Imperfect Competition and Regulation

        Brander, Chs. 10-14*
        Averch and Johnson, "Behavior of the Firm under Regulatory Restraint," <u>AER</u>, 52, 1962, 1058-9
        Stigler, "The Theory of Economic Regulation," <u>Bell Journal of Economics</u>, Spring 1971, 3-21
        Reschenthaler and Stanbury, "Deregulating Canada's Airlines..." <u>Canadian Public Policy</u>, June 1983, 210-22

    B. International Trade

        Brander, Chs. 8,9*
        Krugman, "New Thinking About Trade Policy," in Krugman (ed), <u>Strategic Trade Policy and the New International Economics</u>, MIT Press, 1986
        Grossman, "Strategic Export Promotion: A Critique," in Krugman
        Spencer, "What Should Trade Policy Target?" in Krugman

    C. Uncertainty, Risk and Insurance

        Ehrlich and Becker, "Market Insurance, Self-Insurance and Self-Protection," <u>JPE</u>, July-August 1972, 623-48
        Marshall, "Moral Hazard," <u>AER</u>, December 1976, 880-890
        Arrow, "Uncertainty and the Welfare Economics of Medical Care," <u>AER</u> December 1963, 941-973
        Pauly, "Taxation, Health Insurance and Market Failure in the Medical Economy," <u>JEL</u>, June 1986
        Lewis and Nickerson, "Self-Insurance against Natural Hazards," UBC Commerce mimeo, 1987
        Akerlof, "The Market for Lemons," <u>QJE</u>, 84, 1970, 488-500

D. Externalities, Public Goods and the Environment

> JHS, Chs. 12,13
> Brander, Ch. 15
> Sandler and Tschirhart, "The Economic Theory of Clubs," <u>JEL</u>, December 1980
> Coase, "The Problem of Social Cost," <u>Journal of Law and Economics</u> 3, 1960, 1-44
> Henry, "Investment Decisions under Uncertainty: the Irreversibility Effect", AER, December 1974, 1006-12.
> Morrall, "Reducing Airport Noise," in Miller and Yandle
> Keeton and Kwerel, "Externalities in Automobile Insurance and the Underinsured Driver Problem," <u>Journal of Law and Economics</u>, 27, 1984, 149-79.

E. Consumer and Worker Health Policies

> Thaler and Rosen, "The Value of Saving a Life: Evidence from the Labour Market," in N. Terleckyj (ed), <u>Household Production and Consumption</u>, Columbia-NBER, 1975.
> Viscusi, "The Impact of Occupational Safety and Health Regulation," <u>Bell Journal of Economics</u>, 10-1, 1979, 111-140.
> Levine, "Labelling Donated Blood," in Miller and Yandle
> Levine, "Exposure to Inorganic Arsenic in the Workplace," in Miller and Yandle
> Hopkins and Threadgill, "Evaluating Crash Protection for Auto Occupants," in Miller and Yandle

F. Agricultural Support and Stabilization Policies

> JHS, Ch. 11
> Newbery and Stiglitz, <u>The Theory of Commodity Price Stabilization</u>, Oxford, 1981, Chs 2, 15, 23

<u>Lecture and Required Readings Schedule</u>   (Tentative)

Week 1:   Administrative Noise

Week 2:   Policy Analysis, Economics and Public Choice:

> Brander, 1-3
> Friedman, 1
> Schultze

Weeks 3,4: Microeconomics

        Friedman, 2
        Hirshleifer, 3,4,7
        Brander, 4

Weeks 5,6: Normative Role for Government

        Brander, 5
        Friedman 11
        Weimer and Vining 6,7
        Arrow
        Smith

Weeks 7,8: Positive Theory of Goverment

        Brander, 6
        Weimer and Vining, 4

Weeks 9-12: Applications

Columbia University
Graduate School of Business

B6003
Conceptual Foundations of Business
Prof. Eli M. Noam
Course Syllabus

Spring 1990
T., Th.: 10:00-11:20

Office: 809 Uris Hall, 280-4222
Office Hours: To be determined

Course requirements: To be determined

Grading: To be determined

B6003
Conceptual Foundations of Business
Prof. Eli M. Noam
Course Syllabus

Reading materials can be purchased in the case room at the beginning of the term. Each unit of readings corresponds to one class, and consists of articles and excerpts, plus case materials selected to integrate the readings for class discussion.

Overview of the Course

I. THE ECONOMIC SYSTEM

Unit 1: The Genesis of Capitalism and of the Business Firm
     2: Theories of Capitalism's Demise
     3: The Business Corporation and its Governance
     4: Income Distribution

II. BUSINESS AND GOVERNMENT

Unit 5: Regulation
     6: Antitrust
     7: Industrial Policy
     8: Politics and Lobbies

III. BUSINESS AND EMPLOYEES

Unit 9: Unionization
     10: Labor Relations
     11: Civil Liberties in the Workplace
     12: Employment Discrimination

IV. BUSINESS AND SOCIETY

Unit 13: Wall Street
     14: Consumers
     15: The Legal System
     16: The Community
     17: Intellectual Critics
     18: The Media
     19: Pressure Groups
     20: The Developing World

V. PERSONAL AND ORGANIZATIONAL STANDARDS

Unit 21: Ethics and Liabilities
     22:

I. THE ECONOMIC SYSTEM

Unit 1: THE GENESIS OF CAPITALISM AND OF THE BUSINESS FIRM

Behrman, Jack N. and Richard I. Levin, "Are Business Schools Doing Their Job?," The Harvard Business Review, Jan./Feb. 1984.

Braudel, Ferdinand, Wheels of Commerce, Vol. II. NY: Harper & Row, 1982.

Kristol, Irving, "Adam Smith and the Spirit of Capitalism," Reflections of a Neoconservative. NY: Basic Books, Inc., 1983.

Chandler, Alfred Dupont Jr., "The United States: Seedbed of Managerial Capitalism," The Visible Hand. Cambridge, Mass.: Harvard University Press, 1977.

Case Materials:

Rogers, Everett and Susan Larsen, "The True Capitalist--Steven Jobs of Nelson Bunker Hunt?" Silicon Valley Fever. NY: Basic Books, 1984.

Unit 2: THEORIES OF CAPITALISM'S DEMISE

Boulding, Kenneth, "Entropy Economics."

Schumpeter, Joseph, "The Process of Creative Destruction", (Ch. 7); "Growing Hostility" (Ch. 13); "The Destruction of the Institutional Framesork of Capitalist Society", "Crumbling Walls", (Ch. 7); Can Capitalism Survive?", Capitalism, Socialism, and Democracy. NY: Harper & Row, 1950.

Lowi, Theodore, "Origin and Decline of Liberal Ideology in the U.S.", The End of Liberalism. NY: Norton, 1979.

Marx, Karl. "Wage Labour and Capital", The Marx-Engels Reader, Robert C. Tucker, ed. NY: W.W. Norton & Co., 1972.

Bell, Daniel, "Cultural Contradictions of Capitalism," The Public Interest, Fall, 1979.

Olson, Mancur, "The Political Economy of Comparative Growth Rates, 94th Congress Session, U.S. Econ. Growth, 1976-1986: Prospects, Problems and Patterns, Vol. 2, The Factors and Processes Shaping Long-Term Econ. Growth, Nov. 10, 1976, Joint Economic Committee.

Meadows, Donnella, et al, The Limits to Growth, Universe Books, 1974.

Scherer, F.M., *Industrial Market Structure and Economic Performance*. Chicago: Rand McNally, 1980.

Saunders, Dero A., "Sic transit (most) gloria...," *Forbes*, January 14, 1985.

Case Materials: "A Gentle Passing of Capitalism?"

Unit 3: THE BUSINESS COPORATION AND ITS GOVERNANCE

Stone, Christopher, "Corporations and the Law: The First Skirmishes," (Ch. 3), "The Industrial Revolution: The Die is Cast." *Where The Law Ends*. NY: Harper & Row, 1975.

Berle, Adolf and Gardiner Means, *The Modern Corporation and Private Property*. NY: Brace & World, 1968.

Geneen, Harold S., "Why Directors Can't Protect the Shareholders," *Fortune*, Sept. 17, 1984.

Schoenberg, Robert, Letter to the Editor, *Fortune*, Nov. 12, 1984.

Goodwin, John, *Business Law*, Homewood, IL: Richard Irwin, Inc., 1980.

Case Materials: "Corporations as Persons"

Unit 4: INCOME DISTRIBUTION

Thurow, Lester, "The Outcome of the Economic Game." (Ch. 1), *Generating Inequalities*. NY: Basic Books, 1975.

Thurow, Lester, "Direct Redistributional Issues", (Ch. 7), *Zero Sum Society*. NY: Basic Books, 1980.

Friedman, Milton, "The Distribution of Income", (Ch.10), *Capitalism and Freedom*. Chicago: Chicago University Press, 1965.

Okun, Arthur, "Rights and Dollars", *Equality and Efficiency, the Big Tradeoff*. Washington, DC: Brookings Institute, 1975.

Case Materials: "Market Forces and the Losers: ARCO Closes a Mine"

II: BUSINESS AND GOVERNMENT

Unit 5: REGULATION

Friedman, Milton, _Capitalism and Freedom_, (Ch. 1): "The Relation Between Economic Freedom and Political Freedom," (Ch. 2): "The Role of Government in a Free Society." Chicago: University of Chicago Press, 1962.

Hardin, Garrett, "The Tragedy of the Commons," _Science_, vol. 162, Dec. 13,

Kolko, Gabriel, "The Triumph of Conservatism," _Perspectives on the Administrative Process_, Robert Rabin, ed., Little, Brown & Co., Boston, 1979.

Bernstein, M., "Regulatory Business by Independent Commission," _Perspectives on the Administrative Process_, Robert Rabin, ed., Little Brown & Co., Boston, 1979.

Kristol, Irving, _Two Cheers for Capitalism_, (Ch. 14), "Some Doubts about 'Deregulation,'" Basic Books, Inc., New York, 1978.

Case Materials: A Painful Transition for the Transport Industry

Unit 6: ANTITRUST

Shepherd, William and Wilcox, Clair, "Public Policies Toward Business," (Ch. 4), _Antitrust Tasks and Tools_, Homewood, IL: Richard Irwin Co., Inc., 1979.

Smith, Jr., Fred L., "Why Not Abolish Antitrust?", _Regulation_, January/February 1983.

Brozen, Yale, "Mergers in Perspective," (Ch. 6), _Aggregate Concentration: A Phenomenon in Search of Significance_, Washington, D.C.: American Enterprises Institute, 1982.

Bureau of National Affairs, _Antitrust and Trade Regulation Report_, "Merger Guidelines issued by Justice Department, June 14, 1984, and Accompanying Statement," no. 1169, Special Supplement, Jun. 14, 1984.

Case Materials: "The AT&T Antitrust Case: Was it Worth It?"

Unit 7: INDUSTRIAL POLICY

Reich, Robert B., "The Next American Frontier," in _The Atlantic Monthly_, April 1983.

Hayek, Frederich, <u>The Road to Serfdom</u>, (Ch. 4), Chicago: University of Chicago Press, 1956.

Schultze, Charles L, "Industrial Policy: A Solution in Search of a Problem." <u>California Management Review.</u> Summer 1983.

Albraith, J.K., "The Nature of Industrial Planning", (Ch. 3), <u>The New Industrial State</u>, (Ch. 3), Boston: Houghton Mifflin Co., 1971.

Bradshaw, Thornton, "My Case For Planning," <u>Fortune</u>, Feb. 1977.

<u>Case Materials:</u>   "The Japanese Challenge: A Need for Industrial Policy?"

Unit 8:   POLITICS AND LOBBIES

Epstein, "PACs and the Modern Political Process," <u>Political Impact</u>.

Wilson, James Q., <u>American Government: Institutions and Policies.</u> Lexington, Mass.: DC Heath, 1983.

Blumenthal, Michael, <u>Fortune</u>, "Candid Reflections of a Businessman in Washington," Jan. 29, 1979.

<u>Case Materials:</u> "Business in the Political Arena"

II.   BUSINESS AND EMPLOYEES

Unit 9:   UNIONIZATION

Simons, Henry, "Some Refelctions on Syndicalism," <u>Journal of Political Economy</u>, March 1944.

Tawney, R.H., <u>Essays</u>, "The American Labor Movement," New York: St. Martin's Press, 1979.

Brooks, Thomas, "The Bitter Bread of Survival." (Ch.7) <u>Toil and Trouble, A History of American Labor</u>, New York: Dell Publishing, 1971.

Freeman, Richard B. and Medoff, James L., <u>What Do Unions Do?</u>, "The Union Wage Effect," "The Slow Strangulation of Private-Sector Unions," New York: Basic Books, Inc., 1984.

Crowley, Joseph R., <u>Compendium of New York Law</u>, "Labor Law," 1980.

Case Materials: "New Tactics in Unionization Battles"
Including:

Kuhn, James W., "Resisting Union Organization: What Scope, What Purpose?, J.P. <u>Stevens and the Amalgamated Clothing and Textile Workers Union,</u>" New York: Columbia University Graduate School of Business, 1980.

Unit 10: LABOR RELATIONS

Marx, Karl, "Wage Labour and Capital," <u>Marx-Engels Reader</u>, Robert C. Tucker, ed., New York: W.W. Norton & Co., 1972.

Hirschman, Albert, <u>Exit, Voice and Loyalty</u>, "Exit and Voice as Impersonations of Economics and Politics," Cambridge: Harvard University Press, 1970.

Freeman, Richard B. and Medoff, James L., <u>What Do Unions Do?</u>, "Unionism: Good or Bad for Productivity?", "But Unionism Lowers Profits," "Blemishes on the Two Faces," New York: Basic Books, 1984.

Case Materials: "Management--Employee Relations"
Including:

Peters, Thomas J. and Waterman, Robert H., Jr., <u>In Search of Excellence</u>, (Ch. 8), "Productivity Through People," New York: Warner Books, 1982.

Terkel, Studs, <u>Working</u>, "Gary Bryner," pp. 187-94, New York: Pantheon Books, 1974.

Unit 11: CIVIL LIBERTIES IN THE WORKPLACE

Ewing, David, "Constitutionalizing the Corporation," <u>Corporations and Their Critics</u>, Thornton Bradshaw and David Vogel, eds., NY: McGraw Hill, 1981.

Martin, Donald, "Is an Employee Bill of Rights Needed?," <u>Individual Rights and the Corporation</u>, A. Westin and Stephen Salisbury, eds., New York: Pantheon Books, 1981.

Westin, Alan F., "The Problem of Employee Privacy Still Troubles Management," <u>Individual Rights in the Corporation</u>, A. Westin and Stephen Salisbury, eds., Pantheon Books, NY, 1980.

Lynd, Staughton, "Company Constitutionalism?" <u>Individual Rights in the Corporation</u>, Editors: Westin, Alan F., and Stephan Salisbury New York: Pantheon Books, 1980.

7

ys, Max, "The Myth of the 'Oppressive Corporation,'" <u>Individual
ights and the Corporation</u>, A. Westin and Stephen Salisbury, eds., New
ork: Pantheon Books, pp. 79-82.

etten, Wayne N. and Kinigstein, Noah A. "Discipline and Discharge"
nd "Privacy", <u>The Rights of Employees: ACLU Handbook</u>. Toronto:
antam Books, 1983.

se Materials: "A Whistleblower's Rights and the Organizational
rerogatives."

llert, Dan, "Insisting on Safety in the Skies," <u>Whistleblowers</u>, Alan
estin, (ed.). New York: Mcgraw-Hill Book Company, 1981.

it 12: EMPLOYMENT DISCRIMINATION

omas Sowell, "The Economics of Discrimination", (Ch.2), <u>Markets and
inorities</u>, NY: Basic Books, 1981.

ttenberg, Ben. J., <u>The Good News Is the Bad News Is Wrong</u>, (chaps. 27
 31), NY: Simon & Schuster, 1984.

ul Baran & Paul Sweezy, "Monopoly Capital and Race Relations", (Ch.9)
onopoly Capital, NY: Modern Reader Paperbacks, 1966.

man, Cynthia M., "The Manager's Introduction To Equal Employment
pportunity & Affirmative Action," Stanford University.

se Materials: "Comparable Worth"

vin, Michael, "Comparable Worth: The Feminist Road to Socialism,"
ommentary, Sept. 1984.

. BUSINESS AND SOCIETY

it 13: WALL STREET

it 14: CONSUMERS

ethro Lieberman, <u>The Litigious Society</u>, (chaps. 1 & 2), NY: Basic
Books, 1983.

ichael Pertschuk, "On the Side of the Angels," <u>Revolt Against</u>

8

143

Regulation, Berkeley: University of California Press, 1982.

Paul n. Bloom and Stephen A. Greyser, "The Maturing of Consumerism," Harvard Business Review, Nov.-Dec. 1981.

Case Materials: "The Dalcon Shield"

Unit 15: THE LEGAL SYSTEM (in preparation)

Unit 16: THE COMMUNITY

Milton Friedman, "The Social Responsibility of Business is to Increase its Profits," New York Times Magazine, Sept. 13, 1970.

Christopher D. Stone, "Why Shouldn't Corporations be Socially Responsible?" Where the Law Ends, NY: Harper & Row, 1975.

George Cabot Lodge, "The Connection Between Ethics and Ideology," Proceedings of the First National Conference on Business Ethics, W. Michael Hoffman, ed., Waltham, Mass: The Center for Business Ethics, Bentley College, 1977.

Case Materials: "A Local Bank and the Community"

Unit 17: INTELLECTUAL CRITICS

Richard Hofstadter, "Business and Intellect", Anti-intellectualism in American Life, (chap. IX), NY: Alfred A. Knopf, 1964.

Bell, Daniel, "From the Protestant Ethic to the Psychedelic Bazaar", The Cultural Contradictions of Capitalism, NY: Basic Books, Inc.

Kristol, Irving, "The Adversary Culture of Intellectuals", Reflections of a NeoConservative: Looking Back, Looking Ahead, (chap. 3), NY: Basic Books, 1984.

Case Materials: "Intellectuals and the Commisioned Productions of Ideas"

Unit 18: THE MEDIA

Banks, Louis. "Memo to the Press: They Hate You Out There." The Atlantic Monthly, April 1978, pp. 35-42.

Compaine, Benjamin M., Who Owns the Media? White Plains: Knowledge Industry Publications, Inc., 1982, pp. 458-460.

Hartley, Robert L. "The News Business and Business News." What's News?: The Media in American Society, Elie Abel, ed., New Brunswick, NJ: Transaction Books, 1981.

Welles, Chris, "The Bleak Wasteland of Financial Journalism," Columbia Journalism Review, July/August 1973, pp. 42-45.

Case Materials: "Love Canal and the Press"

Unit 19: PRESSURE GROUPS

Vogel, David. "Polticizing the Corporation" (ch. 11); "The Resurgence of Shareholder Participation" (ch. 3); "Corporate Conduct Abroad," Lobbying the Corporation: Citizen Challenges to Business Authority, NY: Basic Books, 1978.

Herman, Edward S., "Power, Responsibility, conflict," Corporate Control, Corporate Power, NY: Cambridge University Press, 1981.

Case Materials: "The Nestle Boycott"
Including:

Sethi, S. Prakash and James E. Post. "The Marketing of Infant Formula in Less Developed Countries." Business Ethics, Hoffman and Mills Moore, eds, NY: Mcgraw Hill, 1984.

Unit 20: THE DEVELOPING WORLD

Veronon, Raymond. "National Elites, Ideologies and Culture" (Ch.6), Sovereignty at Bay: The Multinational Spread of US Enterprises, NY: Basic Books, 1971.

Gilpin, Robert. US Power and the Multinational Corporation, NY: Basic Books, 1975.

Nora, Simon and Minc, Alain. "Introduction." The Computerization of Society, Cambridge, MA: MIT Press, 1981.

Nye, Joseph. "Multinational Corporations in World Politics," Foreign

Affairs, Oct. 1974.

Case Materials: "Dresser Industries and US Foreign Policy in South Africa and in Eastern Europe."

V. PERSONAL AND ORGANIZATIONAL STANDARDS

Unit 21: ETHICS AND LIABILITIES

Drucker, Peter, "Ethical Chic," *Forbes*, Sept. 14, 1981.

Bok, Sissela, "Lies Protecting Peers and Clients" (ch. 11), *Lying: Moral Choice in Public and Private Life*, NY: Random House, 1979.

Kant, Immanuel, "On a Supposed Right to Lie From Altruistic Motives," *Critique of Practical Reason and other Writings in Moral Philosophy*, Chicago: University of Chicago Press, 1949.

Arrow, Kenneth, "Business Codes and Economic Efficiency." *Ethical Theory and Business*, Beauchamp and Boyd, eds., NY: Prentice Hall, 1979.

Clinard, Marshall B., "Why Some Corporations are More Ethical Than Others" (ch. 4), *Corporate Ethics and Crime*, Beverly Hills: Sage Publ., 1983.

Case Materials: "Personal and Organizational Responsibility" Including:

Farley, Dean, "But Who Guards the Guards? -- The SEC Investigates Allegations Against Citibank."

WASHINGTON UNIVERSITY

MANAGEMENT 100 - THE MANAGERIAL ENVIRONMENT

Fall, 1989 Professor Seth W. Norton

Course Objectives

This course attempts to provide students with background knowledge on American business institutions and practices. The intent is to develop a framework for future courses and to develop an appreciation of important aspects of modern American enterprise.

Administrative Items

Office: Simon 228

Telephone: 889-6368

Office hours: Open

I am usually in my office Monday through Thursday, 1:00-2:30 P.M. If you have an important reason to see me, it is probably best to make an appointment. You may schedule appointments with my secretary in Room 220, phone number 889-6381.

Required Materials

- Packet of readings

- Alfred Chandler, The Visible Hand

- Additional readings, news items, and articles may be distributed during the course. These materials will also be considered required reading.

Grades

Grades will generally be computed based on the following weights:

25% Class participation (including quizzes)

40% Topical exams

35% Final exam

Exceptions will occur when students persistently miss class or exhibit behavioral problems in the class. In the cases of exceptions, the grade will be arbitrarily determined by the Professor.

Integrity

Students are encouraged to study together and discuss course questions together. However, students are expected to complete all written assignments and tests independently.

SYLLABUS - MANAGEMENT 100

Tardiness, Absenteeism, and Classroom Behavior

Students are expected to attend all classes. Ordinarily, there will be no make-up on quizzes or topical exams. A make-up final examination will not be given. If you miss the examination, you can take the exam the next time I teach the course.

All students are expected to be enthusiastic, cordial, orderly, and respectful in all classroom discussions. Exceptions will not be tolerated.

TOPICS

I. The Nature of Economic Organization

   A. Topics

      1. Functions of Economic Systems
      2. Types of Economic Systems
      3. Markets versus Firms as Coordinators
      4. Entrepreneurs

   B. Academic Readings

      1. Adam Smith, The Wealth of Nations, pp. Volume 1, Book I, pp. 5-23.

      2. D. Gale Johnson, "Economic Reforms in the People's Republic of China," Economic Development and Cultural Change, 1988, S225-S245.

      3. Ronald Coase, "The Nature of the Firm," Economica, November, 1937.

      4. James H. Madison, "The Evolution of Commercial Credit in Nineteenth-Century America, Business History Review, Summer, 1974.

      5. Alfred Chandler, The Visible Hand, pp. 1-80.

      6. Leslie Hannah, "Entrepreneurs and the Social Sciences," Economica, 1984, pp. 219-234.

   C. Business Press Readings

      NOTE: TE = The Economist

              WSJ = Wall Street Journal

      1. Luther Calvin Gorbachev, TE, June 25, 1988.

      2. East Germany's Sad Miracle, TE, July 30, 1988.

      3. Gorbachev's Leveraged Buy-Out, TE, November 26, 1988.

4. Why Half-Reformed Communism Isn't Working, TE, May 28, 1988.

5. Martin Feldstein, "Why Perestroika Isn't Happening," WSJ, April 20, 1989.

6. Eyeing the Consumer, TE, April 22, 1989.

7. The Year of the Brand, TE, December 24, 1988.

8. Going for the Golden Arches, WSJ.

I. Business Application: Marketing as Entrepreneurship

   A. Academic Readings

      1. Jerry Kirkpatrick, "Theory and History in Marketing," Managerial and Decision Economics, 1983.

      2. Lynn W. McGee and Rosann L. Spiro, "The Marketing Concept in Perspective," Business Horizons, May-June, 1988.

   B. Business Press Readings

      1. From Little Bricks Great Houses Grow, TE, August 27, 1988.

      2. Complaints? I Love 'Em, TE, November 5, 1988.

III. Technology and Growth

   A. Topics

      1. Two Economic Revolutions
      2. Sources of Economic Development
      3. Cases in American Business History

   B. Academic Readings

      1. Douglas C. North, "Institutions, Transactions Costs and Economic Growth," Economic Inquiry July, 1977.

      2. Alfred Chandler, The Visible Hand, pp. 81-283.

      3. Richard B. DuBoff, "Business Demand and the Development of the Telegraph in the United States, 1844-1860, Business History Review.

      4. Steve Pejovich, "Freedom, Property Rights and Innovation in Socialism," Kyklos, 1987.

      5. Edwin Mansfield, "Technological Creativity: Japan and the United States," Business Horizons, March-April, 1989.

SYLLABUS - MANAGEMENT 100

C. Business Press Readings

1. Fat Boys Have More Fun, <u>TE</u>, April 29, 1989.
2. Whose Idea Is It Anyway?, <u>TE</u>, November 12, 1988.
3. The End of the Independent Farmer, <u>TE</u>, March 4, 1989.
4. An Informed Way to Grow, <u>TE</u>, February 18, 1989.
5. East Africa, <u>TE</u>, June 20, 1987.
6. Nobody to Blame, <u>TE</u>, April 30, 1988.

IV. Business Application: Why Do Accountants Exist?

A. Academic Readings

1. Ross L. Watts and Jerold L. Zimmerman, "Agency Problems, Auditing and the Theory of the Firm: Some Evidence," <u>Journal of Law and Economics</u>, October, 1983.
2. H. Thomas Johnson, "Management Accounting in an Early Multidivisional Organization: General Motors in the 1920's," <u>Business History Review</u>, Winter, 1978.

B. Business Press Readings

1. Uncovering a Company's Costs, <u>TE</u>, June 11, 1988.

V. Demography and Employment

A. Topics

1. Population and Labor Markets
2. Demographic Trends
3. Employment Trends
4. Management and Workers
5. The Role of Unions

B. Academic Readings

1. Alfred Chandler, <u>The Visible Hand</u>, pp. 285-483.
2. James P. Smith and Michael Ward, "Women in the Labor Market and in the Family," <u>Journal of Economic Perspectives</u>, 1989.
3. William G. Ouchi, "Markets, Bureaucracy, and Clans, <u>Administrative Science Quarterly</u>, 1980.

SYLLABUS - MANAGEMENT 100

4. Henry Mintzberg, "The Managers Job: Folklore and Fact," Harvard Business Review, July-August, 1975.

5. William E. Gallagher, Jr., and Hillel J. Einhorn, "Motivation Theory and Job Design," Journal of Business, 1975.

6. Richard B. Freeman, "Contraction and Expansion: The Divergence of Private Sector and Public Sector Unionism in the United States," Journal of Economic Perspectives, 1988.

7. Melvin W. Reder, "The Rise and Fall of Unions: The Public Sector and the Private," Journal of Economic Perspectives, 1988.

C. Business Press Articles

1. The Poor Die Younger, TE, December 24, 1988.

2. Needed: Human Capital, Business Week, September 19, 1988.

3. Putting the Poor to Work, TE, November 26, 1988.

4. A Work-Out for Corporate America, TE, January 7, 1989.

5. The Folly of Raiding the Piggy-Bank, TE, April 9, 1989.

6. Japanese Women, TE, May 14, 1988.

7. New Blood, TE, December 24, 1988.

VI. Government and the Economy

A. Topics

1. Property Rights and Legal Institutions

2. Market Failure: Regulation for the "Public Interest"

3. Captive Regulation: Regulation for Self-Interest

4. Free Riders and the Logic of Collective Action

B. Academic Readings

1. R.H. Coase, "The Problem of Social Cost," The Journal of Law and Economics, October, 1960.

2. W. Lee Hoskins, "Property Rights in a Global Economy," Business Economics, January, 1989.

SYLLABUS - MANAGEMENT 100

3. Peter George and Philip Sworden, "The Courts and the Development of Trade in Upper Canada, 1830-1860," <u>Business History Review</u>, Summer, 1986.

4. Bernard H. Siegan, "Economic Liberties and the Constitution," <u>Business Economics</u>, January, 1989.

5. George Stigler, "The Theory of Economic Regulation," <u>Bell Journal of Economics and Management Science</u>, 1971.

6. Lord Kilmuir, "The Shaftesbury Tradition in Conservative Politics," <u>Journal of Law and Economics</u>, October 1960.

C. Business Press Readings

1. The City, the Commuter, and the Car, <u>TE</u>, February 18, 1989.

2. Profits from the Wild, <u>TE</u>, October 22, 1988.

3. The Greening of the Invisible Hand, <u>TE</u>, December 24, 1988.

4. How Brazil Subsidizes the Destruction of the Amazon, <u>TE</u>, March 18, 1989.

5. Pricing the Privatised, <u>TE</u>, July 30, 1988.

6. The Regulatory Two-Step, <u>TE</u>, January 21, 1989.

7. False Security, <u>TE</u>, December 17, 1988.

8. Sam Peltzman, "By Prescription Only ... or Occasionally," Regulation, 1987.

VII. Business Application: The Governance of Marketing Channels - An Example of Private Regulation

A. Academic Readings

1. Valentine F. Ridgeway, "Administration of Manufacturer - Dealer Systems," <u>Administrative Science Quarterly</u>, 1957.

2. Robert D. Buzzell, "Is Vertical Integration Profitable," <u>Harvard Business Review</u>, January-February, 1983.

3. Thomas G. Marx, "The Development of the Franchise Distribution System in the U.S. Automobile Industry," <u>Business History Review</u>, 1985.

4. Stewart Macauley, "Non-Contractual Relations in Business: A Preliminary Study," <u>American Sociological Review</u>, 1963.

SYLLABUS - MANAGEMENT 100

- B. Business Press Readings

    1. Cheaper Shopping Japan, TE, January 29, 1989.
    2. Franchisees Win New Legal Protection, WSJ, 1988.
    3. Burger King May Be a Whopper To Digest.

VIII. International Trade

- A. Topics

    1. Reasons for International Trade
    2. Trends in U.S. Trade and Investment
    3. The Multinational Enterprise

- B. Academic Readings

    1. Bela Balassa, "The Lessons of East Asian Development: An Overview," Economic Development and Cultural Change, 1988.
    2. David J. Teece, "The Multinational Enterprise: Market Failure and Market Power Considerations," Sloan Management Review, Spring, 1981.

- C. Business Press Readings

    1. Homage to a Liberal, TE, December 25, 1989.
    2. The Ravishing of Trade, TE, March 25, 1989.
    3. The Birth of a Bad Trade Bill, TE, April 30, 1989.
    4. Protectionism Gets Clever, November 12, 1988.
    5. "The Trade Bill Fluffs Its Feathers," TE, March 19, 1988.
    6. Come Back Multinationals, TE, November 26, 1988.
    7. Passing the Buck, TE, February 11, 1989.
    8. Pardon Me Sir, Is That Ouagadougou Choo-Choo?,
    9. The Stubborn Strains of Nationalism, TE, October 22, 1988.
    10. Feeling Poor in Japan, TE, June 11, 1988.

SYLLABUS - MANAGEMENT 100

IX. Social Ethos, Ethics, and Economic Behavior

   A. Topics

      1. Ideology, Religion and Economic Behavior
      2. Business Ethics

   B. Academic Reading

      1. Ronald Coase, "Adam Smith's View of Man," Journal of Law and Economics, October, 1976.

      2. Thomas R. Rohlen, "Spiritual Education in a Japanese Bank," American Anthropologist, 1973.

      3. Robert Nisbet, "The Twilight of Authority," The Public Interest, Spring, 1969.

      4. Daniel Bell, "The Cultural Contradictions of Capitalism," The Public Interest, 1970.

      5. Peter Drucker, "What Is Business Ethics," The Public Interest, Spring, 1981.

   C. Business Press Readings

      1. Thatcher: Sow, and Ye Shall Reap for All, WSJ, May 31, 1988.

      2. Smaller Savings for Rainy Days, TE, March 19, 1988.

      3. A New Victorian Value, TE, January 14, 1989.

      4. The Decline of Drugged Nations, WSJ.

      5. "Waiting for What?", TE, November 26, 1988.

      6. On the Take, TE, November 19, 1988.

NEW YORK UNIVERSITY
Graduate School of Business Administration

B.97. 3301-33   Fall 1989

The Non-Market Context of Employment Decisions

   This course, a course in the Legal and Social Environment group that is a requirement for MBA candidates who choose the Business Policy Course as their graduating option, focuses on

"non-market" - the legal, social, political and ethical - aspects of business decisions in general and of employment related decisions in particular.

Instructors:

O. Ornati - 9/10 -10/24   M 505 Wed. 5 to 7   Phone # 285-6060
L. Zicklin -10/31-12/13   M 509 Wed. 5 to 7   # 285-6055

Course Description:

   The Course' <u>primary aim</u> is to make future senior executives or entrepreneurs aware of the non-market limits, i.e. the legal, social and political constraints and considerations, surrounding normal business decisions as well as those surrounding labor market decisions; to expose the students to some of the "new institutional economics" and to the regulatory consequences associated with market inadequacies and buyer or seller "disappointments".

   The Course's <u>secondary aim</u> is to increase the student's awareness of his or her own ethical standards. This course is neither a course in "Business Ethics" nor in "Corporate Social Responsibility" in which instructors preach to students about "what is the right thing to do !"
   In this term the course is taught by two instructors representing two integrated and overlapping orientations:

1.) the first half - 9/13 to 10-25 will be taught by Ornati who will focus on the analysis of markets and regulations from the point of view of the academic economist concerned with regulatory policy and its development in labor markets;

2.) the second half - 10/31 to 12/13 will be taught by Zicklin from the point of view of the legally trained practicing senior executive concerned with daily decision making, firm policy and climate and with the future of a business society. To maximize the advantage of the joint teaching opportunity, the course stress will be on class discussion and class "exercises" and will throughout presume that the students will do the assigned reading.

Books:

1. A. M. Okun, Equality and Efficiency Brookings 1975.
2. R.Lindsay "Market Inappropriateness and Inadequacy" (A small Packet of materials)
3. "The Blue Book" The American Legal System Wiesen *et.al.*
4. J.Ledvinka, Federal Regulation of Personnel and Human Resource Management. Kent 1982.
5. P. H. Werhane, Persons, Rights, and Corporations. Prentice-Hall 1985.

(4 and 5. Can be bought later as 4 will not come into play before October 3rd. and 5 is the reading underpinning the Zicklin part of the course.)

Calendar and Reading assignments:

I. Sept. 13:   The Panalba *Case*
                Lecture Introduction Ornati
                Market "Appropriateness" and the meaning of "rights"
                Okun Chapter 1 and 2, Lindasy all
                Homework Ass 1 given out

II Sept 20:   Market "Inadequacies" **Lecture and class discussion**
                Market Disappointments and The American Legal Framework
                Wiesen Part A. Pp.4-41: "The System etc.".
                Homework Ass 1 turned in/ Homework Ass 2 given out.

II	Sept 27:	Product Liability **Cases and discussion**

Wiesen Part B. Pp. 42- 86 : *Cases:* "Henningsen..",
"Greenman..", "La Gorga.." * "Caterpillar v. Beck".
Common Law Duties/ Loyalty and Care. Wiesen Part C. Pp. 87- 123
Cases: "Vokes...", "Meinhardt".
Homework Ass 2 due

IV Oct. 4 :   External and Internal Labor Markets **Lecture**
Inappropriateness, Inadequacies and Employment Law
Ledvinka, Pp.1-16, 135-155, 244-260. Okun Chapter 2 and 3.

V. Oct 11:   Employment Contracts: Implicit and Explicit. **Discussion**
Class Handouts on Labor regulations
Labor law, the right to organize and the duty to negotiate. Class Handouts ;

VI. Oct.18   The "compliance" environment **Class discussion**
Ledvinka Pp.17-134. Ornati "On Sex Harassment" Class Handout
Homework Ass 3 given out

VII Oct. 25:   **Mid-course Enved I Lecture / Discussion**
Ornati & Zicklin
Labor markets, is their regulation enough?
Ledvinka Finish the book.
Homework Ass 3 turned in.

VIII Nov. 1 & 8:   **Presentation** Introduction   Zicklin
Insider Trading: the Process and the Law;
Wiesen Part D Pp. 124-133,180- 202 *Cases* :" Baush & Lomb"."Dirks"
who are the regulators, who are the "insiders"?
Case Discussion

IX Nov. 15:   Fraud. Wiesen Pp. 134-179 *Case:* "Escott v. Barchris

Construction"..
Corporate Take-overs: Selling to raiders (or any one else)
The investment mangers dilemma : Fiduciary responsibility
Conflicts of interest
Case Discussion

X Nov. 22: Bribery
The variety of forms,
Corporate managements' dealing with the problem,
"Are we all a little guilty ?"
Class Handouts. Case Discussion

XI Nov 29: **Presentation and Class Discussion**
Rule 405- are there different rules for different buyers?
"Vokes " revisited in the stock market, in employement
Class Handouts. Case Discussion

XII Dec. 6 The direction of the employees as seen from the top!
The duties and the rights of employers
Finish the Verhane book.
The Ethics of buying securities:
Tobacco, South-Africa, Anti-labor policies, Environmental Issues

XIII Dec. 13 **Final Envoi I Lecture / Discussion**
Zicklin & Ornati
Rights and Duties: of Individuals and of
Corporations, the same or different ?

Deliverables, Grading and other Administrative Issues

I. **Deliverables** :

   A. Three homework assignments; due Sept 20, 27 and October 25th.

   B. Class participation in case discussions

   C. A major paper describing how a publicly held corporation has dealt with at least one major non market happening over the most recent 10 years. This is to be a serious 10 page effort in which the students are to show their ability to deal thoroughly and reasonable elegantly with complex matters.

   A detailed set of instructions will be distributed in class on October 4th; the instructor will be available for discussion and advice about the paper after October 25th; due December 5th in Prof. Ornati's Office (Yes Virginia this is when Mr. Zicklin is teaching)

II. **Grading** :

   A. The first half of this course presents a model with which to analyze the "social, political and ethical consequences of market decision" therefore all written deliverables are keyed to measuring the MBA candidates' understanding and applications of this model.

            Homework 1.   2%
            Homework 2. 10%
            Homework 3. 18%
            Paper   40%

   B. Participation in case discussion is very hard to assess in an equitable and scientific manner. Nevertheless 20 % of the final grade will be given for it; the instructors will measure particularly how carefully a student has read the case and his or her ability to apply the market appropriateness/inadequacy model.

   C. Given the importance of case discussion and analysis attendance is required. 10% of the final grade will be given to attendance! For your own protection and to save embarrassment please make a readable sign with your name on it, display it always, sit in the same seat all the time.

   D. Except for Homework Ass. 1, which is a very early effort, we expect to give A's for outstanding work only and therefore presume that there will be about 5% A's;   very good work will get A- and we expect to pass out about 18 to 20 % A's and A-'s. Papers and Class performance significantly above average performance either in terms of effort or outcome will get a B+; average and somewhat below average work will get B's and B-; experience has shown that in most classes these last two grades are the fate of about > 50 % of the students. Although this is a course that comes near the end of the MBA program we have often found it necessary to give a few C's and C-'s.

Good Luck. We hope you will enjoy the Course !

THE PENNSYLVANIA STATE UNIVERSITY AT HARRISBURG
THE CAPITAL COLLEGE
School of Business Administration
Middletown, Pennsylvania 17057

BUS 584.1

SPRING 1990   Instructor: Dr. Kurt Parkum
Class Time: Wed., 6:00-8:30 PM   Office E-355, Olmsted Bldg.
Class Room: E-311   Office Phone: 948-6144
                                     Office Hours: MW 1:50 to 2:30 P.M.
                                     Also after class and by appointment

BUSINESS IN A GLOBAL SOCIETY

Texts:

Kenneth R. Andrews, **Ethics in Practice. Managing the Moral Corporation.** Boston, Mass.: Harvard Business School Press (1989)

Graham K. Wilson, **Business and Politics. A Comparative Introduction.** Chatham, N.J.: Chatham House Publishers, Inc. (1985)

Barbara Taffle, **Tough Choices. Managers Talk Ethics.** New York, NY, John Wiley & Sons (1986)

Business Week; The Wall Street Journal; The New York Times (Business Section).

Course Objective:

The course objective is to increase awareness and to develop analytical skills regarding the following topics: business sector and society relations; international and cultural issues; corporate values and ethics; relationship to stakeholders; social, political, legal issues.

Course Requirements:

Students are expected to regularly participate in class discussions. Each student will furthermore be assigned major responsibility for preparing notes on one ethics-related topic (about 5 pages) and write a country-specific paper (about 15 pages) on a business and society-related topic. This written material will form the basis for class presentation.

BUS 584.1   K. Parkum   Page 2

Grading:

    Exams   20%
    Ethics Review (and presentation)   20%
    Main Paper (and presentation)   50%
    General Class Participation   10%
                                  TOTAL   100%

COURSE OUTLINE

January 10   Course Objective. Assignments.
                American Capitalism: Issues and Values (Lecture)
                Wilson, Chapter 1
                Library Orientation 8 P.M.

January 17   Aspects of Past Corporate Social Policies (Lecture)
                Gellerman: "Why Good Managers Make Bad Ethical
                Choices."
                Case: Michael Williams

January 24   Managerial Theory and Corporate Social Responsibility
                (Lecture)
                Carr: "Can an Executive Afford A Conscience?"
                Norris: "Moral Hazards of an Executive."
                Cases: Harold Lightner (p. 71)
                       Charles Warren

January 31   Unions and Corporate Social Responsibility (Lecture)
                Learned et al: "Personal Values and Business
                Decisions."
                Ohman: "Skyhooks"
                Cases: Jeffrey Lovett
                       Wendell Johnson

February 7   Corporations as Social and Political Institutions
                (Lecture)
                Cadbury: "Ethical Managers Make Their Own Rules."
                Coles: Storytellers' Ethics."
                Cases: Jackson Taylor
                       Ronald Harris (p. 119)

February 14   Nineteenth Century Ideology (Lecture)
                Goodpaster: "Note on the Corporation as a Moral
                Environment."
                Carr: "Is Business Bluffing Ethical?"
                Cases: Tom Benjamin
                       Carol Miller

| February 21 | Ideological Changes in the American Capitalist Class (Lecture)
Blodgett: "Showdown on Business Bluffing."
Brenner and Molander: "Is the Ethics of Business Changing?"
Cases: Mark Hoffman
       Evelyn Grant |

February 28 **SPRING VACATION**

March 7 **MIDTERM EXAM**

| March 14 | Recent and Current Developments in the United States (Lecture)
Sherwin: "The Ethical Roots of the Business System."
Goodpaster and Matthews: "Can a Corporation Have a Conscience?"
Cases: Ronald Harris (p. 171)
       Frank McGraw |

| March 21 | Business and Politics in the U.S.A. (Discussion)
Wilson, Chapter 2
Jackall: "Moral Mazes: Bureaucracy and Managerial Work."
Sonnenfeld and Lawrence: "Why Do Companies Succumb to Price Fixing?"
Cases: Peter Lathan
       William Robertson |

| March 28 | Business and Social Institutions in West Germany (Discussion)
Wilson, Chapter 3
McCoy: "The Parable of the Sadhu."
Goodpaster: "Ethical Imperatives and Corporate Leadership."
Cases: Robert McDonald
       James Gordon |

| April 4 | Business and Social Institutions in Great Britain (Discussion)
Wilson, Chapter 4
Ewing: "Case of the Rogue Division."
Nash: "Ethics Without the Sermon."
Cases: Harold Lighter (p. 235)
       Robert Smith |

| April 11 | Business and Social Institutions in France (Discussion)
Wilson, Chapter 5
Andrews: "Can the Best Corporations Be Made Moral?"
Collier: "Business Leadership and a Creative Society
Case: Arnold Rowan |

BUS 584.1   K. Parkum   Page 4

April 18   **PAPER DUE**
              Cultural Differences (Lecture)
              Business and Social Institutions in Japan (Discussion)
              Wilson, Chapter 6
              Case: Richard Manzini

April 25   Neo-corporatist Nations and Current Developments in
              Europe (Discussion)
              Wilson, Chapter 7
              Multinational Corporations and Developing Countries
              (Discussion)
              Wilson, Chapter 8

May 2   **FINAL EXAM**

KP/eal 12/21/89

BUS 584.1. Spring 1990

SIGN-UP SHEET

Case Assignments	Macro Discussions
Jan. 17 (1)	Mar. 21 - U.S.A. (4)
Jan. 24 (2)	
Jan. 31 (2)	Mar. 28 - West Germany (4)
Febr. 7 (2)	
Febr. 14 (2)	Apr. 4 - Great Britain (4)
Febr. 21 (2)	
Mar. 14 (2)	Apr. 11 - France (4)
Mar. 21 (2)	Apr. 18 - Japan (4)
Mar. 28 (2)	
Apr. 4 (2)	Apr. 25 - Scan./Austria (3)
Apr. 11 (2)	
April 18 (2)	

Queen's University
School of Business

MBUS 988/Comm 377   B. Pazderka
Winter 1990

ECONOMICS AND PUBLIC POLICY
COURSE OUTLINE AND READING LIST

Subject of the Course

Analysis of selected aspects of the legal and institutional framework in which Canadian business operates, and a critical evaluation of government involvement in the market mechanism. The specific forms of the interaction between private and public interests covered in this course include Canadian competition policy, regulation of natural monopolies, public enterprise and privatization, marketing boards, government subsidies, regional economic development programs, the Canada-U.S. free trade debate, environmental policies, the economics and management of health care, and science and technology policy.

Course Format

Combination of lectures and seminar discussions. There will be three short home assignments (group projects) and an individual term paper (about 20-30 typed pages).

Evaluation Scheme

```
Term paper......................50%
Home assignments................30%
Class participation.............20%
```

Office Hours

My office is in Dunning Hall, Room 218. I will be available for consultations as follows:

```
Tuesday     2:00 - 4:00
Friday      9:00 - 10:00
            2:30 - 4:00
```

Other times can, of course, be arranged as required.

The Text:

It is strongly recommended that all of you purchase the following publication:

J.A. Brander, <u>Government Policy Toward Business</u>, Butterworths, 1988.

The textbook and the readings listed below will be regularly supplemented by current newspaper clippings, excerpts from recent government documents and other material to provide an up-to-date context for class discussions.

The Term Paper

A list of topics suitable for term papers is distributed separately. A few recent references will be provided for each topic to facilitate initial stages of your research.

Topics and Readings

1) Background to Economic Policy-Making in Canada.

    (Economic efficiency and equity; opportunity cost; theoretical reasons for government intervention; the theory of government and bureaucracy; theory and practice of lobbying.)

    Readings:

    Brander, Chs. 1 - 4.

    W.T. Stanbury, Business-Government Relations in Canada, Ch.2, "A Framework for Analyzing Business-Government Relations in Canada", pp. 20-47; excerpts from Ch.4, "The Public Choice Approach", pp. 127-157. [Douglas Library Reserve P.PRE 889088 and Law Library K587.A2.S784].

    Case Discussion: Modification of the patent legislation related to prescription drugs.
    A package of newspaper clippings will be distributed in class.
    Also see Case 32 in M.C. Baetz and P.W. Beamish, Strategic Management. Canadian Cases, Irwin, 1987, pp. 632-652.

    Visiting Speaker: A representative of a public relations firm in Ottawa.

2) The Canadian Business Environment

    (Market structure and economic performance; main macro-economic developments; the international market trends.)

    Readings:

    Brander, Chs. 5-6, Ch.15.

    Handout: The Canadian economy: selected statistics.

3) **Freer Trade Between the U.S. and Canada**

(Benefits from trade; international trade policy and institutions; problems of adjustment and rationale for government intervention.)

Readings:

Brander, Chs. 7-8.

Economic Council of Canada, Venturing Forth. An Assessment of the Canada-U.S. Trade Agreement, Ottawa: Supply and Services Canada, 1988 [Documents Library CA1 EC88 V22].

Handout: A selection of clippings from Canadian newspaper on the "free trade debate."

4) **Canadian Competition Policy**

(Historical development of Canadian legislation; the economics of anticompetitive practices and selected court cases; the new approach under the Competition Act of 1986.)

Readings:

Brander, Chs. 9-10.

G. Kaiser & Ian Nielsen-Jones, "Competition Law", Ottawa Law Review, Vol. 18, No. 2, 1986, pp. 405-406, 408-410, 412-424, 428-439, 445-446, 457-458, 468-473, 481-482, 494-496, 498-499.

P. Foster, "Takeover Horror" Report on Business Magazine, May 1989.

Case Discussion: Three recent mergers (beer, airlines, oil). Based on above readings plus supplementary material distributed in class.

Visiting Speaker: A representative of the Bureau of Competition Policy, Ottawa.

5) **Direct Regulation of Entry, Price, and Rate of Return**

(The various forms of government regulation and their rationale; price discrimination, peak-load pricing, and cross-subsidization; regulation of energy, telephones, airlines, and financial institutions; deregulation.)

Readings:

Brander, Chs. 11-12.

Visiting Speaker: A member of the Ontario Energy Board

6) Public Enterprise

(Scope of public enterprise in Canada; Crown corporations as a policy tool; privatization; comparative efficiency of public and private enterprise.)

Readings:

Brander, Ch. 13.

Economic Council of Canada, Minding the Public's Business, Ottawa: Supply and Services Canada, 1986, pp. 5-9 and 21-28 [Documents Library, CA1 EC86 M36].

A.E. Boardman, A.R. Vining, "Ownership and performance in competitive environments. A comparison of the performance of private, mixed, and state-owned enterprises", Journal of Law and Economics, Vol. 32, April 1989, pp. 1-33.

7) Environmental Policies

(Externalities and market failure; property rights; policy approaches; Canadian policy record.)

Readings:

Brander, Ch. 14.

R.W. Hahn, "Economic prescriptions for environmental problems: How the patient followed the doctor's orders", Journal of Economic Perspectives, Vol. 3, No.2, Spring 1989, pp. 95-114.

Visiting Speaker: A representative of the Ontario Ministry of the Environment.

8) Research and Development and Canadian Science and Technology Policy

(Technical change and its impact on productivity; diffusion and adaptation of technology; the role of government; measurement of profitability of innovation; determinants of success of innovation.)

Readings:

Economic Council of Canada, The Bottom Line, Technology, Trade and Income Growth, Ottawa: Supply and Services Canada, 1983, Ch. 3, pp. 25-33 [Documents Library CA1 EC 83 B53; Douglas Library HC 120 I 52 E36].

K.S. Palda, Industrial Innovation, Its Place in the Public Policy Agenda, Vancouver: The Fraser Institute 1984, Ch. 4, pp. 47-66 [Douglas Library HC 120 T4 P34].

Adjusting to Win, Report of the Advisory Committee on Adjustment (Grandpré Committee), Chapter 10, "Technological Innovation," pp. 71-88, Ottawa: Supply and Services Canada, 1989 [Documents Library CA1 Z3 88A24].

9) **The Canadian Tax Reform**

   (Tax system and its efficiency, neutrality, equity, visibility and stability; issues in the current tax reform debate; federal sales tax and goods and services tax.)

   Readings:

   Economic Council of Canada, *The Taxation of Savings and Investment*, Ottawa: Supply and Services Canada, 1987, pp. 1-14. [Documents library, CA1 EC87 T17].

   Canada Department of Finance, *Tax Reform 1987, Sales Tax*, Ottawa: Department of Finance, June 18, 1987, pp. 2-16 and excerpts from the August 1989 *Technical Paper*.

   Handout: Newspaper clippings on the 1989 GST debate.

10) **The Economics and Management of the Canadian Health Care System**

    (Trends in health care spending; comparison of the U.S. and Canadian systems; the role of the public and private sectors; ethical issues in rationing of access to health care.)

    Readings:

    Handout: Review of the literature on Factors Affecting the Demand for Health Care.

    Visiting Speaker: A representative of a Kingston hospital management team.

11) **Ethics and Public Policy**

    (Distributive justice and procedural fairness; assumption of utility maximization and its limitations; corporate social responsibility and business ethics.)

    Readings:

    Brander, Ch. 16.

    Handout: Alternative Perspectives on Business and Economics.

6

<u>Case Discussion</u>: The Union Carbide pesticide plant in Bhopal, India.

Based on above readings plus material from

M.G. Velasquez, <u>Business Ethics, Concepts and Cases</u>, Second Edition, Prentice-Hall, 1988 [Douglas Library HF 5387 V44].

UNIVERSITY OF CHICAGO
Graduate School of Business

Bus. 306/Econ. 381   Mr. Peltzman
Economics of Regulation

Reading List and Course Outline

No text Required. A packet of recommended readings is available from the bookstore. These readings are preceded with (P) in the reading list. Other recommended readings are denoted (*), and are on reserve in the library.

The course uses economic theory to explain the behavior of regulatory agencies and regulated firms. The history, legislation and institutional organization of the various types of economic regulation are treated only briefly. Background material on these subjects may be found in Kahn, The Economics of Regulation, Phillips, The Economics of Regulation or Wilcox, Public Policies Toward Business. Somewhat more specialized treatments are:

　　Garfield and Lovejoy, Public Utility Economics.
　　Clemens, Economics and Public Utilities.
　　Locklin, Economics of Transportation.
　　Neale, The Antitrust Laws of the U.S.
　　Gordon, Reforming the Regulation of Public Utilities
　　Fisher, Resource & Environmental Economics

If you are unfamiliar with this background material, you should at least sample some of these books.

The following journal and publisher abbreviations are used:

　　　　　AER --American Economic Review
　　BJ or RJ --Bell Journal of Economics and Mgt. Science (now RAND Journal)
　　　　　 ET --Econometrica
　　　　　 EA --Economica
　　　　　JLE --Journal of Law and Economics
　　　　　JPE --Journal of Political Economy
　　　　　RES --Review of Economics and Statistics
　　　　　QJE --Quarterly Journal of Economics
　　　　　AEI --American Enterprise Institute
　　　　　 BR --Brookings Institution
　　　　　 PC --Public Choice

I. Introduction

　　1. The Classic Case for Economic Regulation

　　　　a. Natural Monopolies
　　　　　　Troxel, Economics of Public Utilities.

　　　　　　Lyon and Abramson, Government and Economic Life (chapter on "Public Utilities").

2. The Breakdown of the Classic Case

   (P) Stigler & Friedland, "What Can Regulators Regulate? The Case of Electricity," JLE, Oct. 62.

   * Moore, "The Effectiveness of Regulation of Electric Utility Prices," Southern Econ. Journal, 1970.

   (P) Hilton, "The Consistency of the Interstate Commerce Act," JLE, 1966.

   (Above articles are also cited in subsequent sections.)

   Gray, "The Passing of the Public Utility Concept," in American Economic Association, Readings in the Social Control of Industry.

3. Towards a New Theory of Regulation

   a. Consumer vs. Producer Protection

   (P) Stigler "The Economics of Regulation," BJ, Spring 71.

   (P) Posner, "Taxation by Regulation," BJ, Sp. 71.

   Posner, "Theories of Economic Regulation," BJ, Aut. 74.

   (P) Peltzman, "Pricing in Public and Private Enterprise," JLE, Apr. 71.

   (P) _____, "Towards a More General Theory of Regulation," JLE, Aug. 76.

   (P) Hilton, "The Basic Behavior of Regulatory Commissions," AER, May 72.

   (P) Jordan, "Producer Protection, . . ." JLE, Apr. 72.

   Posner, "The Behavior of Administrative Agencies," J. of Legal Studies, June 72.

   Owen & Braetigum, The Regulatory Game.

   Niskanen, "Bureaucrats and Politicians," JLE, Dec. 75.

   Goldberg, "Regulation and Administered Contracts," BJ, Aut. 76.

   Migué, "Controls v. Subsidies," JLE, Apr. 1977.

   Lee, "A Theory of Just Regulation," AER, Dec. 80.

   * Noll & Joskow, "Regulation in Theory and Practice," in Fromm (ed.) Studies in Public Regulation. (A review of the literature.)

Noll & Owen, *The Political Economy of Deregulation*, AEI, 1983.

* Becker, "A Theory of Competition Among Pressure Groups," QJE, August 1983.

  Keeler, "Theories of Regulation and the Deregulation Movement," PC, 1984 (v. 44, n. 1).

II. Public Utility Regulation: Electricity, Gas, Telecommunication, Broadcasting

1. The Natural Monopoly Rationale for Regulation (see readings in I. 1)

   a. Evidence on Economies of Scale

   Boiteaux, "Electric Energy: Facts, Problems and Prospects," in J. R. Nelson (ed.) *Marginal Cost Pricing in Practice*.

   * Nerlove, "Returns to Scale in Electricity Supply," in C. Christ et al., *Measurement in Economics*.

   Dhrymes & Kurz, "Technology and Scale in Electricity Generation," ET, 1964.

   Sudit, "Additive Non-homogeneous Production Function in Telecommunications," BJ, Aut. 73.

   * Christensen and Greene, "Economies of Scale in the U.S. Power Industry, JPE, July 76.

   Gordon, *Reforming the Regulation of Public Utilities*

2. The Welfare Economics of Rate Regulation--what is the "correct" regulated price?

   a. Marginal or Average Cost Pricing

   * Hotelling, "The General Welfare in Relation to Problems of Taxation and Railway and Utility Rates," ET, July 38.

   Coase, "The Marginal Cost Controversy," EA 1946.

   Coase, "The Theory of Public Utility Pricing and Its Application," BJ, Sp. 70.

   Ruggles, "Recent Developments in the Theory of Marginal Cost Pricing," *Review of Econ. Studies*, 1949-50.

   Henderson, "The Pricing of Public Utility Undertakings," *Manchester School*, 1947.

   b. Multipart Pricing and Price Discrimination

   Bonbright, *Principles of Public Utility Rates*.

   Phillips, *Economics of Regulation*, ch. 8-11.

Taylor, "The Demand for Electricity," BJ, Sp. 75.

* Panzar and Willig, "Free Entry and the Sustainability of Natural Monopoly," BJ, Sp. 77.

* Baumol and Bradford, "Optimal Departures from Marginal Cost Pricing," AER, June 70.

c. Peak Load Pricing

Steiner, "Peak Loads and Efficient Pricing," QJE, Nov. 57.

Hirshleifer, "Peak Loads and Efficient Pricing: Comment," QJE, Aug. 58.

Boiteux, "Peak Load Pricing," Journal of Business,, Apr. 60.

Wenders and Taylor, "Experiments in Seasonal-Time-of-Day Pricing of Electricity," BJ. Aut. 76.

Wenders, "Peak Load Pricing", BJ, Sp. 76.

Brown and Johnson, "Public Utility Pricing and Output Under Risk," AER, Mar. 1969.

Mitchell, Manning, Acton, Peak Load Pricing.

Acton and Mitchell, "Evaluating Time-of-Day Electric Rates". Mitchell and Kleindorfer, Regulated Industries and Public Enterprise.

3. The Effects of Regulation

    a. On Rates

    (P) Stigler and Friedland, "What Can Regulators Regulate?"

    * Moore, "The Effectiveness of Regulation of Electric Utility Prices."

    * Jarrell, "The Demand for State Regulation of Electricity," JLE, Oct. 1978.

    Moore, C. G., "Has Electricity Regulation Resulted in Higher Prices?" Economic Inquiry, June 75.

    Mann, "User Power and Electricity Rates," JLE, Oct. 74.

    (P) Peltzman, "Pricing in Public and Private Enterprise."

    DeAlessi, "An Economic Analysis of Government Ownership," PC, Fall, 74.

Joskow, "Inflation and Environmental Concern: Structural Change in Public Utility Regulation," JLE, Oct. 74.

Fournier and Martin, "Does Government Restricted Entry Produce Market Power? The Market for TV Advertising," <u>BJ</u>, Sp. 83.

b. On the Allocation of Resources in Production

(P) Averch and Johnson, "The Behavior of the Firm under Regulatory Constraint," AER, Dec. 62.

Baumol and Klevorick, "Input Choices and Rate of Return Regulation," BJ, Aut. 70.

Spann, "Rate of Return Regulation and Efficiency in Production," BJ, Sp. 74.

Boyes, "An Empirical Examination of the Averch-Johnson Effect," <u>Econ. Inquiry</u>, 3/76.

* Courville, "Regulation and Efficiency in the Electric Utility Industry," BJ, Sp. 74.

Baron and Taggart, "A Model of Regulation under Uncertainty and a Test for Regulatory Bias," BJ, Sp. 77.

Petersen, "An Empirical Test of Regulatory Effects," BJ, Spring 75.

Meyer, R. A., "Publicly Owned v. Privately Owned Utilities," RES, Nov. 75.

Neuberg, L. G., "Two Issues in the Municipal Ownership of Electric Power," BJ, Sp. 77.

* Hendricks, "Regulation and Labor Earnings," BJ, Aut. 77.
Ehrenberg, <u>The Regulatory Process and Labor Earnings</u>.
Davies, "The Efficiency of Public v. Private Firms," JLE, Apr. 71.

Norton, "Regulation and Systematic Risk: The Case of Electric Utilities," JLE, Oct. 85.

4. Alternatives to Regulation

* Coase, The Federal Communications Commission.

(P) Demsetz, "Why Regulate Utilities?" JLE, 1968.

Williamson, "Franchise Bidding," BJ, Sp. 76.

Schmalensee, <u>The Control of Natural Monopolies</u>, ch. 5.

Schultz, "Conditions for Franchise Bidding in W. Germany", in Mitchell and Kleindorfer, "Regulated Industries and Public Enterprise.

Baumol, Panzar & Willig, Contestable Markets.

Primeaux, "A Reexamination of the Monopoly Market Structure in Electric Utilities," in Phillips, ed., Promoting Competition in Regulated Industries, BR, 1975.

Primeaux, "Determinants of Regulatory Policy toward Competition in Electric Utilities," PC, 1984 (v. 43, n. 2).

Loeb and Magat, "A Decentralized Method for Utility Regulation," JLE, Oct. 1979.

Vogelsang and Finsinger, "A Regulatory Adjustment Process," BJ, Sp. 79.

5. Natural Gas and Petroleum

Breyer and MacAvoy, Energy Regulation by the Federal Power Commission.

MacAvoy, Price Formation in Natural Gas Fields.

Gerwig, "Natural Gas Production: A Study of the Costs of Regulation," JLE, Oct. 62.

MacAvoy, "The Regulation Induced Shortage of Natural Gas," JLE, Apr. 71.

_____ and Pindyck, Price Controls and the Natural Gas Shortage, AEI.

* Helms, Natural Gas Regulation, AEI.

Kitch, "Regulation of the Field Market for Natural Gas," JLE Oct. 68.

Erickson & Spann, "Supply Response in a Regulated Industry: The Case of Natural Gas," BJ, Sp. 71.

Mitchell, U.S. Energy Policy: A Primer, AEI.

Federal Energy Administration Regulation, AEI.

III. Transportation Regulation

A. Surface Freight

1. The Origins of Regulation

   a. The Interstate Commerce Act.

   (P) Hilton, "The Consistency of the Interstate Commerce Act."

   * MacAvoy, *The Economic Effects of Regulation: The Trunkline Railroad Cartels* . . .

   * Kolko, *Railroads & Regulation*.

   Locklin, *The Economics of Transportation*.

   b. Are Railroads a Natural Monopoly?

   (P) Spann & Erickson, "The Economics of Railroading," BJ, Aut. 70.

   * Keeler, "Railroad Costs Returns to Scale and Excess Capacity," RES, May 74.

   Harris, "Economies of Traffic Density in Rail Freight," BJ, Aut. 77.

2. The Effects of Regulation and Deregulation

   * Meyer, et al., *The Economics of Competition in Transport Industries*.

   * Friedlaender, *The Dilemma of Frieght Transport Regulation*.

   (P) Sloss, "Regulation of Motor Freight Transportation," BJ, Aut. 70.

   National Bureau of Economic Research, *Transportation Economics*, (see esp. articles by Nelson and Roberts).

   * Moore, *Freight Transportation Regulation*, AEI.

   Moore, "Deregulating Surface Freight Transportation," in Phillips (ed.), *Promoting Competition in Regulated Markets*, BR.

   _____, "The Beneficiaries of Trucking Regulation," JLE, Oct. 78.

   Kim, "The Beneficiaries of Trucking Regulation Revisited," JLE April '84.

178

Robinson & Tomes, Union Wage Differentials in the Public & Private Sector. *Journal of Labor Economics*, Jan. '84.

Friedlaender, "The Social Costs of Railroad Regulation," AER, May 71.

Moore, *Trucking Regulation*, AEI.

Friedlaender and Spady, "Hedonic Cost Functions for Trucking," BJ, Spring, 78.

Friedlaender and Spady, *Freight Transport Regulation*.

MacAvoy, *Regulation of Entry and Pricing in Truck Transportation*, AEI.

Winston, "Welfare Effects of ICC Regulation Revisited," BJ, SP 81.

(P) Boyer, "Minimum Rate Regulation and the Railroad Problem," JPE, June 1977.

Boyer, "Equalizing Discrimination in Transport Rate Regulation", *JPE*, Apr. 81.

Levin, "Allocation in Surface Freight Transportation," BJ, Spring 1978.

Levin, "Railroad Rates, Profitability and Welfare Under Deregulation," BJ, SP 81.

Levin, "Regulation Barriers to Exit and Investment Behavior in Railroads," in Fromm *Studies in Public Regulation*.

Breen, "The Monopoly Value of Household Goods Carrier Operating Certificates," JLE, Apr. 1977.

Frew, "The Existence of Monopoly Profits in the Motor Carrier Industry," JLE, Oct. 81.

Dougan, "Railway Abandonments and the Theory of Regulation", *PC*, 1984 (v. 44, n. 1).

Daughety, "Regulation and Industrial Organization," *JPE,*, Oct. 84.

B. Airlines

Caves, *Air Transport and Its Regulators*.

Keyes, *Federal Control of Entry into Air Transportation*.

(P) Keeler, "Airline Regulation and Market Performance," BJ Aut. 72.

* Jordan, *Airline Regulation in America*.

* Douglas and Miller, *Economic Regulation of Domestic Air Transport*.

  Douglas and Miller, The CAB's Domestic Passenger Fare Investigation, BJ Sp. '74.

  Gronau, "Effect of Travel Time on the Demand for Transportation, JPE, Mar. '70.

  De Vaney, "The Effect of Price and Entry Regulation on Airline Output and Efficiency," BJ, Sp. 75.

  CAB Practices and Procedures, U.S. Senate Subcte. on Administrative Practice, Cte. on Judiciary, 1975.

  Eads, "Competition in the Airline Industry," in Phillips, ed., *Promoting Competition in Regulated Markets*.

  MacAvoy, *Regulation of Passenger Fares and Competition among Airlines*, AEI.

* Keeler & Call, "Airline Deregulation, Fares and Market Behavior" (mimeo).

* Bailey, Graham and Kaplan, *Deregulating the Airlines*.

  Graham and Sibley, "Efficiency and Competition in the Airline Industry," BJ, Sp. 83.

  Spiller, "The Differential Impact of Airline Regulation on Individual Firms," JLE, 10/83.

  Meyer and Oster, *Deregulation and the New Airline Entrepreneurs*.

  Morrison & Winston, *The Economic Effects of Airline Deregulation*, BR.

  Moore, "U.S. Airline Deregulation: Its Effects on Passengers, Capital and Labor," JLE, 4/86.

C. Miscellaneous

   Kitch, "The Regulation of Taxicabs," JLE, Oct. 71.

   Eckert, "The Los Angeles Taxi Monopoly," *Southern Cal. Law Review*, 1970.

   _____, and Hilton, "The Jitneys," JLE, Oct. 72.

   Pashigian, "Consequences and Causes of Public Ownership of Urban Transport," JPE, Dec. 76.

        Keeler and Small, "Optimal Peak Load Pricing on Urban Expressways," JPE, Feb. 77.

        Smith, "Franchise Regulation: An Economic Analysis of State Restrictions on Automobile Distribution", JLE Apr. 82.

IV. Environmental Protection

A. Externalities and the Rationale for Regulation

        Pigou, *The Economics of Welfare*, Pt. II, Ch. 9.

        Buchanan and Stubblebine, "Externality," EA 1962.

Turvey, "On Divergence between Social and Private Cost," EA 1963.

(P) Coase, "The Problem of Social Cost," JLE, 1960.

Demsetz, "When Does the Rule of Liability Matter?" J. of Legal Studies, 1972.

Baumol and Oates, *The Theory of Environmental Policy*, pt. I.

Lave and Seskin, "Acute Relationships Among Daily Mortality, Air Pollution and Climate," in Mills, ed., *Economic Analysis of Environmental Problems*.

Fischer, *Resources and Environmental Economics*, Ch. 6.

B. Implementation of Regulation

* Dales, *Pollution, Property, and Prices*.

* Kneese and Bower, *Managing Water Quality: Economics and Technology*.

(P) Kneese, "Environmental Pollution Economics and Policy," AER, May 71.

Ridker, *Economic Costs of Air Pollution: Studies in Measurement*.

Ridker and Hemming, "The Determinants of Residential Property Values," RES, May 71.

Crocker, "Externalities, Property Rights, and Transaction costs," JLE, Oct. 71.

Baumol and Oates, *Theory of Environmental Policy*, pt. II.

Oates and Baumol, "Instruments for Environmental Policy," in Mills, *Economic Analysis of Environmental Problems*.

Harrison, Who Pays for Clean Air?

Siegan, "Non-zoning in Houston," JLE, Apr. 70.

Rueter, "Externalities in Urban Property Markets," JLE, Oct. 73.

Peskin, Portney, Kneese, Environmental Regulation and the U.S. Economy (discusses current policy issues).

Maloney and McCormick, "A Positive Theory of Environmental Quality Regulation," JLE, Apr. 82.

Leone and Jackson, "The Political Economy of Federal Regulatory Activity: Water Pollution," in Fromm, editor, Studies in Public Regulation.

Graves and Krumm, Health and Air Quality, AEI.

White, Regulation of Air Pollution from Motor Vehicles, AEI.

Pashigian, "Effect of Environmental Regulation on Optimal Plant Size," JLE, April '84.

* _____, "Environmental Protection: Whose Self Interests are being Protected?" Econ. Inquiry, 10/85.

V. Consumer Protection: Safety and Fraud

Nelson, "Advertising as Information," JPE, July-Aug. 74.

* Klein and Leffler, "The Role of Market Forces in Assuring Contractual Performance", JPE, Aug. 81.

Schmalensee, "Advertising and Product Quality", JPE, Jun. 78.

* (P) Akerlof, "The Market for Lemons," Quarterly J. of Econ., Aug. 70.

(P) Darby and Karni, "Free Competition and the Optimal Amount of Fraud," JLE, Apr. 73.

Grossman, "The Informational Role of Warranties and Private Disclosure about Product Quality", JLE, Dec. 81.

Calabresi, The Costs of Accidents.

Oi, "The Economics of Product Safety," BJ, Sp. 73.

Epple and Raviv, "Product Safety . . .," AER, Mar. 1978.

Leland, "Quacks, Lemons and Licensing," JPE, Dec. 79.

a. Effects of Regulation in Specific Industries

   1. Finance and Securities

      (P) Stigler, "Public Regulation of the Securities Markets," <u>J. of Business</u>, Apr. 64.

      (See also articles by Friend and Herman, Robbins and Werner, and reply by Stigler in <u>J. of Bus.</u>, Oct. 64.)

      * Jarrell, "The Economic Effects of Federal Regulation of the Market for New Security Issues", JLE, Dec. 81.

      Beaver, "The Nature of Mandated Disclosure," <u>Report of Advisory Committee on Corporate Disclosure to SEC</u>, 1977, v. 1.

      Schwert, "Public Regulation of National Securities Exchanges: A Test of the Capture Hypothesis," BJ, Sp. 77.

      Horwitz and Kolodny, "Line of Business Reporting," BJ, Aut. 1977.

      (P) Benston, "Required Disclosure and the Stock Market," AER, Mar. 1973.

      Tinic and West, "The Securities Industry Under Negotiated Rates." BJ, Sp. 80.

      Jarrell, "Change at the Exchange: The Causes and Effects of Deregulation," JLE, Oct. '84.

      Stoll <u>Regulation of Security Markets</u>.

      Crafton, "The Effects of Usury Laws," JLE, Apr. 80.

      Barth, "Benefits and Costs of Legal Restrictions in Personal Loan Markets," JLE, 10/86.

   2. Advertising

      Peltzman, "The Effect of FTC Advertising Regulation", JLE, Dec. 81.

      Benham, "The Effect of Advertising on the Price of Eyeglasses," JLE, Oct. 72.

      Bond, "A Direct Test of the Lemons Model: Used Pickup Trucks," AER, Sept. 82.

   3. Health Care and Pharmaceuticals

      * Kessel, "Price Discrimination in Medicine", JLE, Oct. 58.

      Benham and Benham, "Regulating Through the Professions," JLE, Oct. 75.

Haas-Wilson, "The Effect of Commercial Practice Restrictions: The Case of Optometry," JLE, 4/86.

Baily, M. N., "R and D Costs and Returns: The U.S. Pharmaceutical Industry," JPE, Jan. 72.

(P) Peltzman, "An Evaluation of Consumer Protection Legislation: The 1962 Drug Amendments," JPE, Sept. - Oct. 73.

Grabowski, <u>Drug Regulation and Innovation</u>, AEI.

Grabowski and Vernon, The Regulation of Pharmaceuticals, AEI.

* Leffler, "Physician Licensure," JLE, Apr. 78.

Noether, "The Effect of Policy Changes on the Supply of Physicians," JLE, 10/86.

Shepard, "Licensing Restrictions and the Cost of Dental Care," JLE, Apr. 78.

DeVany, Gramm et al. "The Impact of Input Regulation: the U.S. Dental Industry," JLE, Oct. 82.

Sloan and Steinwald, "Effects of Regulation on Hospital Costs," JLE, Apr. 80.

4. Product and Workplace Safety

Peltzman, "The Effects of Automobile Safety Regulation," JPE, Aug. 75.

Arnould and Grabowski, "Auto Safety Regulation," BJ, Sp. 81.

Gaston and Caroll, "Occupational Restrictions and Quality of Service Received," <u>Southern Economic Journal</u>, Apr. 1, 1981.

* Viscusi, "The Impact of OSHA," BJ, Sp. 79.

Viscusi, "Consumer Behavior and the Safety Effects of Regulation," <u>JLE</u>, Oct. 85.

Schneider, Klein, Murphy, "Governmental Regulation of Cigarette Health Information", JLE, Dec. 81.

Jarrell & Peltzman, "The Impact of Product Recalls on the Wealth of Sellers", <u>JPE</u>, June 85.

Neumann and Nelson, "Safety Regulation and Firm Size: Effects of the Coal Mine Health and Safety Act of 1969," JLE, Oct. 82.

  * Staten and Umbeck, "Information Costs and Incentives to Shirk: The Air Traffic Controllers," AER, 12/82.

  Crandall and Lave, <u>The Scientific Basis of Health and Safety Regulation</u>, BR, '81 (case studies of Air Bags, Saccharin, cotton dust, etc.).

  Viscusi, "The Lulling Effect of Safety Regulation," AER May '84.

5. Food and Beverage

  Kwoka, "Pricing under Federal Milk Market Regulation," <u>Economic Inquiry</u>, July 1977.

  <u>Federal Milk Marketing Orders</u>, AEI.

  Ippolito and Masson, "Social Cost of Milk Regulation," JLE, Apr. 78.

  Smith, "An Analysis of State Regulation of Liquor Store Licensing," JLE, Oct. 82.

6. Insurance

  Munch and Smallwood, "Solvency Regulation in Insurance," BJ, Sp. 80.

  Ippolito, "Price Regulation in Auto Insurance," JLE, Apr. 80.

VI. Consumer Protection: Antitrust

1. Origins and Purpose

  Bork, "Legislative Intent and Policy of the Sherman Act," JLE, Oct. 66.

  Neale, <u>Antitrust Laws of the U.S.</u>

  Williamson, "Economies as an Antitrust Defense," AER, Mar. 68.

  Kaysen and Turner, <u>Antitrust Policy: An Economic and Legal Analysis</u>.

2. Effects of Antitrust

  * Stigler, "Economic Effects of the Antitrust Laws," JLE, Oct. 66.

  * Posner, "A Statistical Study of Antitrust Enforcement," JLE, Oct. 70.

Elzinga, "The Antitrust Law: Pyrrhic Victories," JLE, Apr. 69.

Block et al., "The Deterrent Effect of Antitrust Enforcement," JPE, June 81.

VII. Patents and Innovation

1. Rationale: Public Goods and Free Riders

* Plant, "Economic Theory Concerning Patents for Invention," EA, 1934.

Plant, "Economic Aspects of Copyrights in Books," EA, 1934.

Scherer, "Research and Development Resource Allocation under Rivalry," Quarterly J. of Econ., Aug. 67.

Machlup, An Economic Review of the Patent System (U.S. Senate Judiciary Committee, Subcom. on Patents, 1958).

Sappington, "Optimal Regulation of R & D," BJ, Aut. 82.

2. Alternatives to Patents

Arrow, "Economic Welfare and the Allocation of Resources to Invention," in National Bureau of Economic Research, Rate and Direction of Inventive Activity.

Hirshleifer, "The Private and Social Value of Information," AER, Sept. 71.

Demsetz, "Information and Efficiency," JLE, Apr. 69.

a. The Role of Market Structure and Regulation

Schumpeter, Capitalism, Socialism and Democracy, Ch. 7-8.

Boulding, "In Defense of Monopoly," QJE, 1945.

Villard, "Competition, Oligopoly, and Research," JPE, 1958.

Stigler, "Industrial Organization and Economic Progress," in State of the Social Sciences.

Abramovitz, "Monopolistic Selling," QJE, 1938.

Mansfield, Industrial Research and Technological Innovation, Ch. 5.

Nutter, "Monopoly, Bigness and Progress," JPE, 1956.

Sherer, "Firm Size, Market Structure and the Output of Patented Invention," AER, Dec. 1965.

Schmookler, *Invention and Economic Growth*.

Williamson, "Innovation and Market Structure," JPE, Feb. 1965.

Mansfield, "Industrial Research and Development," JPE, 1964.

Mansfield, "Rates of Return from Industrial Research and Development," AER, May 65.

Oster and Quigley, "Regulatory Barriers to the Diffusion of Innovation," BJ, Aut. 77.

Your grade will be based on a final exam and term paper. The paper will account for 35 percent of the grade. It is recommended that the paper be a replication and/or extension of past studies of the causes or effects of regulation, such as those on the reading list. However, any paper topic relevant to the subject matter of the course is acceptable. The paper should contain results of empirical work you have conducted. Please discuss the paper with me before you begin working on it. Each student will have available a limited amount of time on the university's computer and the GSB's computer. (Use of this time may be arranged in W309.)

The final exam will be given on Wednesday, March 18 from 2 to 4:40. There will be no make-up or other nonscheduled exam for any student for any reason. If you do not take the final exam, or hand in your paper before the end of the quarter, you may petition for a grade of "I", which can be removed by taking the exam the next time the course is offered or when you complete the paper.

You will, however, be charged interest for late papers: all papers are graded on a scale $A = 4$, $B = 3$, etc. If you submit your paper late, your numerical grade will be divided by $(1 + .015\sqrt{t})$ where t = number of days from the end of the quarter to the day you submit your paper.

The prerequisites for the course are Bus. 300 and Bus. 370 (or Econ. 300) or equivalent. However, knowledge of basic statistics, including interpretation of multiple regression analyses, will be helpful.

DUKE UNIVERSITY

Business Ethics
BA 342 - Fall 1989
Reading Assignments

Professor William A. Sax

Text: <u>Business Ethics</u>, by Norman Bowie (Prentice-Hall, 1982).

Sept. 4 Introduction: Public perceptions of business ethics.

Format: Guest speaker:

Read: <u>Note on Opinion Research in Business Ethics: The YSW Corporate Priorities Reports</u>, (Harvard Business School, 9-387-081).

Sept. 11 Individual dilemmas: Conflicts between employees and the organization, employees and external constituencies, employees and colleagues, employees and supervisors, employees and subordinates.

Format: Film (Propmore).

Read: <u>Propmore Corporation Case-Situation (I, II and III)</u>, <u>Dilemma of An Accountant</u> (Harvard Business School, 9-380-185), <u>Ethical Quagmire</u>, (Harvard Business School, 9-384-036), <u>Peter Green's First Day</u> (Harvard Business School, 9-380-186 and <u>William Kelp (A)</u>[1], (Harvard Business School, 9-483-018).

Sept. 18 Relations with Less Developed Countries.

Format: Film (Export of Pesticides to the Third World).

Read: <u>Note on the Export of Pesticides from the U.S. to Developing Countries</u> (Harvard Business School, 384-097) and <u>The Agent (A)</u> (Harvard Business School, 9-484-026).

Sept. 25 Relations with customers: Product safety.

Format: Film (Firestone 500), class discussion.

Read: <u>Managing Product Safety-The Case of the Firestone 500</u> (Harvard Business School, 9-383-130), <u>Managing Product Safety-The Ford Pinto</u> (Harvard Business School, 383-129), <u>Managing Product Safety-The Case of the Procter & Gamble Rely Tampon</u> (Harvard Business School, 9-383-131), or <u>Johnson and Johnson-The Tylenol Tragedy (A)</u> (Harvard Business School, 9-583-043).

Oct. 2	Relations with community: Corporate impact on neighborhoods, plant closings.

Format: Film (Poletown).

Read: <u>The Poletown Dilemma</u>[1] (Harvard Business School, N9-389-017) and <u>Shutting it Down: A Test for Management</u> by Anthony C. LaRusso (Business Horizons/July-August, 1989).

Oct. 9	No class.
Oct. 16	No class.
Oct. 23	Viewing of video segments from CBS 60 Minutes and Illinois Power reply in preparation for session on ethics in the media. This deals with Nuclear Power Plant.

Read: <u>Turned Off-Why Executives Distrust TV Reporters</u> by Herbert Schmertz (Washington Journalism Review: July/August 1984, pp. 45-47).

Oct. 30	Ethics in the media.
Nov. 6	Ethical issues in finance: Insider trading.

Read: <u>Don't Mess with RICO-Congress Should Spurn Effort To Curb It</u>, (Barron's: July 3, 1989, pp. 12 & 15), <u>Insider Trading Case Set for Federal Court</u>, (Wall Street Journal, September 18, 1989- p. B8) <u>Insider Trading</u>, (Except, Committee, Report, Insider Trading and Security Fraud Enforcement Act of 1988, H. Rep. No. 100-910, 100th Congress 2nd session, 1988), <u>Recent SEC Enforcement Developments: Insider Trading</u>, (by Gary G. Lynch, Director; Joseph I. Goldstein, Associate Director; Juan M. Marcelino, Branch Chief; Jacob S. Frankel, Attorney; and Robert L. Walker, Attorney, all with the Division of Enforcement, Security and Exchange Commission, Copyright, 1988) and <u>Unfair Shares, Writers Who Profit From Wall Street's Pipeline</u> (Business and The Press, Washington Journalism Review,July/August, 1984).

Nov. 13	Ethical issues in finance: Mergers, acquisitions, and hostile takeovers.

Read: <u>Shame on You, Henry Kravis</u>, by Abraham J. Briloff (Barron's, March 6, 1989, pp. 18-21). <u>Ambiguity, Ethics, and the Bottom Line</u>, by James R. Davis (Business Horizons, May-June, 1989), <u>Buyout at RJR Nabisco: Ethics and the Board of Directors</u>, by Richard O. Mason, Southern Methodist University, August 18, 1989- Not Published. <u>Business's Bottom Line: Ethics</u>, John S.R. Shad, Copyright 1987 New York Times, <u>Roundtable-The Wider Vistas for Commercial Banks of M&A</u>, (Mergers & Acquisition Magazine, pp. 26-36, July/August, 1987), <u>The Fast Buck or Faith in the Future? The Ethics of Corporate Restructuring</u>, Edward G. Hennessy, Jr. Chairman of the Board and CEO Allied-Signal. <u>The Often Overlooked Ethical Aspect of Mergers</u>, (Journal of Business Ethics, 1988 pp. 359-362 by Klower Academic Publishers).

Nov. 20   Ethics of high-consequence technologies: Operating and regulating aviation, nuclear power, genetic engineering, and chemical industries.

Format: Film (The Challenger space shuttle).

Read: <u>Research in Nearly Failure-Free, High Reliability Organizations: Having the Bubble</u>, (IEEE Transactions of Engineering Management Vol. 36, No. 2 May, 1989), <u>American Cyanamid Company</u> (Harvard Business School, 9-181-131), and <u>Collaborative Research, Inc</u>. (Harvard Business School, 9-386-100).

Nov. 27   Organization ethical climate.

Format: Case discussion, lecture, film (H.J. Heinz), Defining Issues Test of ethical reasoning.

Read: <u>H.J. Heinz case: The Administration of Policy (A&B)</u>, Harvard Business School (Cases 382-034 and 382-035) and <u>Weyerhaeuser: Dialogue Over Business Conduct</u>, (Corporate Responsibility Planning Service August 26, 1977 #413).

Dec. 4   Corporate Philanthropy.

Read: <u>Zimbardo's Stanford Prison Experiment</u> and <u>The Relevance of Social Psychology for Teaching Business Ethics</u> by F. Neil Brady and Jeanne M. Logsdon, (Journal of Business Ethics pp. 703-710, 1988).

NORTHWESTERN UNIVERSITY

SYLLABUS

ORGANIZATIONAL CHALLENGES AND DECISIONS
D75 Policy and Environment Department

Spring Quarter 1989

Professor: Walter D. Scott
Office: Leverone Hall - Room 6-111
Telephone: (312) 491-2686
Office hours: Tuesdays 9:00-11:00 a.m.

Course Description:

This course examines some of the significant issues that shape the essential character of an organization as it interacts with society, the marketplace and internally. These will be examined from a variety of perspectives in order to explore both their complexity and the process by which they are resolved by senior managers. Discussions are intended to provide an understanding of these critical issues and improve students' abilities to think through them independently.

The role of senior managers in making these key decisions will be emphasized in order to capitalize on the backgrounds of the instructor and guest lecturers. In addition to emphasis on the decision making process, the means by which decisions are translated into actions will receive attention.

A better understanding of how issues are resolved by senior managers will help students perform more effectively in future jobs. This will improve their abilities to contribute to the overall success of their organizations and help prepare them for expanded managerial responsibilities.

Understanding of these issues will be developed based primarily on readings, lectures, cases and discussions. The practical experiences of guest lecturers and the instructor will be emphasized.

This course is intended for students who have completed all of their core courses. These core courses should provide a helpful framework for getting the most out of Organizational Challenges and Decisions. Enrollment by other students requires prior permission of the instructor.

Page 4

Class Sessions:

3/30/89 Creating an Organizational Vision
Class 1

> Guest lecturer: James F. Bere, Chairman, Borg-Warner Corporation.
>
> Readings:
> *Thriving on Chaos.* Thomas J. Peters. Alfred A. Knopf. 1988. Chapter L-2.
> "Vision and Leadership." Frederick W. Gluck. *Readings On Strategic Management.* Edited by Arnoldo C. Hax. Ballinger Publishing Company. 1984. Chapter 2.
> "Corporate Mission - The Intangible Contributor to Performance." Jerome H. Want. *Managerial Review.* August, 1986.
> "Corporate Soul - Searching." James K. Brown. *Across the Board.* March, 1984.
> "The Beliefs of Borg-Warner." Davidson and Goodpaster. Harvard Business School. 1983.
> "Our Credo." Johnson & Johnson.
> "Mission and Values." The Pillsbury Company.
> "Statement of Philosophy." Dayton-Hudson Corporation.
> (1) *Management: Tasks, Responsibilities, Practices.* Peter F. Drucker. Harper & Row. 1974. Chapters 7 and 8.
> (2) "The Seven Keys to Business Leadership." Kenneth Labich. *Fortune.* October 24, 1988.

4/6/89 The Role of the Corporation in Society
Class 2

> Guest lecturer: Dennis W. Bakke, President, Applied Energy Services, Inc.
>
> Readings:
> "The Social Responsibility of Business Is to Increase Its Profits." Milton Friedman. *New York Times Magazine.* September 13, 1970.
> "Owing Your Soul to the Company Store." Nader and Green. *The New York Review of Books.* 1973.
> *Business Environment and Public Policy.* Rogene A. Buchholz. Prentice Hall. Third Edition. 1989. Chapter 2.

(1) Optional readings - on reserve.
(2) Optional readings - enclosed with case packet.

Page 5

> *Public - Private Partnerships: New Opportunities for Meeting Social Needs.* Edited by Brooks, Liebman and Schelling. Ballinger Publishing Co. 1984. Chapter 10.
> *Management: Tasks, Responsibilities, Practices.* Peter F. Drucker. Harper & Row. 1974. Chapters 25 and 26.
>
> Case:
> "The Poletown Dilemma." Joseph Auerbach. *Harvard Business Review.* May - June 1985.
> Questions:
> -Who are the key constituencies and what do they have to gain or lose?
> -What alternative roles might General Motors have chosen? What would the implications of each have been?
> -Was the process an effective one (for GM and others) or should it have been modified? If so, in what ways?
> -Should Poletown have been given a stronger voice in the process? If so, what voice and what would have been the implications?

4/13/89 The Ethics of the Organization
Class 3
> ASSIGNMENT OF FIRST GROUP PAPER WILL BE GIVEN.
>
> Readings:
> "Organizational Statesmanship and Dirty Politics: Ethical Guidelines for the Organizational Politician." Velasquez, Moberg, Cavanagh. *Organizational Dynamics.* Autumn 1983.
> "Ethics Without the Sermon." Laura L. Nash. *Harvard Business Review.* November-December 1981.
> *Corporate Ethics: A Prime Business Asset.* The Business Roundtable. 1988. Chapters 1, 5 and 10.
> "Is Business Bluffing Ethical?" Albert Z. Carr. *Harvard Business Review.* January-February 1968.
> *"Why 'Good' Managers Make Bad Ethical Choices." Saul W. Gellerman. *Harvard Business Review.* July-August 1986.
> * "Ethical Managers Make Their Own Rules." Sir Adrian Cadbury. *Harvard Business Review.* September-October 1987.

* Optional readings.

Case:
"United Brands" (A). James C. Shaffer. Northwestern University. 1975.
Questions focus on the Honduran bribe:
-Who are the key players and what were their interests in the situation?
-Where were their interests in conflict with those of others?
-How did the outcome affect each?
-Analyze the bribe from a Utilitarian, Justice and Rights posture.
-What alternatives existed for United Brands? What would have been the implications of each alternative?
-What should Wallace Booth do to establish ethical standards for the company and what should those standards be?

4/20/89　The International Organization
Class 4

Guest Lecturer: Robert W. Galvin, Chairman of the Board, Motorola Inc.

Readings:
"Entering a New Age of Boundless Competition." Richard I. Kirkland, Jr. _Fortune._ March 14, 1988.
"How to Be a Global Manager." Andrew Kupfer. _Fortune._ March 14, 1988.
International Business and Multinational Enterprises. Robock and Simmonds. Irwin. 1989. Chapter 9.
Thriving on Chaos. Thomas J. Peters. Alfred A. Knopf. 1988. Chapter C-5.
"Motorola and Japan." Yoffie and Coleman. Harvard Business School. 1987.
*"Do You Really Have a Global Strategy?" Hamel and Prahalad. _Harvard Business Review._ July-August 1985.
*"How Global Companies Win Out." Hout, Porter and Rudden. _Harvard Business Review._ September-October 1982.

Case:
"Lotus Development Corp.: Entering International Markets." Yoffie and Coleman. Harvard Business School. 1987.
Questions:
-What are the key success factors for Lotus in the U.S. and do they carry over into foreign markets?
-What are the major issues facing the company which need to be addressed in expanding overseas?
-What would you recommend as the right course of action to address each of these issues and why?

Page 7

4/27/89 The External Environment-Communications and Media
Class 5   Relationships

FIRST GROUP PAPER DUE

Readings:
"Communications and Strategy: The CEO Gets the
    Message." James E. Arnold speech. 1987.
Media coverage of business. Series of articles.
    Los Angeles Times. 1980.
* Effective Public Relations. Cutlip, Center and
    Broom. Prentice Hall. Sixth Edition. 1985.
    Chapter 17.

Case:
Illinois Power Company/"60 Minutes" - video will be
    shown in class.

5/4/89 The External Environment - Government Relationships
Class 6

Guest lecturer: Robert H. Malott, Chairman and
    Chief Executive Officer, FMC Corporation.

Readings:
Business Environment and Public Policy. Rogene A.
    Buchholz. Prentice Hall. Third edition. 1989.
    Chapters 17 and 18.
"Note on Corporate Strategy and Politics." Joseph L.
    Badaracco, Jr. Harvard Business School. 1982.
"Bob Malott and Product Liability Law Reform."
    Martha Weinberg. Harvard Business School. 1985.
"The Political Education of Bob Malott. CEO."
    Martha Weinberg. Harvard Business School. 1988.

Case:
"Allied Chemical Corporation" (B). Harvard Business
    School. 1982 (revised).
Questions:
-What problems do government regulators face?
-Does Allied's approach and organization structure
 for government relations make sense? Why?
-What actions should Allied take with regard to alum
 and ammonium sulfate, Red Dye #40 and airbags and
 why?

* Optional reading - on reserve.

195

5/11/89 Acquisitions/Divestitures/Restructuring
Class 7

ASSIGNMENT OF SECOND GROUP PAPER WILL BE GIVEN

Readings:
The Mergers and Acquisitions Handbook. Edited by
   Milton L. Rock. McGraw-Hill. 1987. Chapters 1
   and 28.
Management: Tasks, Responsibilities, Practices.
   Peter F. Drucker. Harper & Row. 1974. Chapter
   56.

Case:
"The Pillsbury Company." The Strategy Process.
   Quinn, Mintzberg and James. Prentice Hall.
   1987.
Questions:
-What role did acquisitions and divestitures play in
 the reshaping of Pillsbury?
-Evaluate the company's strategy on acquistions and
 divestitures.
-How effective was the company in making acquistions
 and assimilating them into the organization?
-What role did Chairman Bill Spoor play in the
 acquisition process and was it an appropriate one?
-Should Pillsbury's acquisition strategy for the
 future be altered and, if so, why?

Class 8   Turnaround Management
5/18/89

Guest lecturer: John A. Koskinen, President, The
   Palmieri Company.

Readings:
"When the Mighty Stumble." Charles M. Williams.
   Harvard Business Review. July-August 1984.
"Turnaround Management Every Day." John O. Whitney.
   Harvard Business Review. September-October 1987.
"Designing Turnaround Strategies." Charles W. Hofer.
   Business Policy and Strategic Management.
   W. F. Glueck. McGraw-Hill. 1980.
"Managing the Turnaround." Harvard Business School.
   1988.

Page 9

> Case:
> *Iacocca.* Iacocca and Novak. Bantam. 1984.
>   Chapters XIV-XVI and XX-XXII.
> Questions:
> -What is your appraisal of the steps needed to turn
> Chrysler around?
> -Should additional actions have been taken to turn
> the company around?
> -Was a government loan necessary?
> -To what do you attribute the success of the
> survival efforts? Could the lessons be applied in
> other turnarounds?

5/25/89 Management Succession
Class 9

> ### SECOND GROUP PAPER DUE
>
> Readings:
> "Management Succession: A Hard Game to Play." *Dun's Review.*
> "Secrets of Succession Planning." Stephen W. Quickel. *Business Month.* June, 1988.
> "The Dark Side of Management Succession." Manfred F.R. Kets De Vries. *Harvard Business Review.* January-February 1988.
> "Muscle Build the Organization." Andrall E. Pearson. *Harvard Business Review.* July-August 1987.
>
> Case:
> "Debate at Wickersham Mills." Abram T. Collier. *Harvard Business Review.* September-October 1986.
> Questions:
> -Analyze the present business situation and
> challenges facing Wickersham Mills.
> -What are the future needs of Wickersham Mills in
> terms of executive leadership?
> -Which of the candidates would you choose and why?
> -Was the selection process fair and likely to lead to
> the best selection? If not, how would you change
> it?

6/2/89 Impediments to Successful Management and Reflections
Class 10 on the Role of Senior Management

> ### BRIEFING ON FINAL EXAMINATION

Page 10

Readings:
"Capital Markets and Competitive Decline." Richard R. Ellsworth. Harvard Business Review. September-October 1985.
"Kaisha - Why Growth Not Profits Drives Japan, Inc." Abegglen and Stalk.
"Managing as if Tomorrow Mattered." Hayes and Garvin. Harvard Business Review. May-June 1982.
"Yes, You Can Manage Long Term." Gary Hector. Fortune. November 21, 1988.
"A New Scorecard for Management." Peter F. Drucker. The Wall Street Journal. September 24, 1976.
"Management and the World's Work." Peter F. Drucker. Harvard Business Review. September-October 1988.

Week of 6/5/89 FINAL EXAMINATION

THE UNIVERSITY OF BRITISH COLUMBIA
FACULTY OF COMMERCE AND BUSINESS ADMINISTRATION

COURSE OUTLINE AND READING LIST

COMMERCE 594

Section 1

BUSINESS-GOVERNMENT RELATIONS IN CANADA: A STRATEGIC APPROACH

January - April 1990

Time: Tuesday and Thursday, 2:30 - 4:00 p.m.
Place: Henry Angus 308

Instructor: W.T. Stanbury, UPS Foundation Professor of Regulation and Competition Policy

Office: Angus 369
Phone: 224-8525

RATIONALE: Governments have a large amount of influence on economic activity in Canada (as in all other Western "mixed economies"). They "intervene" in myriad ways: taxes; direct expenditures (exhaustive and transfers); regulation; loans and guarantees; "tax expenditures"; and through suasion, Crown corporations and mixed enterprises. Given Canadians demonstrated taste for government intervention, it seems unlikely that government activity will shrink noticeably in the foreseeable future (despite the recent rhetoric concerning restraint). Therefore, it is desireable that managers of business enterprises understand how (and why) governments act to influence private-sector economic activity. The reason for doing so is not merely a matter of intellectual interest, nor is it a question of being able to cope with "big government". Rather, managers need to understand government to be able to _influence_ its behaviour in ways beneficial to their firms. In her article "Remaking the management mind" (_Canadian Business_, January 1983), M.S. Wente remarks, "Every business must strike a balance with a variety of constituencies, and that inevitably means interaction with every level of government. Many CEOs still see this process as an intrusive nuisance; [others] define it as a central - and growing - part of the job. [Moreover,] understanding bureaucrats or politicians is one skill that CEOs don't get a lot of training in."

This course seeks to provide some insights into how to deal with government as an important actor in the business environment. In addition, a major part of this course addresses both positive and normative analyses of government intervention and examines the forces that influence the behaviour of politicians and senior public servants. Without an understanding of how public policy is made in Canada, individual and interest groups will find it hard to influence either the process or its outcomes.

REQUIREMENTS/EVALUATION

(a) Mid-term (25%) to be held <u>Tuesday, February 6</u> to cover the work up to session 9.

(b) Group project (50%); for details, see below.

(c) Oral presentation and assessment (25%); for details, see below.

GROUP PROJECT

- The groups are to consist of 2 persons, and are to be self chosen.
- Topic areas include:
  (a) analysis of the social, political and economic forces that brought about a major act of government intervention (or reduction in government activity);
  (b) analysis of the government relations function of a major Canadian corporation;
  (c) analysis of the organization and activities of a major business or non-business interest group, e.g., CFIB, BCNI, Greenpeace, Pollution Probe;
  (d) analysis of a major policy issue in which lobbying by <u>various</u> interests was important, e.g., de-indexation of the old age pensions, creation of Canagrex, changes in the NEP; or
  (e) other topics by permission of the instructor.

In general, see the list of projects done by groups in C594 and C592, the predecessor to C594. It is included in "Bibliography for C594" distributed in class.

REQUIREMENTS

- Each group must prepare a 2 page outline and submit it to the instructor within two weeks. It should specify the topic/issue, the methodology and the names of the members of the group and their telephone numbers.
- The topic must be approved by the instructor.
- It is essential that the projects make use of theory concepts/analyses in the required readings, lectures and items in the Bibliography.
- The final version of the project must be typed and the study must be well documented with references to the sources from which it was obtained.
- Possible topics for C594 projects include (but are not limited to) the following:
  - Lobbying for daycare: the next universal social program?
  - Origins of automobile insurance regulation in Ontario, 1987
  - Business' role in the free trade negotiations and 1988 federal election campaign.
  - Lobbying against the federal regulation of lobbying: the Cooper Committee Report, 1986
  - Lobbying against the 1987 BC labour legislation: Bill 19 (general), Bill 20 (teachers)
  - Comparative study of the regulation of the funding of political parties: e.g., federal, B.C., Ontario and Quebec
  - Lobbying by Canadian groups (including the federal government)

against U.S. trade sanctions, softwood lumber (1983, 1986-7), steel, etc.
- The animal rights lobby: growth, tactics and impact
- Lobbying leading to new federal regulations re smoking and tobacco advertising

ORAL PRESENTATIONS

- Each person will have two tasks:
    (a) a 50 minute oral presentation on the material assigned for the class session and
    (b) an page "instant critique" of 5 to 10 minutes immediately following _another_ group's presentation. Note: the assignment of which group will be doing the critique will not be announced until the day it is to be done. The critique is not to exceed 10 minutes.

- Assignments by the instructor will occur within three weeks.

- Oral presentations will take place beginning with Session #12 on February 8th.

- The oral presentation is to be based on the assigned reading for the session plus any other material that you think should be drawn to the attention of students on the topics to be dealt with that week.

- Students may wish to use the overhead projector, create posters, use the blackboard or use handouts. I can get handouts duplicated if I have them (not more than 5 pages typed up) at least one session in advance.

- Those making presentations and those assessing them will probably want to consider the following non-exhaustive list of factors:

    - the use of visual/learning aids (overheads, posters, handouts),
    - ability to involve all members of the group in the oral presentation,
    - structure/organization of the material presented,
    - eye contact with audience,
    - audibility/dynamic range and effective use of the voice,
    - ability to sense the audience's understanding of the material and to adapt accordingly,
    - timing: pacing of the presentation; sticking to the time limit
    - content: ability to identify and highlight important points. Use of examples; critical commentary on the material; evidence of going beyond the required reading.

REQUIRED READING

- W.T. Stanbury, _Business-Government Relations in Canada: Grappling with Leviathan_ (Toronto: Methuen, 1986). [available in the bookstore]

- A. Paul Pross, _Group Politics and Public Policy_ (Toronto: Oxford University Press, 1986). [available in the bookstore]

Outlines\C594 - Disk 18   Page 4

- D.L. Weimer & A.R. Vining, <u>Policy Analysis: Concepts and Practice</u> (Englewood Cliffs, N.J.: Prentice-Hall, 1989), Chapters 3-5 [included in photocopied material]

- Selected articles and book chapters indicated below. These items are included in the photocopied material that will be sold to each student who wants it. See Session 1. (More generally, see the "Business-Government Relations Bibliography" handed out in class.)

- Newspaper and other short articles on lobbying and other topics and notes by the instructor to be handed out in class.

SCHEDULE

Session 1, January 2 (Tuesday)

- Introduction and overview of the course; review of this outline.
- Organizational details including arrangements for copying required reading.
- Discussion of the requirements for the group project.
- Discussion of the requirements for oral presentations in class.
- Importance of business-government relations in the Canadian context.

Session 2, January 4 (Thursday)

- A framework for analyzing business-government relations.
- Growth and scope of government activity in Canada, including recent developments - regulatory reform and privatization.
- Significance of "Big Government" for business.

Reading

- W.T. Stanbury, <u>Business-Government Relations</u>, Ch. 1, 2, 3.
- W.T. Stanbury, "Reforming Direct Regulation in Canada" in W.T. Stanbury and D. Swann (eds.) <u>The Age of Regulatory Reform</u> (Oxford: Oxford University Press, 1989).
- W.T. Stanbury, "Privatization by the Federal and Provincial Governments in Canada," <u>Canadian Trade and Investment Guide</u>, 1989 (Toronto: Financial Post, 1989).

Session 3, January 9 (Tuesday)

- Rationales for Government Action: Allocative Efficiency (Part 1)

    - Characteristics of an efficient Economy
    - Pricing
    - Public Goods (including common property resources)

Reading

- Weimer & Vining, <u>Policy Analysis</u>, pp. 30-56.

202

Session 4, January 11 (Thursday)

- Rationales for Government Action: Allocative Efficiency (Part 2)

    - Externalities
    - Natural Monopoly
    - Information Asymmetry

Reading

- Weimer & Vining, *Policy Analysis*, pp. 56-75.

Session 5, January 16 (Tuesday)

- Rationales for Government Action: Other Limitations of Markets

    - Few buyers/sellers
    - Unstable preferences
    - Uncertainty
    - Myopia
    - Adjustment costs

Reading

- Weimer & Vining, *Policy Analysis*, pp. 75-89.

Session 6, January 18 (Thursday)

- Rationales for Government Action: Altering the Distribution of Income

    - Dignity
    - Greater Equality of Outcomes
    - Utilitarianism
    - "Basic human needs"
    - Ameliorating poverty
    - Presumption of equality
    - Justice as fairness
    - Meaningful choice
    - Deservingness

Reading

- Weimer & Vining, *Policy Analysis*, pp. 89-93.
- W.T. Stanbury, *The Normative Bases of Government Action*, Research Study No. 15 (Toronto: Ontario Commission of Inquiry into Residential Tenancies, 1985), Ch. 3.

Session 7, January 23 (Tuesday)

- Limits to Public Intervention: Government Failures

    - Problems of Direct Democracy
    - Problems of Representative Government
    - Problems of Bureaucratic Supply
    - Problems of Decentralization

Reading

- Weimer & Vining, <u>Policy Analysis</u>, pp. 95-123.

Session 8, January 25 (Thursday)

- Correcting Market and Government Failures

    - Freeing, Facilitating and Simulating Markets
    - Using Subsidies and Taxes
    - Establishing Rules
    - Supplying Goods Through Nonmarket Mechanisms
    - Providing Insurance and Cushions

Reading

- Weimer & Vining, <u>Policy Analysis</u>, pp. 125-173.

Session 9, January 30 (Tuesday)

- Positive Theories of Government Intervention

    - The public choice approach
    - Policies for snow or symbolic reassurance
    - Policies to create rights

Reading

- W.T. Stanbury, <u>Business-Government Relations</u>, Ch. 4, sections 2-7 only.
- W.T. Stanbury and Peter Thain, <u>Positive Theories of Government Action and a Case Study of Rent Regulation</u> (Toronto: Ontario Commission of Inquiry into Residential Tenancies, 1986), Chapter 4.
- W.T. Stanbury, <u>The Normative Bases of Government Action</u>, Ch. 4.

Session 10, February 1 (Thursday)

- Key aspects of the federal policy making-administrative process in Canada.
- Understanding businessmen, senior bureaucrats and politicians.
- Policy-making and the public interest.

Reading

- W.T. Stanbury, *Business-Government Relations*, Ch. 4, pp. 89-125 and Ch. 9, pp. 395-407.
- W.T. Stanbury, "A Framework for Understanding Business, Bureaucrats and Politicians" (University of B.C., Faculty of Commerce, 1988, mimeo), 4pp.
- W.T. Stanbury, "Notes on the Policy Making Process" (UBC, Faculty of Commerce, 1989, mimeo) [to be handed out in class].
- Department of Justice, *The Federal Legislative Process in Canada* (Ottawa: Minister of Supply and Srevices, 1987), 28pp.
- A.P. Pross, *Group Politics and Public Policy*, Ch. 1-3.

Session 11, February 6 (Tuesday)

- Mid-term examination: to cover the material in sessions 1 to 9 inclusive.

Session 12, February 8 (Thursday)

[This is the first session with a student presentation.]

- Analysis of interest groups: types, functions, motivation for joining, organization, financing
- Role of interest groups in policy making in Canada

Reading

- W.T. Stanbury, *Business-Government Relations...*, Ch. 9, pp. 305-327.
- A.P. Pross, *Group Politics and Public Policy*, Ch. 4, 5, and 8.
- W.T. Stanbury, "Notes on Interest Groups" (UBC, Faculty of Commerce, 1989, mimeo). [to be handed out in class]

Session 13, February 13 (Tuesday)

- Strategic Approach to Government Relations

- The Government Relations Function
    - Growth of the function
    - Activities
    - Degree of involvement in politics
    - Perceived influence of business
    - Conflicts within the business community
    - Strategic issues in government relations

Reading

- W.T. Stanbury, Business-Government Relations, Ch. 5.
- Mark Baetz, "The Organizational Status of the Government Relations Function Among Canada's Largest Firms" (Wilfred Laurier University, School of Business, mimeo, March 1987).
- M.H. Ryan, C.L. Swanson and R.A. Buchholz, Corporate Strategy, Public Policy and the Fortune 500 (Oxford: Basil Blackwell, 1987), pp. 15 ff.

Session 14, February 15 (Thursday)

No class: mid-term break.

Session 15, February 20 (Tuesday)

- Issues Management
  - Issues and publics
  - Issues management process
  - Assessment of issues
  - Forecasting
  - Ranking
  - Analysis
  - Formulating strategy
  - Implementation

Reading

- W.T. Stanbury, Business-Government Relations, Ch. 6.
- S.E. Littlejohn, "New Trends in Public Issue Identification and Resolution," California Management Review, Vol. 29(1), 1986, pp. 109-123.
- W.L. Wartick and P.E. Rude, "Issues Management: Corporate Fad or Function?" California Management Review, Vol. 29(1), 1986, pp. 124-140.
- Edith Weiner and Arnold Brown, "Stakeholder Analysis for Effective Issues Management," Planning Review, Vol. 14, 1986, pp. 27-31.
- M.H. Ryan, C.L. Swanson, R.A. Bucholz, Corporate Strategy, Public Policy and the Fortune 500 (Oxford: Basil Blackwell, 1987), Ch. 3.

Session 16, February 22 (Thursday)

- Lobbying: Targets
  - Identifying the targets
  - Bureaucrats as targets
  - Cabinet ministers as targets
  - Para-political bureaucracy
  - MPs as targets
  - Committees
  - Senate

Reading

- W.T. Stanbury, Business-Government Relations, Ch. 7, pp. 245-286.
- Xeroxed newspaper articles handed out in class.
- A. Paul Press, Group Politics and Public Policy, Ch. 6.

Session 17, February 27 (Tuesday)

- Lobbying: Timing
    - New legislation/amendments
    - Subordinate legislation
    - Expenditures
    - Revenue budget
    - Regulatory agencies
- Regulation of Lobbying

Reading

- W.T. Stanbury, <u>Business-Government Relations</u>, Ch. 7, pp. 286-304 and Ch. 9, pp. 407-419.
- A. Paul Pross, "The Debate Over Lobbying in Canada" (paper presented at the Political Studies Association Annual Meeting, Aberdeen, Scotland, April 7-9, 1987, mimeo).
- John Sawatsky, <u>The Insiders: Government Business and the Lobbyists</u> (Toronto: McClelland & Stewart, 1987), pp. 1-11 and 322-335.
- Xeroxed materials on lobbying handed out in class.

Session 18, March 1 (Thursday)

- Lobbying: techniques and vehicles
    - Nature of lobbying
    - Reciprocity and lobbying
    - Negotiating situations
    - Paralleling public opinion
    - Competition in lobbying
    - Using public opinion polls
    - Forming coalitions
    - Role of trade associations

Reading

- W.T. Stanbury, <u>Business-Government Relations</u>, Ch. 8.
- Xeroxed newspaper articles handed out in class.
- A. Paul Press, <u>Group Politics and Public Policy</u>, Ch. 7, pp. 155-175.

Session 19, March 6 (Tuesday)

- Lobbying: techniques and vehicles (continued)
    - Role of consultants (government relations firms)
    - Role of information in lobbying
    - Dynamics of lobbying and the policy process
    - Dealing with administrative agencies
    - Confrontation or conciliation
    - Characteristics of an effective lobbyist
    - Strategic use of the concept of "the public interest"

Reading

- W.T. Stanbury, Business-Government Relations, Ch. 9, pp. 357-407.
- Xeroxed newspaper articles handed out in class.
- John Sawatsky, The Insiders, Ch. 19, pp. 297-321.
- Stevie Cameron, Ottawa Inside Out (Toronto: Key Porter Books, 1989), Ch. ___ [to be handed out in class].
- W.T. Stanbury, "Notes on Government Relations Firms" (UBC, Faculty of Commerce, 1990) [to be handed out in class].

Session 20, March 8 (Thursday)

- Corporations and Political Contributions, Part 1
    - Contributions prior to the Election Expenses Act of 1974
    - The 1974 legislation
    - Federal party revenues and expenditures, 1974-1988
    - Importance of large contributions, notably from corporations

Reading

- W.T. Stanbury, Business-Government Relations, Ch. 10, pp. 420-460.
- K.Z. Paltiel, "Canadian Election Expenses Legislation, 1963-1985: A Critical Appraisal or Was the Effort Worth It?" in R.J. Jackson et al. (eds.) Contemporary Canadian Politics (Scarborough, Ont.: Prentice Hall Canada, 1987), pp. 228-246.
- W.T. Stanbury, "Data on Political Contributions to Federal Parties in Canada, 1974-1988" (University of B.C., Faculty of Commerce, 1990, mimeo) [to be handed out in class].

Outlines\C594 - Disk 18

Session 21, March 13 (Tuesday)

- Corporations and Political Contributions, Part 2
    - Political resources other than campaign contributions
    - Gaps in the legislation
    - Political corruption
    - Business policy concerning contributions
- Government Financing of Interest Groups

Reading

- W.T. Stanbury, <u>Business-Government Relations</u>, Ch. 10, pp. 460-501.
- Xeroxed newspaper articles handed out in class.
- W.T. Stanbury, "Notes on Government Financing of Interest Groups" (UBC, Faculty of Commerce, 1990, mimeo) [to be handed out in class].

Session 22, March 15 (Thursday)

- Business and the Media, Part 1
    - Importance of the mass media
    - Critical characteristics of the media

Reading

- W.T. Stanbury, <u>Business-Government Relations</u>, Ch. 11, pp. 502-523 & 546-47.
- Mary Anne Comber and R.S. Mayne, <u>The Newsmongers: How the Media Distort the Political News</u> (Toronto: McClelland and Stewart, 1986), pp. 145-154.
- Allan Fotheringham, <u>Birds of a Feather: The Press and Politicians</u> (Toronto: Key Porter Books, 1989), pp. ___ [to be handed out in class].

Session 23, March 20 (Tuesday)

- Business and the Media, Part 2
    - Effective use of the media in government relations
    - Handling the media interview

Reading

- W.T. Stanbury, <u>Business-Government Relations</u>, Ch. 11, pp. 524-545.
- Anne Collins, "You're On," <u>Canadian Business</u>, March 1987, pp. 38-44, 115, 117.
- Paul Malvern, <u>Persuaders</u> (Toronto: Methuen, 1985), Ch. 12, pp. 287-301.
- Excerpts from a new book on dealing with the media [to be handed out in class].

Session 24, March 22 (Thursday)

- Advocacy Advertising, Part 1

    - Definition
    - Growth
    - Distinctions
    - Why advocacy ads are needed
    - When to use advocacy ads
    - Types of ads and their posture
    - Targets
    - Types of creative strategies
    - Execution/implementation
    - Purposes/examples
    - Gulf Canada's Campaign

Reading

- W.T. Stanbury, Business-Government Relations, Ch. 12, pp. 549-598.
- Xeroxed material on advocacy advertising handed out in class.

Session 25, March 27 (Tuesday)

- Advocacy Advertising, Part 2

    - Normative framework
    - Unresolved issues of public policy
    - Public perceptions and attitudes toward advocacy advertising
    - Growth
    - Diversity of sponsorship
    - Conceptual framework
    - Implementation strategies
    - Measuring effectiveness

    - Canadian Petroleum Assoc. campaign re the NEP

Reading

- S.P. Sethi, Handbook of Advocacy Advertising (Cambridge, Mass.: Ballinger, 1987). Ch. 1, pp. 3-94; Ch. 11, pp. 337-364.
- Xeroxed material on advocacy advertising handed out in class.

Session 26, March 29 (Thursday)

- Counter Strategies for Bureaucrats and Politicians in Dealing with Interest Groups

    - analyzing the power of interest groups
    - general approaches
    - alternative strategies
    - government funding of interest groups

Reading

- W.T. Stanbury, "Notes on Business-Government -Interest Group Relations: A Bureaucrat's Perspective" (University of B.C., Faculty of Commerce, 1989, mimeo) [to be handed out in class].
- A. Paul Pross, *Group Politics and Public Policy*, Ch. 8, pp. 176-207.
- W.T. Stanbury, "Government Funding of Interest Groups" (UBC, Faculty of Commerce, 1990, mimeo) [to be handed out in class].

UNIVERSITY OF CHICAGO

Bus 308 / Econ 384　　　　　　　　　　　　　George J. Stigler
Public Control of Economic Activity　　　　Autumn Quarter 1989

READING LIST

Marginal Notations:
   R - Required reading
   P - In packet

Recommended texts:

   G.J. Stigler, The Citizen and the State, University of Chicago Press, paperback.

   Anthony Downs, An Economic Theory of Democracy, Harper & Row, paperback.

1. **CLASSICAL THEORIES OF THE STATE: EXTERNALITIES**

   　　A.C. Pigou, The Economics of Welfare (4th ed.), Part II, Ch's. 2, 9, 11, 20.

   RP　R. Coase, "The Problem of Social Cost," Journal of Law & Economics, Oct. 1960.

   RP　H. Demsetz, "Why Regulate Utilities?" JLE, 1968.

   　　John Crecine, O. Davis, and J. Jackson, "Urban Property Markets," JLE, 1967.

   　　S.M. Maser, W.H. Riker, and R.N. Rosett, "The Effects of Zoning and Externalities on the Price of Land," JLE, April 1977.

   　　S. Cheung, D. Johnson, and J.R. Gould, three articles on bees and orchards, JLE, April 1973.

2. **CLASSICAL THEORIES OF THE STATE: PUBLIC GOODS**

   R　P. Samuelson, "Diagrammatic Exposition of a Theory of Public Expenditure," Review of Economics and Statistics, Nov. 1985. Also in Readings in Welfare Economics, ed. Arrow and Scitovsky.

   　　C.M. Tiebout, "A Pure Theory of Local Expenditures," Journal of Political Economy, Oct. 1956.

3. **THE SPECIAL CASE OF KNOWLEDGE**

    K. Arrow, "Economic Welfare and the Allocation of Resources for Invention," in *The Rate and Direction of Inventive Activity* (National Bureau of Economic Research, 1962).

    H. Demsetz, "Information and Efficiency: Another Viewpoint," *JLE*, April 1969.

    G. Stigler, "The Economics of Information," *JPE*, 1961; also in *Organization of Industry*.

    G. Akerlof, "The Market for 'Lemons'," *Quarterly Journal of Economics*, 1970.

P   K.B. Leffler, "Persuasion or Information: The Economics of Prescription Drug Advertising," *JLE*, April 1981.

    W.K. Viscusi and W.A. Magat, *Learning about Risk* (Harvard University Press, 1987).

4. **ECONOMIC THEORIES OF THE POLITICAL PROCESS; THE THEORY OF REGULATION**

    J. Buchanan and G. Tullock, *The Calculus of Consent*, Ch's. 2, 6, 7, 8, 10.

R   A. Downs, *An Economic Theory of Democracy*, Parts I, IV.

    D. Friedman, "A Theory of the Size and Shape of Nations," *JPE*, Feb. 1977.

    G. Becker, "Competition and Democracy," *JLE*, Oct. 1958.

    M. Olson, *Logic of Collective Action*.

    Y. Barzel and E. Silberberg, "Is the Act of Voting Rational?" *Public Choice*, Fall 1973.

RP   G. Becker, "A Theory of Competition among Pressure Groups for Political Influence," *QJE*, Aug. 1983.

RP   W. Allen Wallis, "Political Entrepreneurship and the Welfare Explosion," in *Welfare Programs: An Economic Appraisal*, ed. Tobin and Wilson (American Enterprise Institute, 1969).

    J.B. Kau and P.H. Rubin, "Self-Interest, Ideology, and Log-rolling in Congressional Voting," *JLE*, Oct. 1979.

RP   G. Stigler, "Director's Law of Public Income Redistribution," *JLE*, April 1970.

P   G. Stigler, "Economic Competition and Political Competition," <u>Public Choice</u>, Aug. 1972.

W. Niskanen, <u>Bureaucracy and Representative Government</u>, Ch's. 4-7.

RP   B.R. Weingast, K.A. Shepsle, and G. Johnson, "The Political Economy of Benefits and Costs," <u>JPE</u>, Aug. 1981.

5. THE INDUSTRY IN POLITICS; THE "FREE" RIDER PROBLEM

T.N. Tideman and G. Tullock, "A New and Superior Method of Making Social Choices," <u>JPE</u>, Dec. 1976.

RP   G. Stigler, "The Theory of Economic Regulation," <u>Bell Journal</u>, Spring 1971; also in <u>The Citizen and the State</u>.

RP   S. Peltzman, "Toward a More General Theory of Regulation," <u>JLE</u>, Aug. 1976.

J.Q. Wilson, ed., <u>The Politics of Regulation</u>, Ch. 10.

6. THE QUALITATIVE STUDY OF POLICIES

A. Smith, <u>The Wealth of Nations</u>, Bk. IV, Ch. 11, "Of Restraints upon the Importation..."

R. Coase, "The Federal Communications Commission," <u>JLE</u>, 1959.

7. THE SOURCES AND EFFECTS OF REGULATORY POLICIES

H. Marvel, "Factory Regulation: A Reinterpretation of Early English Experience," <u>JLE</u>, Oct. 1977.

RP   G. Stigler and C. Friedland, "What Can Regulators Regulate?" <u>JLE</u>, 1962.

RP   G. Jarrell, "The Demand for State Regulation of the Electric Utility Industry," <u>JLE</u>, Oct. 1978. See also <u>JLE</u>, Dec. 1981.

W. Jordan, "Producer Protection, Prior Market Structure and the Effects of Government Regulation," <u>JLE</u>, April 1972.

G. Stigler, "Public Regulation of the Securities Market," <u>Journal of Business</u>, April 1964; and subsequent denunciations, Oct. 1964.

G.W. Schwert, "Public Regulation and the Securities Market," <u>Bell J.</u>,

Spring 1977.

W. Landes and L. Solomon, "Compulsory Schooling Legislation," *J. Economic History*, March 1972.

P   R.W. Crandall and J.D. Graham, "The Effects of Fuel Economy Standards on Automobile Safety," *JLE*, April 1989.

P   N.L. Rose, "The Incidence of Regulatory Rents in the Motor Carrier Industry," *Rand Journal*, Autumn 1985.

N.L. Rose, "Labor Rent Sharing and Regulation: Evidence from the Trucking Industry," *Journal of Political Economy*, Dec. 1987.

R. Ippolito, "The Effects of Price Regulation in the Automobile Insurance Industry," *JLE*, Apr. 1979.

G. Daly and T. Mayor, "Estimating the Value of a Missing Market: The Economics of Directory Assistance," *JLE*, Apr. 1980.

G.A. Jarrell, "Change at the Exchange: The Causes and Effects of Deregulation," *JLE*, Oct. 1984.

P   Chief Economist, S.E.C., "Stock Trading before the Announcement of Trader Offers," Washington: Office of S.E.C., February 1987.

R.E. Baldwin, *The Political Economy of U.S. Import Policy*, Ch. 1, pp. 142-74.

B. Gardner, "Causes of U.S. Farm Commodity Programs," *JPE*, April 1987.

8. **PRODUCT AND JOB SAFETY**

P   W. Kip Viscusi, "Consumer Behavior and the Safety Effects of Product Safety Regulation," *JLE*, Oct. 1985.

R   W. Landes and R.A. Posner, "A Positive Economic Analysis of Products Liability," and P.L. Danzon, "Comments on Landes and Posner," *JLS*, Dec. 1985.

P   G. Jarrell and S. Peltzman, "The Impact of Product Recalls on the Wealth of Sellers," *JPE*, June 1985.

P   S. Peltzman, "The Effects of Automobile Safety Regulation," *JPE*, Aug. 1975.

J. Chelius, "Liability for Industrial Accidents," *J. Legal Studies*, June 1976.

P   W. K. Viscusi, "The Impact of Occupational Safety and Health Regulations," <u>Bell J.</u>, Spring 1979.

      A.P. Bartel and L.G. Thomas, "Direct and Indirect Effects of Regulation: A New Look at OSHA's Impact," <u>JLE</u>, April 1985.

      S. Peltzman, "An Evaluation of Consumer Protection Legislation: 1962 Drug Amendments," <u>JPE</u>, Sept./Oct. 1973.

9. THE ENFORCEMENT OF REGULATIONS

P   G.S. Becker, "Crime and Punishment," <u>JPE</u>, March/April 1968.

      G. Stigler, "The Optimum Enforcement of Laws," <u>JPE</u>, May/June 1970.

      R.A. Posner, "Taxation by Regulation," <u>Bell J.</u>, Spring 1971.

RP   G. Becker and G. Stigler, "Law Enforcement, Malfeasance, and Compensation of Enforcers," <u>JLS</u>, Jan. 1974.

      W.L. Landes and R.A. Posner, "The Private Enforcement of Law," <u>JLS</u>, Jan. 1975.

RP   W.L. Landes and R.A. Posner, <u>The Economic Structure of Tort Law</u>, Harvard University Press, 1987, Chs. 1 and 10.

      R. Smith, "The Legal and Illegal Markets for Taxed Goods," <u>JLE</u>, Aug. 1976.

      O. Ashenfelter and R. Smith, "Compliance with the Minimum Wage Law," <u>JPE</u>, April 1979.

      M.K. Block, F.C. Nold, and J.E. Sidak, "The Deterrent Effect of Antitrust Enforcement," <u>JPE</u>, June 1981.

      C.C. Cox, "The Enforcement of Public Price Controls," <u>JPE</u>, Oct. 1980.

      R.G. Ehrenberg and P.L. Schuman, "Compliance with the Overtime Pay Provisions of the Fair Labor Standards Act," <u>JLE</u>, April 1982.

      Y. Chang and I. Ehrlich, "On the Economics of Compliance with the Minimum Wage Law," <u>JPE</u>, Feb. 1985.

Harvard University
Graduate School of Business Administration
George F. Baker Foundation

The Coming of Managerial Capitalism
Associate Professor Richard S. Tedlow

Spring Semester, 1990

THE COMING OF MANAGERIAL CAPITALISM

Course Outline

I. **Introduction: Forging a National Economy**

1. Benjamin Franklin and the Definition of American Values
   --in Chandler and Tedlow, COMING OF MANAGERIAL CAPITALISM (CMC)
2. Establishing the Political Base; and,   CMC
   John Jacob Astor   CMC
3. The Rise of New York Port; and,   CMC
   The Second Bank of the United States   CMC
4. Slater, Lowell, and the Factory System   CMC

II. **The Revolution in Transportation and Communication**

5. The Coming of the Railroads   CMC
6. The Railroads and the Beginnings of Modern Management   CMC
7. Jay Gould and the Coming of Railroad Consolidation   CMC
8. J.P. Morgan, 1837-1913; and,   CMC
   The Railroad Problem and the Solution   CMC

III. **The Revolution in Distribution and Production**

9. 19th Century Retailing and the Department Store; and,   CMC
   Chain Stores   9-386-127
       Rev. 2/86   1
10. Pure Marketing: The Coke and Pepsi Story   2
11. The Integration of Mass Production and Mass Distribution   CMC
12. The Standard Oil Company   CMC
13. Du Pont: The Centralized Structure   CMC
14. The Multidivisional Enterprise; and,   CMC
    Du Pont: The World War II Years   9-388-074   1
15. The Decline of the British Cotton Industry   9-386-078   1
16. The Decline of the British Economy; and,   8-386-079   1
    Competition and the Workplace, 1945-1988   Seminar Paper   2
17. The Emergence of Managerial Capitalism   CMC

IV. **New Relations of Management and the Work Force**

18. Patterns of Work in 19th Century America; and, excerpts
    from Nathan Irvin Huggins, _Slave and Citizen: The Life
    of Frederick Douglass_ (Boston: Little, Brown and   CMC
    Company, 1980)   2
19. Mass Production and the Beginnings of Scientific Management   CMC
20. Organized Labor and the Worker   CMC
21. From Lean Years to Fat Years: Labor Between the Wars   CMC

CMC--Alfred D. Chandler, Jr. and Richard S. Tedlow, _The Coming of Mana-Managerial Capitalism: A Casebook on the History of American Economic Institutions_ (Homewood, Ill.: Irwin, 1985)

1--Harvard Business School Case. Copies may be obtained through the Publishing Division, Harvard Business School, Boston, MA 02163. (617) 495-6117.
2-- Material distributed in class.

V. The Role of Government

    22. The Antitrust Movement   CMC
    23. The Great Depression: Causes and Impact; and,   CMC
        The Federal Government and Employment   CMC
    24. Regulatory Agencies; and,   CMC
        The Federal Trade Commission and Shared Monopoly   CMC
    25. When America Got It Right: Mobilization during World War II   2

VI. Business Management in the Modern Era

    26. Alfred D. Chandler, Jr., "Managerial Enterprise and Competitive Capabilities," <u>Harvard Business Review</u>, Forthcoming March-April 1990.   2
    27. James Burke: A Career in American Business   9-389-177 (A)   1
    28. Cases accompanied by a videotape of same name 9-390-030 (B)   1
                                                              Rev. 11/89
    29. Production and Distribution: Competition Policy and Industry Structure   2-387-079   1

CMC-- Alfred D. Chandler, Jr. and Richard S. Tedlow, <u>The Coming of Managerial Capitalism: A Casebook on the History of American Economic Institutions</u> (Homewood, Ill.: Irwin, 1985)

1--Harvard Business School Case. Copies may be obtained through the Publishing Division, Harvard Business School, Boston, MA 02163. (617)495-6117.
2--Material distributed in class.

MANAGING IN THE REGULATED ENVIRONMENT

Spring 1990

Course Syllabus

Richard H.K. Vietor

Graduate School of Business Administration

Harvard University

Instructor

Richard H.K. Vietor, Professor, Business, Government, and Competition. Baker Library 213.

Course Form

One credit course, Y-schedule, offered in the SPRING semester.

Target Students

For students interested in issues of public economic policy, and those planning a career in an industry, or with clients that are exposed to economic, structural, or social regulation, or significant regulatory change.

Educational Objectives and Course Organization

Managing in the Regulated Environment will introduce students to an environment in which government regulation distorts competition and significantly alters conventional principles of business management. The perspective is usually a manager's, but occasionally a regulator's.

After an introduction to the scope of regulation, the course is organized in five parts, following the presumptive justifications for regulation: (1) externalities, (2) natural monopolies (and economic rent), (3) excess competition, (4) inadequate information, and (5) public goods.

Case materials explore five broad business sectors -- toxic and hazardous substances, energy (oil-gas-nuclear), transportation, financial services, and telecommunications. They illustrate, in some depth, analytical and decision-making concepts derived from business policy, regulatory theory, institutional history, and industrial organization. Wherever possible, an "inside-outside" approach is utilized to examine the viewpoint of both managers and regulators.

Class Participation

Regulation is a subject matter especially well-suited to vigorous class discussion; preparation is crucial. Accordingly, 60% of the grade for the course will be based on the quality and quantity of a student's participation in discussion. A final exam will constitute the other 40%.

Meetings with the Instructor

Appointments can be scheduled on days that the course meets by contacting Ms. Carmen Abber, at ext. 5-6534.

Course Outline

INTRODUCTION: THE SCOPE OF REGULATION

(1/24)   Commonwealth Edison (A)   *

The perspective here is that of the CEO of a large electric utility faced with the question of whether or not to delay a construction program for six nuclear power plants. Relevant considerations include financial condition, recent rate settlements and cash flow, operating constraints, the regulatory climate at the state and federal levels, and energy market conditions in the recent past and near future.

Discussion Questions:

1. How did Commonwealth Edison get into such a difficult situation? To what extent is this a result of external developments, as opposed to management?

2. Evaluate Jim O'Connor's response to the Illinois Commerce Commission's interim rate decision in 1979.

3. What course of action would you recommend Jim O'Connor take in April 1980, with respect to CWE's nuclear construction schedule and capital budget?

4. Does the nuclear construction program put the interests of ratepayers and stockholders at odds?

(1/25)   Typical Justifications for Regulation   1-384-147

This reading, from Breyer's Regulation and its Reform, summarizes economic rationales for government regulation. As such, it provides a framework for the topical organization of the course.

Discussion Questions:

1. What is the importance for managers, if any, of distinguishing among economic rationales for regulation? For regulators? For legislators?

2. To what extent does the theory of "second best" undermine these economic justifications for regulation?

3. Given these different justifications for regulation, will it be possible to generalize about the process of regulation, much less the task of managing in the regulated environment?

*Strategic Management in the Regulatory Environment, by Richard H.K. Vietor. (Available at the "COOP").

EXTERNALITIES

(2/1) **William D. Ruckelshaus and the Environmental Protection Agency** *

Regulatory Agencies   1-384-150

This case, and the accompanying note by Tom McCraw, focus on the regulatory agency as a bureaucracy, and the problems of organizing a regulatory program.

Discussion Questions:

1. What is the product of this organization? What is the market?

2. What are the managerial constraints and opportunities facing Ruckelshaus, in comparison with those that economic regulators (i.e., Kahn) or business managers of equivalent level?

3. What is Ruckelshaus' strategy? What's your evaluation of his performance during the first six months?

(2/2) **The Work of a Regulatory Agency: The EPA and Toxic Substances**   9-380-081

A Note on Administrative Law   1-384-146

This case focuses on the administrative process of implementing regulatory legislation; imposing standards and choosing the types of products and companies to cover.

Discussion Questions:

1. What is the EPA seeking to accomplish in this case? How would you describe its approach?

2. What are the criteria for implementation?

3. What problems would you anticipate as a chemical-industry manager? As the director of the Office of Toxic Substances? As the policy director of an environmental group?

- 4 -

(2/7)   Note on the Hazardous Waste Management Industry   9-382-146

This note provides an opportunity to analyze the structure of a rapidly growing industry in which the market exists because of regulation and the competing firms are themselves heavily regulated. Financial, operational, and regulatory issues interact in determining competitive advantages.

Discussion Questions:

1. Why is there a market for "hazardous waste management?"

2. What are the characteristics of that market? What does it take to be a successful company in hazardous waste management?

3. What is your evaluation of the major competitors described in the note, with regard to past performance and likely future directions and success?

(2/8)   IT Corporation (B)   *

This is a case on strategy in a heavily regulated, but competitive industry environment. The company has a number of strategic options; the strengths and weaknesses of each are affected by the future course of regulatory policy and implementation.

Discussion Questions:

1. How have regulatory developments since 1981 affected the hazardous waste management business?

2. What is your evaluation of IT's strategy to date? How would you assess the changes in the company's organizational structure since 1981?

3. What changes in strategy, organizational structure, and implementation would you recommend to the company's management team?

225

(2/14)   DuPont Freon® Products Division (A)   8-389-111

Changes in science, like changes in technology, can redefine the premises for regulation or non-regulation. In this case, a DuPont division that manufactures chloroflourocarbons is suddenly confronted by scientific evidence that reshapes the political environment and threatens to undermine the market for its product. Product and research policy in this relatively small division quickly become an issue of corporate responsibility and strategy for DuPont.

Discussion Questions:

1. What are the likely effects of the Montreal Protocol and the report of the Ozone Trends Panel on the market structure of chloroflourocarbons? On the political marketplace?

2. What are the implications for DuPont?

3. What would you recommend that Joe Glas do? Why?

NATURAL MONOPOLIES

(2/15)   El Paso Natural Gas Company and the FPC   *

This case introduces the principles of cost-base, utility rate regulation. El Paso's management must decide if the "just and reasonable" rate is also viable financially. This case introduces a chronological series on regulated energy industries.

Discussion Questions:

1. What is El Paso trying to do, and why do intervenors object?

2. What are the methodological problems and economic implications of cost-base rate regulation?

3. Should Howard Boyd recommend that El Paso accept the FPC's final order, or appeal the FPC's decision in court?

(2/16)   **Marginalism in the State of New York**   *

           Marginal Cost Pricing   8-384-145

   In 1974, the economist, Alfred Kahn, has turned regulator, and
   faces the political and bureaucratic challenges of implementing
   regulatory change. This case and note introduce the concepts of
   marginal cost pricing.

   Discussion Questions:

   1. Evaluate Kahn's strategy for introducing rate reform in New York.
      What might he have done differently?

   2. Is a marginal-cost rate structure really feasible, given the
      technical costs and problems, and the problem of second best?

   3. Is a marginal-cost pricing, in the electric-power sector,
      desirable social policy? Would you generalize on your view, to
      other regulated sectors?

   4. What would you advise Kahn to do at the July 8th meeting?

(2/21)   **Mexican Natural Gas**   9-382-048

   In 1977, Energy Secretary James Schlesinger decides not to allow
   Mexican natural gas to be imported under terms negotiated between
   U.S. firms and Pemex. The case explores issues facing an
   administrative regulator in a market thoroughly distorted by
   regulation.

   Discussion Questions:

   1. What are the economic justifications for Schlesinger's regulatory
      control of gas imports? Why are American companies so interested
      in Mexican gas?

   2. Evaluate the strengths and weaknesses of Diaz Serrano's bargaining
      position with respect to natural gas exports as of August 1977.
      What about Schlesinger's?

   3. From Schlesinger's perspective, evaluate the 1977 deal negotiated
      between Pemex and the Border Gas consortium in terms of (1) its
      potential effects on the other supplemental gas options, and (2)
      other policy criteria of interest to Schlesinger and his boss.

   4. Identify all the constituents involved in the gas negotiations.
      How did Border Gas expect to overcome Schlesinger's opposition to
      their deal?

   5. Considering changes in the U.S. energy situation after 1977, what
      kind of a deal would you expect Schlesinger to accept in September
      1979?

                                                              227

(2/22)   **Bay State Gas**   N2-388-066

The company, a local distribution company in Massachusetts, faces significant challenges both external and internal to its operation. Regulatory changes at both the federal and state level have transformed the natural gas industry from a world of guaranteed franchises and stable prices to a deregulated environment. The CEO is attempting to chart a new strategic course--one based on an increased emphasis on cost containment and new marketing initiatives--a far cry from the status quo perpetuated by "cost plus" regulation.

Discussion Questions:

1. How has regulatory reform at the state and federal level affected Bay State Gas?

2. Identify and evaluate Bay State Gas's strategy since 1984.

3. What would you recommend that Roger Young do now?

(3/1)   **Commonwealth Edison (B)**   9-389-211

By the Spring of 1988, Commonwealth Edison has completed its nuclear-plant construction program, but the Illinois Commission appears unwilling to accept either a deregulatory structural solution or traditional rate-base treatment that would require a rate hike of $1.4 billion. The Federal Energy Regulatory Commission, meanwhile, has tentatively proposed regulatory initiatives that would encourage competitive cogeneration and unbundle power generation from transmission and distribution.

Discussion Questions:

1. What combination of factors have caused the situation that O'Connor faces in 1988?

2. What course of action would you recommend to Jim O'Connor in the spring of 1988? Explain how your recommendations will address CWE's immediate problems, while anticipating likely developments in energy markets and regulation over the longer term?

3. What solutions, in your view, would best serve the "public interest?"

EXCESS COMPETITION

(3/2)   Bailey & Baumol, <u>Deregulation and the Theory of Contestable Markets</u>

By challenging conventional concepts of oligopolistic behavior, this reading provides a frame of reference for discussion of airlines, telecommunications and banking in the next two sections of the course.

Discussion Questions:

1. Does the theory of contestable markets have any more to do with the real world than the theory of perfect competition? Do you think it provides more useful criteria for antitrust policy than does perfect competition?

2. Would the FPC or the Justice Department have reassessed the El Paso-PNW Merger in light of contestable-market theory?

3. How would you reassess <u>Exxon et al.</u>, in light of contestable-market theory? Would it affect your choice of remedy?

4. Do you agree that contestability theory can help "determine appropriate boundaries between regulated and unregulated portions of an industry"? (p.137)

(3/7)   <u>Senator Kennedy and the CAB</u>   9-378-055

This case describes the strategy and tactics of Senator Kennedy and Steven Breyer in initiating a legislative drive towards regulatory reform. Selection of the airline industry as a political target, the organization of legislative hearings, and the committee's recommendations are discussed.

Discussion Questions:

1. Why is this happening in 1975? Why did Kennedy and Breyer choose the CAB as a target? What other candidates might have been suitable?

2. What is your appraisal of the Kennedy/Breyer strategy? How should each of the major participants have responded?

(3/8)   **Chicago-Midway (A): Alfred Kahn at the CAB**   9-384-156

This case takes the view point of a key regulator in the process of implementing regulatory changes that affect the entire market structure of the regulated industry. Kahn must formulate a multi-part regulatory strategy in a precedent-setting situation of reducing entry barriers.

Discussion Questions:

1. As Alfred Kahn, what is your decision in the Chicago-Midway Low Fare Route Proceeding? Specifically, which applicants are allowed entry? How are the routes allocated? What minimum fare and service conditions do you require? How should the incumbents be restricted?

2. How would you justify the above decision, in terms of the public interest?" Is "contestability" useful?

3. As an administrative situation, how is this different for Alfred Kahn than rate-reform at the NYPSC in 1974?

4. As an executive for (a) a new-entrant airline, (b) an incumbent airline, (c) Amtrack, and (d) the Illinois Department of Transportation, how would you respond to the decision above?

(3/21)   **American Airlines (A)**   *

In July 1980, Robert Crandall is appointed president of American Airlines, after a first half operating loss of $120 million. American's past strategy and structure were products of a regulated environment, now changed. The case explores the effects of regulation on American's operations, the impact of deregulation, and the strategic options for adjustment.

Discussion Questions:

1. How had regulation affected the strategy and structure of American Airlines? What were American's strengths and weaknesses with respect to deregulation?

2. What are Bob Crandall's strategic options?

3. What strategy (addressing the major operational issues) would you recommend?

(3/22)   **Note on Freight Transportation and Regulation**   *

This note describes the evolution of surface-transport markets, the railroad and motor carrier industries, and their regulatory environment. It is designed as a vehicle for exploring the causes of regulation and deregulation over nearly a century and its impact on industry structure, and performance.

Discussion Questions:

1. What were the original justifications for regulation of surface-freight transportation? How valid were they in the 1880s? In the 1930s?

2. In the three-and-a-half decades after 1940, how did regulation shape the structure of markets for surface-freight transportation?

3. What, if anything, had reduced the appropriateness of regulation by 1980?

4. What are the major impacts of the Staggers Act and the Motor carrier act on market and industry structure?

5. The Reagan administration has proposed abolishing the ICC; do you agree?

(3/23)   **CSX**   *

By 1985, CSX, a holding company for two of the nation's largest railroads and a major gas pipeline company, has made significant progress since Congress initiated deregulation in 1980. Still, the company's chairman, Hays Watkins, realizes that more needs to be done if the railroads are to earn their cost of capital in an intensely competitive and declining market.

Discussion Questions:

1. In what ways has deregulation since 1980 affected CSX competitive environment?

2. What is your evaluation of CSX management's response, to date?

3. What changes in strategy, organizational structure, and implementation would you recommend to Hays Watkins, as of mid-1985?

INADEQUATE INFORMATION

(3/28)   Regulation and Competition in Commercial Banking   *

This notes describes the origins of banking regulation in the United States, its effects on the structure of financial-services markets, and recent regulatory changes that are redefining the commercial-banking industry.

Discussion Questions:

1. What were the assumptions underlying banking legislation and regulation during the Depression Era? How did this public policy framework affect market structure? To what extent are those public policy goals still valid today?

2. What forces have changed the market for financial services? How have these changes impacted the price, product, and geographic dimensions of bank regulation?

3. How has the business of banking evolved during this period of change? What are the strategic implications of this regulatory transition?

4. Are banks special? Is further deregulation inevitable? Desirable?

(3/29)   The Comptroller and Non-Bank Banks   *

The Comptroller of the Currency is considering whether or not to extend his moratorium on approval of applications from "non-bank banks." Congress has been unable to resolve issues of industry definition and entry, and the Comptroller has been managing a fragile balance between regulation and politics.

Discussion Questions:

1. What are the public-policy issues behind this non-bank bank controversy? Who are the stakeholders in the issue? Do non-bank banks pose a clear threat to the financial system?

2. What was the Comptroller trying to achieve? How has Congress responded? The Fed? State banking commissions?

3. Why are non-bank banks being established? Should the Comptroller end the moratorium? What would be the reaction?

- 12 -

(3/30)   S&L Crisis   8-389-159

This case describes the S&L crisis and the regulatory and economic circumstances that precipitated it. It is accompanied by a series of supplements, each representing an important interest group's perspective on the situation. Each student will receive the base case and one supplement. These materials are designed to facilitate a discussion of the political process from which the bailout and re-regulation policy emerged.

Discussion Questions:

1. What caused the S&L Crisis? Was regulation the problem, or deregulation?

2. What's your evaluation of the Bush administration's proposal?

   a. What are its implications for market structure in financial services? Does this best serve the "public interest?"

   b. Does the plan seem feasible, politically?

3. What is the particular perspective expressed by the interests represented in your supplement? Do you find it reasonably convincing?

(4/12) TO BE ANNOUNCED

PUBLIC GOODS

(4/13)   Telecommunications in Transition   *

This note, describes the evolution of regulation in the telecommunications industry since 1913, its impact on organization, market structure, and political interests, potential consequences for users, and threats and opportunities to firms in the industry.

Discussion Questions:

1. How did the public interest come to be defined during the first half of the 20th century?

2. How did regulation shape the structure of telecommunications markets and the telephone industry? What roles were played by different political institutions?

3. Why did this system undergo dramatic change during the period 1959-1983? How did this regulatory transition affect the structure of the industry and the market for telecommunications?

4. How is the public interest in telecommunications now defined? What has changed? What public issues does this change imply?

(4/18) **US West** 9-386-082

This case explores the organizational problems of a holding company determined to be involved in both regulated and non-regulated, competitive businesses. It raises some difficult questions about management functions under two different regimes, and about the economic implications of mixed systems.

Discussion Questions:

1. How serious are the restrictions still imposed on US West after divestiture?

2. Analyze US West's strategy, organization, and behavior from the perspective of Judge Greene. From the perspective of a Colorado public utility commissioner?

3. In light of technological and regulatory trends affecting the Telecommunications industry, what is your evaluation of US West's strategy and organization?

4. How should Jack MacAllister respond to Judge Greene's Opinion?

(4/19) **AT&T and the Access Charge** *

This case examines the potential economic impact of a complex regulatory change on an array of public and private stakeholders, the motives and relative political leverage of each, and AT&T's options for managing the political process.

Discussion Questions:

1. How does the Access Charge Plan work? What are its objectives? What alternatives might there have been for accomplishing the same general objectives?

2. How does the Plan affect each of the stakeholders, as among user groups, political interests, and supplier interests? What were their positions on the policy issues, and what role did each see for AT&T in a competitive environment?

3. In the political discourse over access charges, how might AT&T have managed stakeholders differently?

4. In view of the delay and pending legislation and regulatory action (as of February 15, 1984) what are AT&T Communications' strategic options? What option would you recommend?

- 14 -

(4/20) General Telephone of the Northwest   *

The CEO of a telephone operating company must implement a new strategy to contend with the economic and political implications of regulatory change. This case brings home to the general manager the lessons of MRE.

Discussion Questions:

1. What are the key issues facing Kent Foster?

2. What are the company's principal strengths and weaknesses as it prepares for competitive markets?

3. What is Foster's strategy, and what should he do first to implement it? Develop an integrated plan, with consideration to regulatory affairs, marketing and customer service, public affairs, human resources, operations, finance and control.

(4/25) AT&T and the Regional Bell Holding Companies   1-388-078

This case describes the regulatory developments in telecommunications since divestiture, and how they have affected AT&T's business relationships with its former operating companies. Late in 1987, AT&T's management considers what strategic and organizational changes, if any, would serve the company's long-term interests.

Discussion Questions:

1. How has regulation (through the MFJ, FCC and state PUCs) shaped the structure of the telecommunications market since the breakup of the Bell System? What have been the implications for the business relationships between AT&T and the Bell RHCs?

2. To what extent are these market-structuring regulations likely to change in the near-term (3-5 years) future?

(4/26) AT&T and the RHC's, continued.

3. What is your assessment of AT&T's strategy for managing these relationships over the past three years?

4. What changes in strategy--both substantive and organizational--should Al Partoll consider and recommend to AT&T's Board of Directors in October 1987?

(4/27) Review and summary.

235

SIMON FRASER UNIVERSITY
AT HARBOUR CENTRE

FACULTY OF BUSINESS ADMINISTRATION

MBA 691
BUSINESS, GOVERNMENT & SOCIETY

A. Vining/291-3768
733-5097(home)
Fall 1989

COURSE DESCRIPTION

Purpose

The purpose of this course is to survey what is -- and should be -- the relationship between government and private firms, non-profit institutions and other agencies, such as universities. For most of the course, you will assume the role of a government analyst (i.e., become a "policy analyst") both to learn how such analysts do analysis and to understand their thinking. During the latter part of the course (specifically in the group project), you will adopt the stance of private market participants who have to attempt to convince government why a particular policy would be "optimal" (including from the firm or industry perspective).

Major Elements

The basic components of the course will focus on:

1. <u>The normative rationale for government intervention -- when does the market fail?</u> Market failures will be illustrated with reference to specific industries, e.g., natural monopoly -- power utilities, telephone industry; common property resource problems -- fisheries industry, forestry industry; public goods problems -- broadcasting; as well as problems that have cross-sectoral impacts, e.g., information failure -- consumer product safety and energy efficiency; negative externalities -- pollution control.

2. <u>The alternative to the market is government, whether directly or indirectly. Just as market failure can be systematically analyzed so can "government failure. -- When does government fail?"</u> Government failures will be illustrated with respect to specific industries; e.g., rent-seeking -- auto import restraints; price controls -- NEP.

3. <u>Given the problems of both market and government failure, what are the potential policy alternatives?</u> The use, potential use, and misuse of these policy options will be reviewed in the context of specific industries and cross-sectoral studies; e.g., auctions to allocate natural monopolies, the provision of information to negate information asymmetry, etc.

4. <u>How can the government analyst assess the costs and benefits of government interventions?</u> Cost-benefit, cost-effectiveness and policy analysis as art and craft.

5. The government analyst must learn to combine all the above elements (as must those responding to these analyses). What are "the tricks of the trade" to landing on your feet? Or, how to do policy analysis.

Weekly Schedule

Our tentative schedule (and particular readings) to cover these broad topic areas will be as follows:

Week 1 (September 6)
Course overviews and discussion of administration. The readings for Week 2 will be "The Content and Process of Microeconomic Policy Analysis" and Policy Analysis, Chapter 3, pp 29-56. pp 29-39 is simply a review of basic micro; if you remember all this, skip to p 39.

Week 2 (September 13)
Discussion of the nature of competition and review of basic microeconomic concepts - consumer surplus, producer surplus/economic rent, deadweight loss, compensating variation, ordinary and compensated demand curves. Beginning of Traditional Market Failures: public goods. Readings for Week 3, Policy Analysis, Chapter 3, pp 56-93 and "Information Asymmetry Favoring Sellers: A Policy Framework."

Week 3 (September 20)
"Traditional" Market Failures continued: externalities, information asymmetries, natural monopoly. Reading for next week is Policy Analysis, Chapter 6, pp 179-218. Reread "Content and Process" part pertaining to Figure 4. Groups assigned for group projects (3/4 people).

Week 4 (September 27)
Nontraditional Market Failures: non-independent preferences, uncertainty, intertemporal allocation, adjustment costs. The reading for next week is Policy Analysis, Chapter 4. 1st individual project assigned.

Week 5 (October 4)
Equity and other goals: efficiency is not all. No reading except on first policy analysis.

Week 6 (October 11)
Introduction to Government Failure: The Failures of Direct Democracy and Representative Government. Reading is "Government Production Failure." *1st individual project due.*

Week 7 (October 18)
Conclusion on Government Failure: Bureaucratic Supply and Government Firms, Decentralized Government. Reading is Policy Analysis, Chapter 5.

Week 8 (October 25)
Generic Policy Alternatives. 2nd policy analysis is assigned. Reading is Chapter 7, Policy Analysis (skim).

Week 9 (November 1)
Overview of Cost-Benefit Analysis (1 hour), Group project presentations begin.

Week 10 (November 8)
Topics in Cost-Benefit Analysis (1 hour), *2nd Individual Project due.* Group project presentations. Policy Analysis, Chapter 9.

Week 11 (November 15)
"How to put together a policy analysis" (revisited).

Week 12 (November 22)
Group presentations.

Week 13 (November 29)
Review and wrap-up. *Group Project due.* 1 hour final exam.

Format and Course Requirements

The course will be part lecture, part seminar. As the term progresses, I shall lecture less and you will, hopefully, talk more. Requirements will comprise:
- assigned chapters and readings
- a brief final examination
- 2 individual projects (case studies of government policy)
- 1 group project (to be presented orally in class and in written form).

The proposed weighting of the requirements is as follows:
- final examination   10
- individual projects (2 x 20)   40
- group projects
    oral version   10
    written version   30   40
- class participation   10
- Total   100

Text

David L. Weimer and Aidan R. Vining, Policy Analysis: Concepts and Practice, Prentice-Hall, 1989.

Readings (to be distributed)

Aidan R. Vining and David L. Weimer, "The Content and Process of Microeconomic Policy Analysis."

Aidan R. Vining and David L. Weimer, "Information Asymmetry Favoring Sellers: a Policy Framework". Policy Sciences 21 (1988) : 281-303.

Aidan R. Vining and David L. Weimer, "Government Production Failure: Towards an Analytic Framework".

UNIVERSITY OF CALIFORNIA
Haas School of Business

Course Outline
Fall 1989

B.A.170 - SOCIAL AND POLITICAL ENVIRONMENT OF BUSINESS
Mr. Vogel

Office Hours: Wednesday, 10:00-11:00; 2:00-4:00
Friday, 10:00-11:00
Office: 564 Barrows Hall
Office Phone: 642-5294
Home Phone: 530-5470

Reading Materials

Sinclair, *The Jungle*

Porter, *The Rise of Big Business*

Reagan, *Regulation: The Politics of Policy*

Vogel, *Fluctuating Fortunes*

Abegglen & Stalk, *Kaisha*

Reading Packet (available at Copymat)

Course Requirements

B.A.170 has five requirements. ALL must be satisfactorily completed to receive a passing grade.

(1) Midterm (15%)

(2) Final examination (25%)

(3) Attendance and participation in sections (15%)

(4) Two short essays (five to seven pages) (30%)

Each paper should explicitly demonstrated familiarity with relevant class readings and lectures and should express your own point of view. Papers will be due at the beginning of lecture; later papers will not be accepted. The two paper topics are as follows:

1. Government Regulation

   Summarize and critically evaluate the contemporary debate over the appropriate role of government in regulating corporate behavior.

Limit your paper to either some aspect(s) of economic or social regulation. Please illustrate your position and your argument by reference to a specific policy drawn from either the course materials or other sources with which you are familiar. Whenever appropriate, your paper should draw upon the relevant class readings.

2. <u>International Competition</u>

Choose a particular American industry which is facing international competition. Discuss the nature and causes of the challenges facing the industry, evaluate its performance and discuss the difficulties <u>and</u> the appropriate public and private strategies for improving its global competitiveness. Whenever appropriate, your paper should draw upon the relevant class readings.

(5) A journal based on your regular reading of newspapers and magazines that cover business news. (15%)

Three times during the semester, you will be asked to turn in a three to five page (typed double-spaced) memo based on your reading of either the daily or weekly business press. Each journal should discuss one article or groups of articles on <u>each</u> of the following <u>three</u> different subjects: government regulation (social or economic), business political activity/ business ethics, corporate social responsibility, and America in the world economy.

In your journal, you should briefly cite and summarize <u>each</u> story, assess its significance, evaluate the fairness or political "angle" of the story, examine its relevancy to the course material (when possible) and present your own views on the subject.

In addition, each journal should be based on articles published in more than one source. Appropriate publications include, <u>The Wall Street Journal</u>, <u>Business Week</u>, the <u>Financial Times</u>, <u>The Economist</u>, and major daily newspapers.

I. <u>The Nature of Capitalism</u> (2 Weeks)

Sinclair, <u>The Jungle</u>

George Gilder, Selections from <u>Wealth and Poverty</u>

Michael Waltzer, "In Defense of Equality"

II. <u>Business in America</u> (2 Weeks)

Porter, <u>The Rise of Big Business</u>

David Vogel, "Business Mistrust of Government", <u>Center Magazine</u>

Thomas McCraw, "Business & Government: The Origins of the Adversary Relationship", <u>California Management Review</u>

****
FIRST JOURNAL DUE: Third Week
****

III. <u>Government Regulations of Business</u> (2 Weeks)

   <u>Overview</u>:

   Reagan, <u>Regulation</u>, Chapters I, II

   Vogel, <u>Fluctuating Fortunes</u>, Chapters III - IV

   <u>Economic Regulation</u>:

   Reagan, <u>Regulation</u>, Chapters III, IV

   Gregg Easterbrook, "The Virtues of Competition"

   "Is Deregulation Working", <u>Business Week</u>

   John Curran, "Does Deregulation Make Sense?" <u>Fortune</u>

   <u>Social Regulation</u>:

   Reagan, <u>Regulation</u>, Chapters V, VI, VII

   David Bollier & John Claybrook, "Regulations that Work", <u>Washington Monthly</u>, April 1, 1986

   John Morrell, "A Review of the Record", <u>Regulation</u>, Nov/Dec 1986

   Maraniss & Weisskopf, "Life in the National Sacrifice Zone", <u>Washington Post Weekly</u>

   Specter, "Fear of Frying", <u>Washington Post Weekly</u>

   Jeremy Main, "Here Comes the Big New Clean Up", <u>Fortune</u>

   Vogel, "AIDS and the Politics of Drug Lag", <u>Public Interest</u>

****
FIRST PAPER DUE: Sixth Week
****

IV. <u>Corporate Governance</u> (1 Week)

   T. Boone, Pickens, "Professions of a Short-termer", <u>Harvard Business Review</u>

   W. Law, "A Corporation Is More Than Its Stockholders", <u>Harvard Business Review</u>

   "The Battle for Corporate Control", <u>Business Week</u>

Robert Kuttner, "The Truth About Corporate Raiders", New Republic, Jan 23, 1988

Moria Johnston, "The Takeovers", California Magazine, May 1987

Jonathan Greenberg, "Sold Short", Mother Jones

****
MIDTERM: Eighth Week
****

V. Corporate Social Responsibility and Corporate Philanthropy   (1 Week)

James O'Toole, "Moral Courage"

Milton Friedman, "The Social Responsibility of Business is to Increase Its Profits", New York Times, September 13, 1970

"The Education Crisis: What Business Can Do", Fortune

David Kirp, "Uncommon Decency: Pacific Bell Responds to AIDS", Harvard Business Review

"Privacy", Business Week, March 28, 1988

Michael Unseem, "Patterns of Corporate Contributions", California Management Review, Winter 1988

Messon & Tilson, "Corporate Philosophy: A Strategic Approach to the Bottom Line", California Management Review, Winter 1987

VI. Corporate Crime and Business Ethics   (1 Week)

Russell Mokhiber, "Criminals By Any Other Name", Washington Monthly, January 1988

"Clamor to Make Punishment Fit the Crime", Business Week, February 10, 1986

"The Rationale for Ethical Corporate Behavior", Business Roundtable, Winter 1988

Vogel, "Ethics and Profits Don't Always Go Hand in Hand", L.A. Times

Bunake, "Should We Teach Business Ethics?", Business Horizons

****
SECOND JOURNAL DUE: Tenth Week
****

VII. <u>Corporate Political Activity</u> (2 Weeks)

   Vogel, <u>Fluctuating Fortunes</u>, Review Chapters III-IV
   Read Chapters I, II, V-X

   ****
   THIRD JOURNAL DUE: Twelfth Week
   ****

VIII. <u>America in the World Economy</u> (2 Weeks)

   Abegglen & Stalk, <u>Kaisha</u>

   Additional readings to be assigned

   ****
   SECOND PAPER DUE: Fifteenth Week
   ****

IX. <u>Review</u> (1 Week)

UNIVERSITY OF CALIFORNIA
Haas School of Business

Course Outline
Fall 1989

B.A.207 - BUSINESS AND PUBLIC POLICY
Mr. Vogel

Office Hours: Wednesday, 10:00-11:00; 2:00-4:00
                Friday, 10:00-11:00
Office: 564 Barrows Hall
Office Phone: 642-5294
Home Phone: 530-5470

Reading Materials

Louis Galambos and Joseph Pratt, *The Rise of The Corporate Commonwealth*, Basic

Michael Reagan, *Regulation: The Politics of Policy*, Little Brown

David Vogel, *Fluctuating Fortunes: The Political Power of Business in America*, Basic

Stephen Cohen and John Zysman, *Manufacturing Matters: The Myth of the Post-Industrial Economy*, Basic

Jared Taylor, *Shadows of the Rising Sun*, Quill

Reading Packet

California Management Review, Summer 1989

Course Requirements

Students will be required to write three papers, which collectively will constitute 60% of your grade. There will also be a final, worth 20%. The remaining 20% will be based on class participation.

Paper Topics

1. <u>Government Regulation</u>: Pick an area of government regulatory policy that is currently on the political agenda. Describe the origin of the issue, the arenas in which the policy is being made and the interest or interest groups involved. Evaluate the debate over the policy and state your own view as to both the likely and describable outcomes. This paper should, whenever appropriate, draw on the reading material in Section III.

2. <u>The Management of Corporate Public Affairs</u>: This is a group project. Describe how a particular firm or industry manages its external environment. Your project should include a description of governmental relations, corporate philanthropy, public relations and business ethics as well as an analysis of how your firm or industry has or is addressing a current issue or issues. This essay should draw upon the reading materials in Number V, VI, VII.

3. <u>International Competition</u>: Drawing primarily on the readings in section VIII, describe the competitive challenges confronting American industry, evaluate how well American business and government have responded to these international challenges and suggest areas for improvement. Your analysis should be illustrated by reference to a particularly sector.

I. <u>The Origins and Nature of Capitalism</u> (2 Weeks)

   Michael Waltzer, "Money and Commodities"

   George Gilder, Selections from <u>Wealth and Poverty</u>

   Joseph Schumpter, Selections from <u>Capitalism, Socialism and Democracy</u>

II. <u>Business in America</u> (2 Weeks)

   Galambos and Pratt, <u>The Rise of The Corporate Commonwealth</u>

   David Vogel, "Business Mistrust of Government", <u>Center Magazine</u>

   Thomas McCraw, "Business & Government: The Origins of the Adversary Relationship", <u>California Management Review</u>

III. <u>Government Relations of Business</u> (2 Weeks)

   Background, <u>Reagan</u>, Chapters I & II

   <u>Social Regulation</u>:

   Vogel, <u>Fluctuating Fortunes</u>, Chapters III, IV

   Reagan, <u>Regulation</u>, Chapters V - VII

   David Bollier & John Claybrook, "Regulations that Work", <u>Washington Monthly</u>, April 1, 1986

   Maraniss & Weisskopf, "Life in the National Sacrifice Zone", <u>Washington Post Weekly</u>

   Specter, "Fear of Frying", <u>Washington Post Weekly</u>

   Jeremy Main, "Here Comes the Big New Clean Up", <u>Fortune</u>

   Morrell, "A Review of the Record", <u>Regulation</u>

   David Vogel, "Cooperative Regulation", <u>Public Interest</u>

   David Vogel, "AIDS and the Politics of Drug Lag", <u>Public Interest</u>

<u>Economic Regulation</u>:

    Reagan, <u>Regulation</u>, Chapters IV & V

    Gregg Easterbrook, "The Virtues of Competition"

    "Is Deregulation Working?", <u>Business Week</u>

    John Curran, "Does Deregulation Make Sense?" <u>Fortune</u>

****
FIRST PAPER DUE: Sixth Week
****

IV. <u>Corporate Governance</u> (1 Week)

    T. Boone Pickens, "Professions of a Short-termer", <u>HBR</u>

    W. Law, "A Corporation Is More Than Its Stockholder", <u>HBR</u>

    "The Battle for Corporate Control", <u>Business Week</u>

    George Melloan, "New Debate Over Corporate Governance", "The Backlash Against Corporate Raiders", <u>Wall Street Journal</u>

    "Taking Charge", <u>Business Week</u>

    Sherman, "Pushing Corporate Boards to be Better", <u>Fortune</u>

V. <u>Corporate Social Responsibility and Corporate Philanthropy</u> (1 Week)

    Milton Friedman, "the Social Responsibility of Business is to Increase Its Profits", <u>New York Times</u>, September 13, 1970

    "The Education Crisis: What Business Can Do", <u>Fortune</u>

    David Kirp, "Uncommon Decency: Pacific Bell Responds to AIDS", <u>Harvard Business Review</u>

    Cathy Trost, "Best Employers for Women and Parents", <u>WSJ</u>

    "Privacy", <u>Business Week</u>, March 28, 1988

    Michael Unseem, "Patterns of Corporate Contributions", <u>California Management Review</u>, Winter 1988

    Messen & Tilson, "Corporate Philosophy: A Strategic Approach to the Bottom Line", <u>California Management Review</u>, Winter 1987

VI. Corporate Crime and Business Ethics (1 Week)

   Russell Mokhiber, "Criminals By Any Other Name", Washington Monthly, January 1988

   "Clamor to Make Punishment Fit the Crime", Business Week, February 10, 1986

   James Traub, "Into the Months of Babes", New York Times

   Jim Stone, "Fuzzy Laws help Blur the Boundaries", New York Times

   "The Rationale for Ethical Corporate Behavior", Business Roundtable, Winter 1988

   Vogel, "Ethics and Profits Don't Always Go Hand in Hand", L.A. Times

   Cases in Professional Conduct: Ethical Principles in Business

VII. Corporate Political Activity (2 Weeks)

   Vogel, Fluctuating Fortunes, Review Chapters III-IV
                                  Read Chapters I, II, V-X

   ****
   SECOND PAPER DUE: Eleventh Week
   ****

VIII. The International Economy (3 Weeks)

   O'Reilly, "Corporations, Culture & Commitment", CMR, Summer 1989

   Brown & Reich, "When Does Cooperation Work? - A Look at NUMMI & GM-Van Nuys", CMR, Summer 1989

   Yoffie & Milner, "Why Corporations Seek Strategic Trade Policy?", CMR, Summer 1989

   Hart & Tyson, "Responding to the Challenge of HDTV", CMR, Summer 1989

   Taylor, Shadows of the Rising Sun

WASHINGTON UNIVERSITY

Professor Murray Weidenbaum

Management 515
Management 4581
Spring 1990

BUSINESS AND GOVERNMENT
Course Outline and Reading List

I. **Business As a Political Actor**

    A. **Lobbying**

        Eagleton: "Lobbying"

    B. **Political Action Committees**

        Eagleton: PACs

        Weidenbaum: Chapter 17

II. **The Government's Regulatory Power**

    A. **Introduction to Regulation**

        Weidenbaum: Chapters 1, 2

    B. **Regulation and the Consumer**

        Eagleton: Tobacco Road, Dalkon Shield

        Weidenbaum: Chapter 3

    C. **Environmental Regulation**

        Eagleton: Times Beach

        Weidenbaum: Chapter 4

    D. **EEO and Affirmative Action**

        Weidenbaum: Chapter 5

    E. **Job Safety and Pension Regulation**

        Weidenbaum: Chapter 6

    F. **Traditional Economic Regulation**

        Eagleton: Sports Industry

        Weidenbaum: Chapter 7

- G. Deregulation
  - Eagleton: Airline Deregulation
  - Weidenbaum: Chapter 8
- H. Privatization
  - Eagleton: Privatization
- I. Reforming Government Regulation
  - Weidenbaum: Chapter 9

III. Broader Governmental Powers
- A. Promoting Competitiveness
  - Eagleton: Steel Industry and Industrial Policy
  - Weidenbaum: Chapter 10
- B. Tax Policy
  - Weidenbaum: Chapter 11
- C. Controlling Foreign Trade
  - Weidenbaum: Chapter 12
- D. Directing Foreign Investment
  - Eagleton: Foreign Investment in U.S.
- E. Corporate Bailouts
  - Eagleton: Politics of Bailouts
  - Weidenbaum: Chapter 13
- F. The Military Market
  - Weidenbaum: Chapter 14

IV. Business and Public Policy
- A. Business-Government Relations
  - Weidenbaum: Chapter 15

    B.   <u>Issues Management</u>

          Weidenbaum: Chapter 16

    C.   <u>Corporate Governance</u>

          Weidenbaum: Chapter 18

    D.   <u>Takeovers and Shareholders</u>

          Eagleton: "Wall Street Watch"

          Weidenbaum: Chapter 19

    E.   <u>The Long-Term Outlook</u>

          Weidenbaum: Chapter 20

<u>Required Books</u>

Thomas F. Eagleton, *Issues in Business and Government* (Processed)
Murray L. Weidenbaum, *Business, Government and the Public*, 4th Edition, Prentice-Hall

NEW YORK UNIVERSITY
STERN SCHOOL OF BUSINESS

Market Organization, Antitrust,   Prof. L.J. White
and Regulation
Fall 1989

This is a course in applied microeconomics. The basic principles of micro theory will be used to develop an understanding of the structure, behavior, and performance of firms and markets in the American economy and an understanding of the possible strategies for successful firms in this economy. The course will then examine the major government policies - antitrust and regulation - that are used in the United States to influence this structure, behavior, and performance.

The course requirements are a term paper and a final examination.

There are three books that will be used in this course:

    F.M. Scherer, *Industrial Market Structure and Economic Performance*, 2nd edition (S).

    Michael Porter, *Competitive Strategy* (P).

    Leonard W. Weiss and Michael W. Klass, eds., *Regulatory Reform: What Actually Happened?* (W&K).

Schedule (approximately) of lectures and readings:

Sept. 13:	Introduction and review of micro theory: S, chs. 1-2; P, ch. 1-3.
Sept. 20:	Barriers to entry; the size of firms: S, pp. 81-91, 229-239; P, chs. 14-16.
Sept. 27:	Oligopoly theory: S, chs. 5-7; P. chs. 4-6.
Oct. 4:	Structure: S, chs. 3-4; P, chs. 7-8.
Oct. 11:	Behavior: S, chs. 8, 11-14; P, chs. 9-13.
Oct. 18:	Performance: S, chs. 9-10, 17.
Oct. 25:	Innovation: S, chs. 15-16.
Nov. 1:	Policy: Introduction: S, ch. 18.
Nov. 8:	Antitrust: Sherman Act, Sec. 1.: S, ch. 19 pp. 588-594.
Nov. 15:	Antitrust: Sherman Act, Sec. 2.: S, pp. 527-544.

Nov. 22:	Antitrust: Clayton Act, S, pp. 544-588.
Nov. 29:	Regulation: Overview; economic regulation (easy cases): W&K, intro, cases 1-2, 4-6.
Dec. 6:	Regulation: Economic regulation (hard cases): W&K, cases 3, 7.
Dec. 13:	Regulation: Health-safety-environment regulation: W&K, cases 8-9.

BUSINESS ADMINISTRATION READING LISTS AND COURSE OUTLINES
1990

Compiled by Richard Schwindt, *Simon Fraser University*

Volume 1 ACCOUNTING, 229 pages

Contributors: Ashiq Ali, V. Bernard, W.L. Ferrara, G.T. Gilbert, Robert Hagerman, S. Hamlen, Charles Horngren, Young K. Kwon, Herman Leonard, Laureen Maines, G. Mueller, R.D. Nair, Paul Newman, Pekin Ogan, Alan J. Richardson, Byung T. Ro, H.M. Schoenfeld, Gordon Shillinglaw, Brett Trueman, Ross L. Watts, Roman L. Weil, J.J. Williams, Dave Wright, William F.Wright

Volume 2 MARKETING, 315 pages

Contributors: Erin Anderson, I.E. Berger, Thomas Bonoma, Noel Capon, Douglas J. Dalrymple, Wayne DeSarbo, Jehoshua Eliashberg, Pete Fader, Bruce Fauman, Neil M. Ford, Morris B. Holbrook, Stanley C. Hollander, Wayne Hoyer, Ajay Kohli, Philip Kotler, K. Sridhar Moorthy, K.S. Palda, Gordon Patzer, Vithala Rao, Thomas S. Robertson, D. Sexton, John Sherry, Louis W. Stern, Vern Terpstra, Charles B. Weinberg, Jerry Wind, Russell S. Winer, Ugur Yucelt, Youjae Yi

Volume 3 CORPORATE FINANCE AND INVESTMENTS, 206 pages

Contributors: Franklin Allen, S. Bhattacharyya, L.D. Booth, Peter Carr, Michael Fishman, Steve Foerster, Virginia G. France, N. Bulent Gultekin, Robert L. Hagerman, Milton Harris, Campbell R. Harvey, Michael L. Hemler, Roger Ibbotson, Kose John, Jonathan M. Karpoff, Allan W. Kleidon, Robert Korajczyk, Claudio Loderer, James H. Lorie, John D. Martin, M.P. Narayanan, Andrew Postelwaite, Asani Sarkar, G. William Schwert, Lemma W. Senbet, S.Smidt, Stephen P. Zeldes

Volume 4 FINANCIAL THEORY, INSTITUTIONS AND MONEY MARKETS, 202 pages

Contributors: George P. Baker, George Constantinides, Yoon Dokko, Mark R. Eaker, Robert A. Eisenbeis, Edwin J. Elton, Joel Hasbrouck, Chi-fu Huang, Michael Jensen, Avraham Kamara, Robert Kauffman, Robert Korajczyk, Robert E. Krainer, John D. Martin, Frederic S. Mishkin, I.G. Morgan, Carol Osler, James V. Poapst, Arnold Sametz, Anthony Saunders, G. William Schwert, Jay Shanken, S. Smidt, Lewis Spellman, Hal R. Varian, P. Wachtel, Jerry Warner, S. Wheatley, James A. Wilcox, Ralph Winter

Volume 5 INTERNATIONAL BUSINESS, 268 pages

Contributors: Yair Aharoni, Schon Beechler, Earl Cheit, Kang Rae Cho, Jose de la Torre, Steven Globerman, Leslie E. Grayson, Richard Locke, Richard Lyons, Richard W. Moxon, Thomas P. Murtha, Thomas Pugel, Pierre Regibeau, Tom Roehl, Alan Rugman, J.A. Sawyer, Vern Terpstra, J. Frederick Truitt, Stephen Weiss, David Yoffie

Volume 6 INTERNATIONAL BANKING AND FINANCE, 153 pages

Contributors: Robert Aubey, Catherine Bonser-Neal, Laurence D. Booth, Bhagwan Chowdhry, Gunther Dufey, Bernard Dumas, Mark Eaker, David Eiteman, Holger Engberg, Jack Glen, R.J. Herring, Robert Higgins, Robert J. Hodrick, Philippe Jorion, K. Kasa, Richard Levich, Antonio Mello, Carol Osler, Raman Uppal, Ingo Walter, S. Wheatley, Josef Zechner

Volume 7   ORGAIZATIONAL BEHAVIOR, 265 pages

Contributors: Hugh J. Arnold, Susan Ashford, Ellen Auster, Douglas Austrom, Fred Dansereau, Daniel R. Denison, Randall B. Dunham, Peter Frost, Barrie Gibbs, William Glick, Mary Ann Glynn, John Godard, Dev Jennings, Todd Jick, H. Leblebici, Larry Moore, Trond Petersen, Karlene Roberts, Ben Rosen, James P. Walsh, Ross A. Webber

Volume 8   INDUSTRIAL RELATIONS AND HUMAN RESOURCES MANAGEMENT 266 pages

Contributors: William J. Bigoness, Francine Blau, Mario Bognanno, James G. Clawson, William Cooke, John Crispo, Gerald Ferris, John H. Godard, Wallace Hendricks, Archie Kleingartner, Thomas Kochan, Robert LaLonde, John Lawler, David Levine, David McPhillips, Daniel Mitchell, Larry Moore, Raymond A. Noe, Oscar A. Ornati, Robert Rogow, Denise Rousseau, Richard Rowan, James G. Scoville, K. Taira, Harry Triandis, Anil Verma, James P. Walsh

Volume 9   QUANTITATIVE METHODS, RESEARCH DESIGN AND COMPUTER APPLICATIONS IN BUSINESS, 286 pages

Contributors: Charles Blair, David Blair, Norman L. Chervany, Thomas Cooley, Joseph G. Davis, Sid Deshmukh, Al Dexter, Jehoshua Eliashberg, Gordon C. Everest, Gerald Ferris, Robert M. Freund, William Glick, Terry Harrison, Michael Hottenstein, Ted D. Klastorin, M.R. Leenders, Ting-peng Liang, Henry Lucas, Alan W. Neebe, L. Orman, E.R. Petersen, Trond K. Petersen, Donald Richter, Larry Robinson, Paul Rubin, John Sviokla, Clinton White, Carson Woo, W.T. Ziemba

Volume 10   BUSINESS, GOVERNMENT AND SOCIETY, 252 pages

Contributors: Mitchel Abolafia, James A. Brander, R. Chatov, Earl Cheit, Edwin M. Epstein, Gerald Faulhaber, Murray Frank, Thomas Kerr, George C. Lodge, Alfred A. Marcus, David D. Martin, D. Nickerson, Eli Noam, Seth Norton, O. Ornati, Kurt Parkum, Bohumir Pazderka, Sam Peltzman, William A. Sax, Walter D. Scott, William Stanbury, George J. Stigler, Richard S. Tedlow, Richard Vietor, A. Vining, David Vogel, Murray L. Weidenbaum, L.J. White

Volume 11   BUSINESS POLICY AND STRATEGY, 242 pages

Contributors: David A. Aaker, Anthony Boardman, Bala Chakravarthy, Joseph D'Cruz, Gerald Faulhaber, James Fitzsimmons, Murray Frank, Michael Geringer, Arnoldo C. Hax, R.M. Jalland, Alton C. Johnson, Aneel Karnani, Kenneth MacCrimmon, Will Mitchell, K.S. Palda, Margaret A. Peteraf, Robert S. Pindyck, Michael Porter, Katharine Rockett, T.W. Ruefli, Edward Snyder, Howard H. Stevenson, Valerie Suslow, F. Brian Talbot, David J. Teece, Andrew Van de Ven, R.E. White

Volume 12   RISK, DECISION MAKING AND BARGAINING, 271 pages
Compiled by Richard Schwindt & Tim McDaniels

Contributors: R.J. Aldag, Robert Ashton, Max Bazerman, Lee Roy Beach, David Bell, James H. Berson, Philip Bromiley, Peter Carnevale, Peter Cramton, J. David Cummins, Jose de la Torre, James S. Dyer, Baruch Fischhoff, Leonard Greenhalgh, Robin Gregory, Milton Harris, Terry Harrison, Aron Katsenelinboigen, Gordon Kaufman, L. Robin Keller, Peter Kempthorne, Craig W. Kirkwood, Howard Kunreuther, James D. Laing, Kenneth MacCrimmon, Theodore Marmor, John W. Minton, Barry Nalebuff, John W. Payne, J. Edward Russo, Rakesh K. Sarin, George Strauss, A. J. Taylor, Dean Tjosvold, Larry Tomassini, Paul Vatter, Thomas S. Wallsten, Elke Weber, Robert Witt

Volume 13   ENTREPRENEURSHIP, SMALL BUSINESS AND VENTURE CAPITAL, 221 pages

Contributors: Hugh J. Arnold, Zenas Block, David Brophy, William Bygrave, Neil Churchill, Wendell E. Dunn, A.C. Filley, Eric Flamholtz, Wendy Handler, John Kao, Dennis E. Logue, Ian MacMillan, Edward Marram, Daniel Muzyka, Alfred Osborne Jr., William A. Sahlman, Jeffry A. Timmons, Karl H. Vesper, Steven Wheelwright

Volume 14   MANAGEMENT COMMUNICATION, 125 pages
Compiled by Mary Munter

Contributors: Paul Argenti, Michael Hattersley, H.W. Hilderbrandt, Christine Kelly, Robert Kent, Sherron Kenton, Mary Munter, Martha Nord, Alan Pike, Robert Reinheimer, Priscilla Rogers, Charlotte Rosen, Larry Smeltzer, Joanne Yates

All volumes are priced at $20 each. The complete set is $225. These prices include postage, handling and taxes for DOMESTIC ORDERS. Other postage and handling charges are: foreign surface @ $1/volume; Canada air @ $3/volume; Europe & Latin America air @ $4/volume; Africa, Asia & Pacific air @ $10/volume. Payment accepted in U.S. funds only.

Eno River Press
Box 4900 Duke Station
Durham, N.C. 27706-4900
U.S.A.

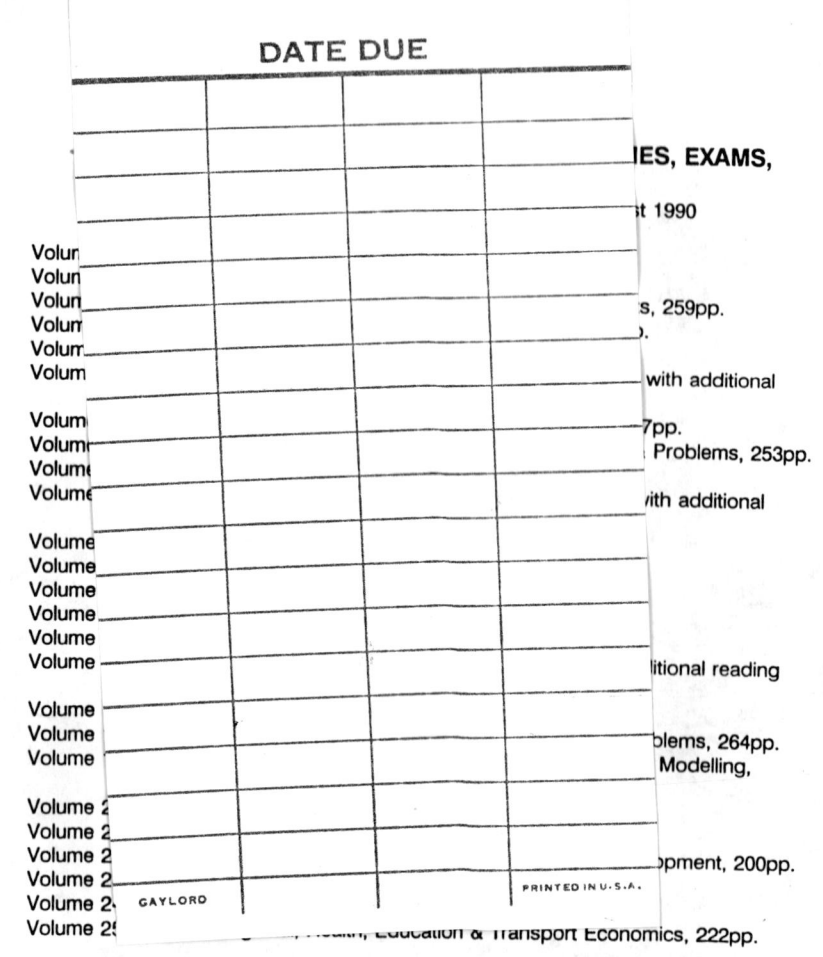

The price of each volume is $20. The discount price for the complete set of 25 Economics volumes is $350. For individuals buying economics volumes, buy 2 volumes at the regular price, and get additional volumes for a special price of $15 each when ordering directly from Eno River Press. These prices include postage and handling for domestic orders only. Other postage charges are: foreign surface @ $1 per volume; Canada air @ $3 per volume; Europe & Latin America air @ $4 per volume; and Asia, Africa & Pacific air @ $10 per volume. U.S. funds only please.

Eno River Press
Box 4900, Duke Station
Durham, N.C. 27706-4900
U.S.A.

GREENVILLE COLLEGE LIBRARY

016.339SCH99   C001
SCHWINDT, RICHARD.
BUSINESS, GOVERNMENT AND SOCIETY   STX

3 4511 00000 4941

016.339
Sch99

123501

DEMCO

Mitchel Abolafia
James A. Brander
R. Chatov
Earl Cheit
Edwin M. Epstein
Gerald Faulhaber
Murray Frank
Thomas Kerr
George C. Lodge
Alfred A. Marcus
David D. Martin
D. Nickerson
Eli Noam
Seth Norton
O. Ornati
Kurt Parkum
Bohumir Pazderka

Sam Peltzman
William A. Sax
Walter D. Scott
William Stanbury
George J. Stigler
Richard S. Tedlow
Richard Vietor
A. Vining
David Vogel
Murray L. Weidenbaum
L.J. White

Eno River Press
Box 4900, Duke Station
Durham, NC 27706-4900
USA

ISBN 0-88024-12

Greenville College Library

GREENVILLE COLLEGE
ILLINOIS

016.339   Sch99

Volume 10

Business, Government and Society

Business Administration
Reading Lists and Course Outlines

Compiled by Richard Schwindt, *Simon Fraser University*,
August 1990